Foreword

Welcome to edition 45 of Medicines, Ethics and Practice (MEP).

The MEP is a professional guide for pharmacists and aspires to support pharmacists to practise confidently and professionally; to use professional judgement and to develop as a professional. It can be used to support practice, learning and CPD. *Please note: the MEP will not always provide a definitive solution to a problem however it can be used to help you identify steps to resolve a problem/issue in practice.*

Where we think it will be helpful we have provided hyperlinks to take you directly to an article or specific part of a website. However, we are aware that links can change. If you have difficulty accessing any links we provide, please go to the organisation's home page or your preferred internet search engine and use appropriate key words to search for the relevant item. All hyperlinks were accessed in April/May 2022.

MEP evolves and develops with the support and collaboration of members through the advice and expertise of the MEP Advisory Panel and through feedback received from members between editions.

The Advisory Panel is composed of pharmacists and aspiring pharmacists from different sectors, different stages of practice and across Great Britain who have volunteered their time to provide advice to the RPS on the development of the MEP.

This edition of MEP has been edited by Rakhee Amin, Senior Professional Standards Pharmacist.

We welcome volunteers from all sectors and stages of practice willing to commit time to help us develop MEP and also appreciate comments and feedback; these can be sent to the RPS Professional Support service support@rpharms.com

Copies of MEP are available for general purchase at a cost of £55.00 and are available from the Pharmaceutical Press website at www.pharmpress.com or from Pharmaceutical Press c/o Macmillan on tel: 01256 302 600.

Please note: Details of any corrections to MEP after publication can be found on the RPS website www.rpharms.com/publications/the-mep.

Disclaimer

This publication is intended as a guide and may not always include all information relating to its subject matter. You should interpret all information and advice in light of your own professional knowledge and all relevant pharmacy and healthcare literature and guidelines. Nothing in this publication constitutes legal advice and cannot be relied upon as such. Whilst care has been taken to ensure the accuracy of content, the Royal Pharmaceutical Society excludes to the fullest extent permissible by law any liability whether in contract, tort or otherwise arising from your reliance on any information or advice.

Contents

Changes to this edition

The following amendments and additions have been made for Edition 45

NEW SECTIONS

2.5.4
RISK MANAGEMENT

This section provides information on what risk management is in pharmacy practice and the principles of risk assessment

2.7
SUSTAINABILITY

Includes detailed signposting to RPS policies on Sustainability to help pharmacists and their teams to reduce impact of medicines and the services they provide on the climate

3.3.1
GENERAL PRESCRIPTION REQUIREMENTS

Information on Homecare prescriptions including signposting to RPS Professional Standards for Homecare services , Handbook on providing homecare services in England and Wales and the Hackett Report

3.5.6
SELLING VETERINARY MEDICINES ON THE INTERNET

Includes signposting to VMD guidance on the requirement for selling veterinary medicines over the internet and information on the Accredited Internet Retailer Scheme (AIRS)

3.7.16
NEEDLE SYRINGE PROVISION

Highlights importance of being aware of National and Local guidelines available when delivering this service and having the appropriate training

---

UPDATED SECTIONS

2.1.4
STANDARDS AND GUIDANCE

Updated RPS Standards and Guidance list

2.2.2
DEVELOPMENT FRAMEWORKS AND RECOGNITION

Information on RPS Consultant Credentialing Service has been updated to reflect the credentialing process

2.2.3
PHARMACIST PRESCRIBING

Includes information on the new GPhC Standards for the Initial Education and Training of Pharmacists (2021)

Information on Prescribing Case Studies has been removed and replaced with information on the new RPS Independent Prescriber Guide detailing what the guide contains

2.6.7
PATIENT CONSULTATIONS

Information on conducting remote consultations

3.3.1
GENERAL PRESCRIPTION REQUIREMENTS

Consider prescribing restrictions set by the prescriber's regulatory and professional body

Information on the validity of owings for POMS on Pregnancy Prevention Programme (PPP) added to Table 4 : Validity of owings on NHS and private prescriptions

3.3.5
PRESCRIPTIONS FROM THE EEA OR SWITZERLAND

Included information on GPhC update on "Guidance for registered pharmacies providing pharmacy services at a distance, including on the internet" March 2022

3.3.14
PRESCRIBER TYPES AND PRESCRIBING RESTRICTIONS

Updated on table 6 that EEA or Swiss registered approved health professional can prescribe off – label medicines

3.3.16
PRESCRIBING AND DISPENSING FOR THE SAME PERSON

Signposting to RPS Independent prescribers guide for information on exceptional circumstances to consider when the same pharmacist is responsible for prescribing and supplying

3.5
VETERINARY MEDICINES

Information updated on Table 9 that NFA-VPS medicines are not accessible to public in the pharmacy

CHAPTER 5
ROYAL PHARMACEUTICAL SOCIETY CODE OF CONDUCT

Updated to include information on complaints about members using social media

CHAPTER 6
PHARMACIST SUPPORT

Information on the services and support Pharmacist Support offers has been updated with the help from Pharmacist Support . Information on what the charity's ACTNow campaigns addresses on stress in workplaces for pharmacists , students and trainees has been included

---

REMOVED SECTIONS

APPENDIX 6
GPhC guidance on responding to complaints and concerns

Core concepts and skills

2.1
Professional Conduct

Pharmacy is a profession and pharmacists are professionals who exercise professionalism and professional judgement on a day-to-day basis.

The concepts of a 'profession', a 'professional' and 'professionalism' are not rigidly defined. However, these are concepts that are important for any pharmacist, including those who work in non-patient facing roles.

A **profession** can be described as an occupation that:

- Is recognised by the public as a profession
- Has a recognised representative professional body
- Benefits from professional standards and codes of conduct
- Is regulated to ensure the maintenance of standards and codes of conduct

A **professional** can be described as:

- A member of a profession
- A member of a professional body
- An individual who:
  - Behaves and acts professionally
  - Exercises professionalism and professional judgement
  - Undertakes continuing professional development
  - Has professional values, attitudes and behaviours.

2.1.1
PROFESSIONALISM

Pharmacy professionalism can be defined as a set of values, behaviours and relationships that underpin the trust the public has in pharmacists.

Examples of these are:

- Altruism
- Appropriate accountability
- Compassion
- Duty
- Excellence and continuous improvement
- Honour and integrity
- Professional judgement
- Respect for other patients, colleagues and other healthcare professionals (including listening to and acting on feedback when needed)
- Working in partnership with patients, doctors and the wider healthcare team in the patient's/public's best interest
- Work within competence
- Ensure patient is placed at the centre of all decision making
- Being honest about scope of practice
- Knowing when to seek support.

Many of these values, attitudes and behaviours are also reflected in the mandatory GPhC Standards and are relevant to all pharmacy professionals including pharmacy students.

Pharmacists who are working in industry should also adhere to the Association of the British Pharmaceutical Industry (ABPI) Code of Practice for the Pharmaceutical Industry.

FURTHER READING

Association of British Pharmaceutical Industry
ABPI Code of Practice for the Pharmaceutical Industry. 2021.
www.abpi.org.uk

General Pharmaceutical Council
Standards for pharmacy professionals. 2017.
www.pharmacyregulation.org
(see MEP Appendix 1)

PROFESSIONAL JUDGEMENT

Professional judgement can be described as the use of accumulated knowledge and experience, as well as critical reasoning, to make an informed professional decision – often to help solve a problem, or in relation to, a patient; or policies and procedures affecting patients. It takes into account the law, ethical considerations, relevant standards and all other relevant factors related to the surrounding circumstances. Furthermore, it will resonate with the core values, attitudes and behavioural indicators of professionalism.

Many pharmacists exercise their professional judgement instinctively, but it may be helpful to break the process down into smaller steps:

Diagram 1:
Exercising professional judgement

1. IDENTIFY THE ETHICAL DILEMMA OR PROFESSIONAL ISSUE

e.g. deciding whether to supply a medicine or not

↓

2. GATHER ALL THE RELEVANT INFORMATION AND RESEARCH THE PROBLEM

i.e. obtain the following:

- Facts
- Knowledge
- Laws
- Standards
- Good practice guidance
- Advice from support services, head office, line managers or colleagues

↓

3. IDENTIFY ALL THE POSSIBLE SOLUTIONS

- Consider and act in the best interests of the patient
- Consider and manage appropriately any personal interests or organisational goals, incentives or targets

↓

↓

4. WEIGH UP THE BENEFITS AND RISKS OF EACH OPTION

Consider the advantages and disadvantages of each of the possible options you have identified

↓

5. CHOOSE AN OPTION – ENSURING YOU CAN JUSTIFY THE DECISION

It's important you can justify the decision you have made because often the ethical dilemma or professional issue means you are weighing up conflicting obligations which could be genuine patient interest, legal obligations, professional standards, public interest, contractual terms of service and company procedures

↓

6. RECORD THE DECISION-MAKING PROCESS

- Include your reasons leading to a particular course of action where appropriate
- This may be a record in the patient's medication record (PMR), medical record, the back of the prescription register or an intervention record book. This is important as evidence of the thought processes leading to the decision

The process of making a professional judgement is underpinned by knowledge. Chapter 3 in MEP provides information on the core knowledge required by pharmacists in their day-to-day practice.

ETHICS AND PROFESSIONAL JUDGEMENT

Professional judgement is key to handling ethical dilemmas. Ethical issues often arise in situations where acting in the patient's best interests may be outside the legal constraints of normal practice.

It is entirely possible for two different pharmacists, faced with the same facts and circumstances, to choose two different courses of action. This is the nature of a finely balanced ethical dilemma. Both options could be justifiable and legitimate choices for a significant proportion of pharmacists if faced with the same dilemma.

It is important to point out that professional judgement is not a blanket defence or a blanket reason to take the most convenient choice.
It must be exercised properly, logically and for valid reasons. If there are mechanisms to achieve the required goal it would be risky to choose an illegal alternative. For example, lending medication would be very difficult to justify if an emergency supply could have been used.

FURTHER READING

Royal Pharmaceutical Society
Professional judgement.
www.rpharms.com

Royal Pharmaceutical Society
RPS guidance on ethical, professional decision making in the COVID-19 Pandemic . 2020

General Pharmaceutical Council
Standards for pharmacy professionals. 2017.
www.pharmacyregulation.org
(see MEP Appendix 1)

Wingfield J, Pitchford K, editors
Dale and Appelbe's Pharmacy and Medicines Law.
12th edition. 2021. London; Pharmaceutical Press.
www.pharmpress.com

2.1.3
PROFESSIONAL EMPOWERMENT

Professional empowerment is about enabling professionalism and professional judgement.

At an individual level for pharmacists and future pharmacists, it is about the development of knowledge; development of skills, experience and confidence; and the cultivation of professional values and behaviours which collectively imbue the pharmacist with authority, empowering and enabling professionalism and the ability to manage ethical dilemmas.

At a wider level it is about creating an environment around an individual which enables all the above.

Professional training starts at university and is enhanced with the Foundation training year by learning, designated supervisors and training programmes. In professional practice it is self-cultivated through revalidation and continuing professional development (CPD), continuing

education, and supported by the RPS through our foundation and advanced practice programmes.

The GPhC standards for registered pharmacies require that staff are empowered and competent to safeguard the health, safety and wellbeing of patients and the public (see Appendix 2 for further information).

The RPS contributes to creating empowerment through guidance, standards, news and alerts; through webinars and our mentoring programme; through our Leadership Development Framework; through influencing policy and embedding and nurturing the right culture.

Our resource *Reducing workplace pressure through professional empowerment* discusses various ways to reduce workplace pressure. The document is designed to help by empowering pharmacists, as individuals, to take action if they are adversely affected by workplace pressures and includes:

- Mechanisms for raising concerns
- Promoting management skills
- Ensuring pharmacists take breaks
- Professionalism and managing commercial pressures
- Job satisfaction.

Employers play a key role by providing structured training resources and events; conferences; opportunity and time for CPD; support from the superintendent's office; company alerts and updates; developing and implementing the right organisation culture which enables professional empowerment.

Other pharmacy organisations, stakeholders and training providers are also integral to enabling professionalism through training, and enabling the right environment for professionalism to flourish, including through *getting the culture right*.

FURTHER READING

Royal Pharmaceutical Society
Leadership development framework and accompanying handbook.
www.rpharms.com

Royal Pharmaceutical Society
Reducing workplace pressure through professional empowerment.
www.rpharms.com

Royal Pharmaceutical Society
Working as a locum in community pharmacy.
www.rpharms.com

General Pharmaceutical Council
Guidance to support the standards for registered pharmacies.
www.pharmacyregulation.org
(see MEP Appendix 2)

General Pharmaceutical Council
Standards for pharmacy professionals.
www.pharmacyregulation.org
(see MEP Appendix 1)

Diagram 2:
Standards and guidance

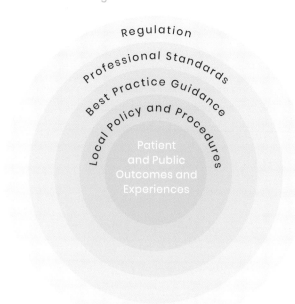

2.1.4

STANDARDS AND GUIDANCE

Regulatory and professional standards and guidance have the same overarching purpose – to provide a framework which helps ensure good care, focussed on patients.

Patient-centred care should be at the heart of everything that pharmacists and pharmacy teams do. Being a pharmacy professional is about having the right skills, knowledge, attitude, behaviour and judgement to help ensure good quality outcomes for patients.

To inform the care you provide and your decision making you should:

- Consider what is in the best interests of the patient
- Be guided by your education and training and ongoing CPD
- Consider the standards and guidance (both regulatory and professional) that are relevant to your situation, and
- Understand the legal framework in which you are operating.

The GPhC and the RPS expect that all pharmacists and pharmacy owners are aware of and use all relevant standards and guidance as part of ensuring safe, effective and high-quality professional practice and care for patients.

Diagram 2 illustrates how regulatory and professional standards, together with guidance, policies and procedures, support positive patient outcomes.

GPHC STANDARDS AND GUIDANCE

The regulatory standards produced by the GPhC for pharmacy professionals and pharmacies are statements of what people have the right to expect when they use pharmacy services. They also reflect what pharmacy professionals should expect of themselves when delivering high standards of care.

The GPhC has also produced guidance which provides additional information to help pharmacy professionals meet their standards.

Regulatory standards must be met by all pharmacy professionals and owners of registered pharmacies.

The following GPhC regulatory standards and guidance have been reproduced, with the permission of the GPhC, as Appendix 1–5.

- Standards for pharmacy professionals
- Standards for registered pharmacies
- Guidance on confidentiality
- Guidance on consent
- Guidance on raising concerns

These documents are subject to change and review by the GPhC and the latest versions can be obtained from the GPhC website www.pharmacyregulation.org or via the app.

Additional standards and guidance can be obtained from the GPhC website or via the app including the following:

- Conflicts of interest
- Duty of candour
- Female genital mutilation: mandatory duty for pharmacy professionals to report
- Pharmacist prescribers
- Preparing unlicensed medicines
- Professionalism online
- Providing pharmacy services at a distance, including on the internet
- Maintaining clear sexual boundaries
- Religion, personal values and beliefs
- Safe and effective pharmacy teams
- Standards for the initial education and training for pharmacists

RPS PROFESSIONAL STANDARDS AND GUIDANCE

The professional standards produced by the RPS provide a framework to support pharmacists and their teams, working in a variety of settings and roles, to develop their professional practice, improve services, shape future services, and deliver high quality patient care.

Professional standards are supportive and enabling whilst also professionally challenging, describing and building on good practice to support pharmacists with achieving excellence in professional practice. They provide a broad framework to support pharmacists and their teams to develop their professional practice, improve services, shape future services and deliver high quality patient care across all settings and sectors.

While professional standards are not mandatory, they are developed and owned by the profession. They set out what constitutes 'good' in terms of practice, systems of care, and working practices. Pharmacy professionals that are following professional standards set by the RPS can have confidence that they are meeting the regulatory standards set by the GPhC.

RPS professional standards and frameworks include:

- Competency framework for prescribers
- Competency framework for designated prescribing practitioners
- Error reporting standards
- Homecare services standards
- Hospital pharmacy standards
- Optimising medicines in secure environments (1: Immigration removal centres; 2: Prisons, young offenders institutions and secure training centres)
- Polypharmacy
- Safe and secure handling of medicines

RPS guidance covers a wide range of topics – including:

- Administration of medicines
- Antimicrobial Stewardship
- Compliance aids (MCA) best practice
- Controlled drugs
- Emergency Supply
- Homeopathic and Herbal medicines
- Independent prescribers
- Medical Devices
- Poisons
- Professional Judgement
- Prescription from EEA or Switzerland
- Pregnancy Prevention Programmes
- Preparing for Day one guides (community pharmacy, hospital pharmacy, pharmaceutical industry, working as a locum)
- Reclassified medicines
- Return to practice
- Research
- Revalidation
- Safeguarding
- Wellbeing
- Working in guides (GP practice, care homes, urgent and emergency care)
- Veterinary medicines

An A-Z index of our key publication topics can be found on the RPS website: www.rpharms.com alternatively you can search by topic area.

CONFLICTS OF INTEREST

It is important to declare conflicts of interest appropriately whether they are actual or potential.

An actual conflict of interest is when one or more interests materially conflict.

A potential conflict of interest is where there is a possibility of a conflict between one or more interests in the future.

Some examples of conflicts of interest include:

- Having another job or receiving consultancy fees (i.e. having an outside employment) which impacts upon another role

- Receiving or being offered gifts from patients or suppliers to the NHS or your employer

- Receiving or being offered hospitality such as travel, accommodation, meals or refreshments e.g. in relation to attending a meeting, conference or training event

- Receiving or being offered sponsorship for events, research grants or posts

- Owning shares in a company whose value could be influenced by your role

- Having an indirect interest or non-financial interest e.g. if a spouse, close relative, business partner or close friend has an interest

- Receiving any other payments or 'transfers of value'.

Declarations will most commonly be made to:

- Your employer through a line manager, governance or conflict lead

- Someone commissioning your services

- A chairperson at the meetings which you attend.

A declaration of an interest does not necessarily prevent an individual from carrying out a role, but it ensures that there can be no perception that they are seeking to influence decisions improperly.

FURTHER READING

General Pharmaceutical Council
Joint statement from the Chief Executives of statutory regulators of health and care professionals
www.pharmacyregulation.org

NHS England
Managing conflicts of interest in the NHS.
www.england.nhs.uk

INTERFACE BETWEEN PERSONAL AND PROFESSIONAL LIVES

Managing the interface between personal and professional life is one of the most common causes of conflicts of interest or ethical dilemmas you are likely to come across; it is also one you are most likely to come across early in your career. Your friends and family may not always understand how being a healthcare professional – even a healthcare-professional-in-training – affects what you can say and do, and how you may apply your knowledge.

The nature of pharmacy means that it is likely you will, at some stage, be asked to provide pharmacy services or advice for family or close friends. This is not necessarily a bad thing; many people prefer to ask for (or accept) advice from someone they already know and trust (and who knows them). However, there are likely to be times when your instincts and duties as a healthcare professional conflict with your instincts and duties as a friend or family member.

As a healthcare professional, you may also be seen as a convenient source of information not only regarding a person's own health, but also regarding things they may have heard about other people. Non-healthcare professionals may not always understand that your duty of confidentiality does not only apply at work, and also applies to people who may not be 'officially' your patients.

Providing pharmacy services* or advice to family/ friends relies upon you being able to apply your professional judgement and remain objective within the situation. This is notoriously difficult, especially if the situation is complex. It is therefore important to stop and think about whether it is appropriate for you to be involved, and if so, what you should do.

Pharmacy services includes the dispensing of prescriptions, providing advanced and locally commissioned/enhanced professional pharmacy services and providing advice.

Before providing pharmacy services to family/ friends, consider the following:

- Is the situation an emergency - where not advising or dispensing a prescription could put the person at risk of serious harm?

- Could the person be easily signposted to an alternative appropriate healthcare provider? Would it be more appropriate to do so?

- Are you able to maintain objectivity and exercise professional judgement?

- Is maintaining confidentiality an issue? Does the person who is asking the question have a right to know the answer?

- Are you fully aware of all of the care currently being provided?

- Do you have **all** of the necessary information to professionally and confidentially provide the pharmacy service/information - can you advise accurately and appropriately with the information that you have?

- Is what you are being asked for within the bounds of your professional competence?

- Can you demonstrate transparency – personal and professional boundaries should be maintained to prevent any conflict of interest arising?

- Do you have access to Summary Care Records (or equivalent, as appropriate)?

- Are you able to make appropriate records (where required)?

- Will providing the service/advice affect the person's relationship with their usual healthcare provider(s), and if so, how?

- Do you need to inform anyone else of what you have done/advised?

- What is in the best interests of the patient, all factors considered?

- Remember, even if you a providing pharmacy services (such as advice) outside the work environment, you are still expected to provide it to the same standard as you would at work, and your liability if anything should go wrong is likely to be the same.

- Ensure that you know what your employer's policies are regarding providing services to friends and family.

See also section 3.3.17: Dispensing self-prescribed prescriptions and prescriptions for close friends and family.

SOCIAL MEDIA

Pharmacists and aspiring pharmacists who use social media* and social networking should do so responsibly and with the same high standards which they would apply in face to face interactions.

It is important to maintain proper professional boundaries in relationships and interactions with patients and at all times to respect the confidentiality of others, including patients and colleagues.

Be aware of the potential audience of your online activity, that this may be publicly accessible, circulated and shared beyond your control. This activity could impact upon your professional image and the reputation of the profession as a whole.

Organisations may use social media, such as WhatsApp, to communicate with healthcare professionals in other departments (i.e between wards), instead of bleeping them. It is important pharmacists understand and follow their company or NHS Trust policies on this practice.

*Social media includes blogging, web forums including professional web forums, Twitter, Facebook, WhatsApp messaging and virtual networks (this list is not exhaustive).

FURTHER READING

British Medical Association
Social media, ethics and professionalism.
www.bma.org.uk

General Pharmaceutical Council
Demonstrating professionalism online. 2016.
www.pharmacyregulation.org

General Pharmaceutical Council
Guidance on patient confidentiality. 2018.
www.pharmacyregulation.org
(see MEP Appendix 3)

Health and Care Professionals Council
Guidance on the use of social media.
www.hcpc-uk.org

NHS Digital
Social Media guidance.
www.digital.nhs.uk

PROFESSIONAL INDEMNITY

It is a requirement if you are registered with the GPhC that you have professional indemnity insurance in place before you start working in your role. The GPhC has advised

"that the professional indemnity arrangement you have in place provides appropriate cover. This means that the cover needs to be appropriate to the nature and extent of the risks involved in your practice."

Further information and useful FAQs can be viewed on the GPhC website: www.pharmacyregulation.org

Please contact the RPS Professional Support team if you want to discuss further.

2.2
Professional Development

Professional development describes the manner by which pharmacy professionals maintain and enhance their knowledge, skills and personal qualities throughout their professional careers.

All pharmacy professionals undergo professional development – whether as part of their GPhC revalidation; or by undertaking training to develop core workplace skills or advanced practice; or by using frameworks and tools to gain advanced skills or professional recognition.

2.2.1
REVALIDATION

The GPhC standards require pharmacy professionals to maintain, develop and use their professional knowledge and skills.

Revalidation helps pharmacy professionals to:

- Keep their professional skills and knowledge up to date
- Reflect on how to improve
- Demonstrate to the public and patients how they provide safe and effective care.

To revalidate, pharmacy professionals must submit the following records each year:

- Four continuing professional development (CPD) records (at least two planned)
- A peer discussion
- A reflective account.

The RPS can support you with all aspects of revalidation. www.rpharms.com.

Further details, including templates and case studies are available on the GPhC website: www.pharmacyregulation.org

2.2.2
DEVELOPMENT FRAMEWORKS AND RECOGNITION

RPS POST-REGISTRATION FOUNDATION PHARMACIST CURRICULUM

The RPS Post-registration Foundation Pharmacist Curriculum sets out the knowledge, skills, behaviours and level of performance for early career pharmacists working in patient-focussed roles across community pharmacy, primary and secondary care.

The curriculum includes independent prescribing to reflect the core changes in pharmacist practice which are incorporated into the new GPhC Standards for the initial education and training of pharmacists. It will also develop leadership, management, education and research capabilities. Training programmes aligned to this curriculum will support pharmacists developing the skillset to progress to the RPS advanced credentialing pathways.

RPS ADVANCED CREDENTIALING SERVICE

The RPS is developing a prospective assessment service to credential advanced pharmacist practice in patient-focused roles.

A core advanced credential is being developed to assure the practice of pharmacists who demonstrate the knowledge, skills, behaviours and experience to be credentialed as ready to practise at an advanced level in any patient focussed role or setting.

Detailed information on this service can be viewed on RPS website www.rpharms.com

RPS CONSULTANT CREDENTIALING SERVICE

The RPS Consultant Pharmacist credentialing process will help you to understand the requirements to enter consultant-level pharmacy practice. It sets out the entry-level knowledge, skills, behaviours and levels of performance expected of consultant pharmacists. These form the basis of the assessment, which you will be credentialed against. This credential allows pharmacists to demonstrate their entry-level competence to practice in a consultant pharmacist post.

DEVELOPING LEADERSHIP

We have published a Leadership Development Framework for pharmacists and pharmaceutical scientists.

The framework is based on the concept of engaging, collective leadership for all, whether in a leadership role or not. It promotes leadership behaviours (the 'how-to-do' of leadership) across all sectors of the profession and encourages a collective responsibility for the success of an organisation and its services. Engaging leadership can come from anyone in an organisation, as appropriate, and at different times, and is an essential element of good practice and professional development.

FURTHER READING

Royal Pharmaceutical Society
Consultant pharmacist credentialing.
www.rpharms.com

Royal Pharmaceutical Society
Post-registration foundation pharmacist training.
www.rpharms.com

Royal Pharmaceutical Society
Leadership development framework.
www.rpharms.com

2

2.2.3
PHARMACIST PRESCRIBING

Pharmacists, nurses, midwives and other allied healthcare professionals (AHPs) who have completed an accredited prescribing course and registered their qualification with their regulatory body, are able to prescribe.

An independent prescriber (IP) is a practitioner, who is responsible and accountable for the assessment of patients with undiagnosed or diagnosed conditions and can make prescribing decisions to manage the clinical condition of the patient.

A supplementary prescriber (SP) is a practitioner who prescribes within an agreed patient specific written clinical management plan (CMP), agreed in partnership with a doctor or dentist.

Further information on what an independent prescriber or supplementary prescriber can prescribe can be found in 3.3.14. Independent/supplementary prescribers should restrict prescribing to their areas of clinical competence.

The new GPhC Standards for the Initial Education and Training of Pharmacists (2021) incorporate the skills, knowledge and attributes for prescribing, to enable pharmacists to independently prescribe from the point of registration. The GPhC has not currently introduced independent prescribing as part of the Foundation training year 2021/2022 and have developed an interim version of learning outcomes of the Standards for the initial education and training. They plan to include the requirement for independent prescribing in later iterations of transitional learning outcomes.

INDEPENDENT PRESCRIBER GUIDE
This guide which can be found on the RPS website www.rpharms.com (search for "Independent prescriber guide") contains guidance for :

- Aspiring pharmacist prescribers on becoming a prescriber & courses available, prescriber role & type, DPP role & training, and finding a DPP.
- Prescribing trainees & Newly qualified prescribers on using tools such as CFAP, deciding the scope of practice, completing portfolio of evidence & personal formularies, managing workload, prescribing safely & legally, support with professional registration & indemnity.

- Practicing & Experienced prescribing practitioners on keeping up to date with practice, maintaining prescribing competencies, supporting others, therapeutic resources, expanding scope of clinical practice. There's also practical guidance and support on prescribing scenarios such as repeat prescribing, prescribing for yourself, close family and friends, prescribing and dispensing or administering for the same person, and prescribing for patients remotely.

COMPETENCY FRAMEWORK FOR ALL PRESCRIBERS
The Prescribers competency framework sets out what good prescribing looks like. It describes the demonstrable knowledge, skills, characteristics, qualities and behaviours for a safe and effective prescribing role. Its implementation and maintenance are important in informing and improving practice, development, standard of care and safety (for both the prescriber and patient). It can be used by any prescriber at any point in their career to underpin professional responsibility for prescribing.

COMPETENCY FRAMEWORK FOR DESIGNATED PRESCRIBING PRACTITIONERS
The Competency Framework for Designated Prescribing Practitioners supports experienced independent prescribers to be effective designated prescribing practitioners by outlining the skills, knowledge, attitudes and behaviours required.

Further information can be found on the RPS website.

FURTHER READING

Royal Pharmaceutical Society
Designated prescribing practitioner competency framework.
www.rpharms.com

Royal Pharmaceutical Society
Independent prescribing of controlled drugs.
www.rpharms.com

Royal Pharmaceutical Society
Independent prescriber guide.
www.rpharms.com

Royal Pharmaceutical Society
A Competency Framework for all prescribers.
www.rpharms.com

General Pharmaceutical Council
In Practice: Guidance for pharmacist prescribers.
2019.
www.pharmacyregulation.org

General Pharmaceutical Council
Standards for the initial education and training of
pharmacists (January 2021)
www.pharmacyregulation.org

General Pharmaceutical Council
Standards for the initial education and training of
pharmacists – Interim learning outcomes (2021).
www.pharmacyregulation.org

2.2.4
MENTORING

Mentoring is a mutually beneficial professional relationship and it is an important part of career development at any stage for any professional, and pharmacists are not an exception. Every pharmacist has skills and experience to offer and everyone can benefit from having a mentor.

The role of the mentor is to support and guide the mentee in their learning and development, to listen and understand their needs, recognise where they are in their career and help them make decisions that will lead to them reaching their goals. It is also a great way to build connections for peer discussions and widen your professional network.

The RPS mentoring platform facilitates easy and appropriate matching of mentor to mentee. All RPS members can join the platform as both mentors and mentees.

FURTHER READING

Royal Pharmaceutical Society
Mentoring platform.
www.rpharms.com

2.3
Research

2.3.1
PHARMACISTS IN RESEARCH

For some pharmacists, particularly those working in industry and academia, research will be a large part of their role, while other pharmacists will be involved to a lesser extent e.g. in research support activities such as recruiting people for clinical trials. All pharmacists, regardless of their sector or level of practice, will have had some experience of using research to inform practice (see Diagram 3).

Diagram 3:
Pharmacists: involvement in research

Using research evidence to inform practice

Supporting research led by others

Collaborating in research as a partner

Leading research

2

RESEARCH ETHICS

It is important that pharmacists have a good understanding of the ethical implications and requirements for research and how these impact on their working practices and study outcomes. This applies whether they are leading the research or being asked to participate in research led by others – research is often a multidisciplinary team activity. Most research studies will require ethical approval by a Research Ethics Committee (REC); a group of experts who hold the responsibility of ensuring research conforms to accepted standards. Professional bodies, such as the Health Research Authority, use these committees to help govern and regulate research in the UK. This helps to protect and promote the interest of patients and the public in health and social care research, ensuring that research is transparent, ethically reviewed, and approved. It is always wise to seek guidance on whether formal REC approval is required, particularly when patient data is involved. When collecting any form of data (be it for research, audit or service evaluation) it is important to involve key stakeholders in your organisation (e.g. your hospital R&D department, or university research office) so that the complex legal and governance requirements are met.

Ethical principles must be considered at all stages of the research process (see Diagram 4) – regardless of whether research ethics and governance approval are required.

Diagram 4:
Steps of the research process

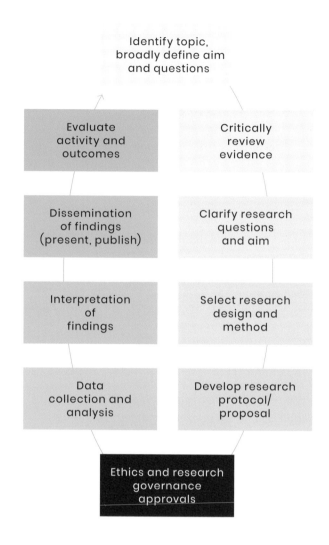

FURTHER READING

Royal Pharmaceutical Society
Research and evaluation guide.
www.rpharms.com

Health and Care Research Wales
healthandcareresearchwales.org

Health Research Authority
www.hra.nhs.uk

National Institute for Health Research
www.nihr.ac.uk

NHS Research Scotland
www.nhsresearchscotland.org.uk

2.4
Patient Or Person-Centred Healthcare

PERSON-CENTRED HEALTHCARE

The concept of patient or person-centred healthcare is important to all health and social care professionals and is integrated into healthcare policy throughout Great Britain.

Common themes are:

- Treating patients as people and as equal partners in decisions about their care
- Putting people at the centre of all decisions
- Respect for patient preferences
- Compassion, dignity and empathy
- Support for self-care, enablement, autonomy and independence
- Patient choice, control and influence
- Good communication

Examples of person-centred healthcare in practice include:

- Introducing yourself (e.g. 'Hello, my name is') and explaining your role clearly and explicitly
- Asking, rather than telling, people to do something
- Helping people to make informed choices
- Ensuring people feel able to speak openly about their experiences of taking or not taking medicines; their views about what medicines mean to them, and how medicines impact on their daily life (this includes any complaints or concerns they have about their medicines/ services received)
- Involving people in decisions about their medicines and self-care

- Being aware of how different aspects of medicine-taking – e.g. quantity, formulation, timing, patient beliefs – impact the individual
- Listening to people when they raise concerns about their medicines/treatment or that of a relative

BEING CULTURALLY INFORMED

In order to provide good care to all patients, you need to be aware of the implications of culture – both for yourself and the patient.

We are all products of our own culture, and this influences the way we see the world, the way we interact with others, and the choices we make. Each person will usually be a member of several groups, all of which have their own culture, for example:

- Age
- Gender
- Ethnicity
- Sexual orientation
- Nationality
- Religion
- Social class
- Profession

Most people will not be fully conversant with the details of every culture they come across, but there are some general pointers which will help you in interacting with people who are in different cultural groups to yourself:

- Check how a person would like to be addressed:
  - Some cultures put the given name after the family name, so you may inadvertently pick the wrong one
  - Some people prefer more formality, e.g. Mr Smith rather than Mike, or even Michael
  - A transgender person may prefer to be addressed by a name that is not on their official documentation (and so may anyone else)
- Create a welcoming environment for people from multiple cultures:
  - Display health information or other information intended for patients from multiple cultures (e.g. medication and fasting in Ramadan, LGBTQ health)

- Display your equality/diversity policy/statement
- Try not to make unwarranted assumptions:
  - Don't assume 'married' or 'single' – '[civil] partnered' is an option for all gender combinations, and an option for 'other' is generally useful
  - Don't assume that membership of a particular cultural group means that a person conforms to all the norms of that group
  - Don't assume that everyone's priorities are the same as yours would be in the same situation
- Ask open questions to give people the opportunity to tell you anything they think you need to know.
  - "Is there anything else you think I need to know?
- Be patient:
  - If a person is a member of a group which has experienced discrimination, they may be less open until they know that they can trust you
  - Being culturally informed goes both ways. When interacting with a person who is a member of a different culture, there is the potential for misunderstanding in both directions: be as understanding if the other person makes a mistake as you would hope that they would be for you.

Remember, if it is apparent that you are making an effort to help them to feel comfortable, most people will be understanding if you make a mistake.

FURTHER READING

Royal Pharmaceutical Society
Your care, your medicines: Pharmacy at the heart of patient-centred care.
www.rpharms.com

General Pharmaceutical Council
Standards for pharmacy professionals.
(See Standard 1.) 2017.
www.pharmacyregulation.org
(see MEP Appendix 1)

General Pharmaceutical Council
Guidance on maintaining clear sexual boundaries. 2020.
www.pharmacyregulation.org

General Pharmaceutical Council
Guidance on religion, personal values and beliefs. 2017.
www.pharmacyregulation.org

Government Equalities Office
LGBT Action Plan 2018: Improving the lives of Lesbian, Gay, Bisexual and Transgender people.
www.gov.uk

Health Foundation
Person-centred care made simple: What everyone should know about person-centred care. 2014.
www.health.org.uk

National Voices
Person-centred care in 2017: Evidence from service users.
www.nationalvoices.org.uk

NHS England
Developing patient-centred care.
www.england.nhs.uk

NHS Scotland
Person-centred care.
www.gov.scot

LGBT Foundation
Pride in Practice.
www.lgbt.foundation

NHS Wales
Person Centred Care.
www.wales.nhs.uk

2.5
Patient Safety

2.5.1
GETTING THE CULTURE RIGHT

We know that it is important for the profession to get the culture right. There have been infamous examples across industries and organisations of the problems caused by the wrong culture, including within the banking industry, the media and within healthcare. The wrong type of culture contributed to the unacceptable failings at Mid-Staffordshire NHS Foundation Trust hospital between 2005 and 2008, those at Orchid View care home and also the abuse at Winterbourne View private hospital.

The types of culture which collectively help us to achieve patient-centred, safe and effective care together with professional empowerment are interlinked and include a culture that is based upon the principles and values of fairness, quality, safety, transparency, learning and reporting.

Underpinning getting the culture right is a 'just culture'. This is a culture based upon fairness and is achieved when attitudes, behaviours and practices are fair.

PROBLEMS WITH A PUNITIVE CULTURE

A **punitive culture** is based upon assigning blame and punishment. It contributes to creating a culture of fear. People and organisations see what happens to others and if what they see is perceived to be draconian or unjust, this leads to fear, stifling reporting and stifling the raising of concerns. We lose the opportunity to learn, and patient safety is

affected. A single instance of perceived punitive action can have a wide effect on how large groups of people choose to act.

Punitive culture:
punishment

↓

Stifles reporting
and learning

↓

Reduction in patient safety and
quality of care

WHY A NO-BLAME CULTURE IS INADEQUATE

A **no-blame culture** may not be better than a punitive culture. It can breed complacency or nonchalance which can also impact upon patient safety. At its worst it can appear unacceptable to society overall due to the immunity from accountability which can also be abused.

For example, there is a perception that at times diplomatic immunity can be unfair and abused.

No blame culture:
blanket immunity

↓

Lack of
accountability

↓

Not acceptable to society. Unfair

THE 'RIGHT CULTURE'

Instead, the **'right culture'** or a **'just culture'** is needed which is a culture based upon the principles of fairness, quality, transparency, reporting, learning and safety. A just culture promotes an open culture (transparency and discussion), a reporting culture (raising concerns), and a learning culture (learning from mistakes).

These cultures support each other to create a **safety culture** – balancing accountability and learning and leading to improved patient safety. It also creates a just and open working environment which is rewarding to work in, fosters professional empowerment, and enhances the quality of service to patients and the patient experience.

```
Just culture: right culture

        ↓

    Open culture;
   reporting culture;
   learning culture

        ↓

 Safety and quality culture;
    balanced accountability
       and learning

        ↓

 Fair working environment,
 improved patient experience,
   improved patient safety
    and quality of care
```

Why do we need a just culture?

When applied to the provision of healthcare and pharmacy services, a just culture means removing fears, increasing sharing and reporting of concerns, being able to learn from mistakes or incidents, being able to share lessons learnt (throughout the profession where appropriate) and using this shared learning to reduce the likelihood of similar mistakes and incidents happening again. This is a vital component contributing to better patient safety. When a mistake or incident occurs, we all want assurances that actions are being taken so that it will never happen again and that there will be fair accountability. It is not possible to stop errors occurring, however, a just culture will contribute to a system that improves continuously which should in time result in fewer errors.

How to achieve a just culture

The journey to achieving the right culture requires the embedding of just culture principles into attitudes, behaviours and practices, and the design of legislation, regulation, standards, policies and systems.

It requires commitment by all stakeholders to apply and 'live' the culture routinely, through all activities and all interfaces and for this to be habitual. It is a continuous and evolving movement and may take years to achieve, but one to which the RPS and others are committed. Policies and procedures for a just and safe culture are simply words on paper if they are not 'lived' in actions and interactions. We all have responsibilities for living the culture and

embedding the habit. Individuals and organisations can do this through strong leadership and educating people about a just and safe culture appreciating when it is in action through reflection, through benchmarking and through commitment of time.

CULTURE AND PATIENT SAFETY INCIDENTS

Patient safety can be improved by the reporting of concerns and learning from incidents. The reporting of concerns will only take place if individuals feel they will not be victimised and that it is 'safe' to report these concerns. To provide assurance and confidence, everybody needs to know where they stand.

The airline industry has been embedding just culture principles into its practices for decades to improve safety. Adapting from what the airline industry has learnt, together with consideration of similar workstreams within the NHS, we believe in the following just culture principles for patient safety incidents:

1   Patient safety is paramount

2   Deliberate harm and unacceptable risk impacting on patient safety must not be tolerated

3   Patient safety is maintained by healthcare professionals being candid and raising concerns and learning from incidents to improve systems, standards, policies, legislation and people

4   To ensure that concerns will be raised and learning from incidents occurs, individual accountability must always be fair and proportionate, and viewed in the context of root cause, system deficiencies, mitigating circumstances and the entirety of contributing factors (i.e. the whole picture).

The NHS has developed an incident decision tree (see Diagram 5) based upon the work of Professor James Reason, an expert on patient safety. This decision-making tool embodies just culture principles and uses a series of tests to decide on the appropriate course of action following an incident.

Based on the NHS Improvement Just Culture Guide.

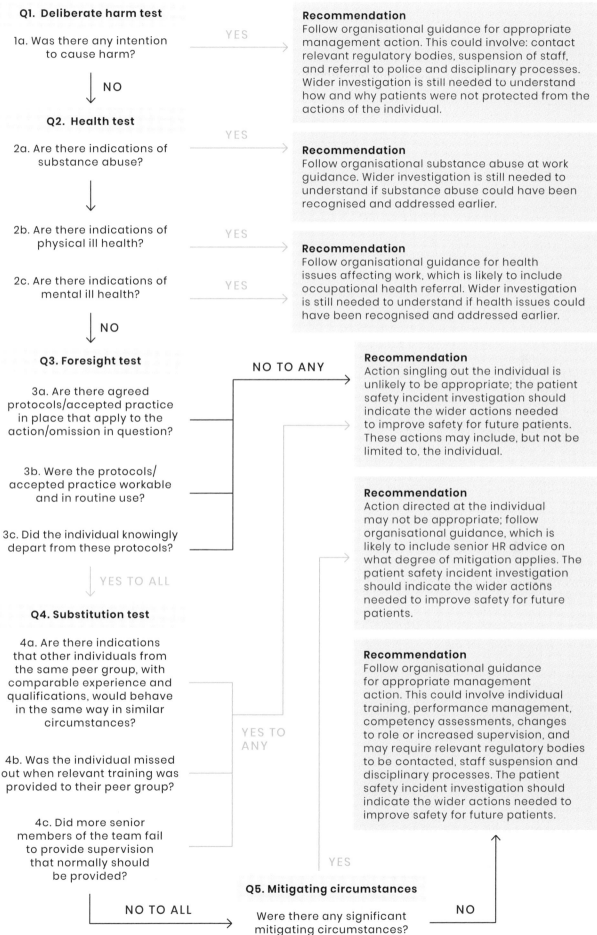

Q1. Deliberate harm test

1a. Was there any intention to cause harm?

YES →

Recommendation
Follow organisational guidance for appropriate management action. This could involve: contact relevant regulatory bodies, suspension of staff, and referral to police and disciplinary processes. Wider investigation is still needed to understand how and why patients were not protected from the actions of the individual.

↓ NO

Q2. Health test

2a. Are there indications of substance abuse?

YES →

Recommendation
Follow organisational substance abuse at work guidance. Wider investigation is still needed to understand if substance abuse could have been recognised and addressed earlier.

2b. Are there indications of physical ill health?

YES →

Recommendation
Follow organisational guidance for health issues affecting work, which is likely to include occupational health referral. Wider investigation is still needed to understand if health issues could have been recognised and addressed earlier.

2c. Are there indications of mental ill health?

YES →

↓ NO

Q3. Foresight test

NO TO ANY →

3a. Are there agreed protocols/accepted practice in place that apply to the action/omission in question?

Recommendation
Action singling out the individual is unlikely to be appropriate; the patient safety incident investigation should indicate the wider actions needed to improve safety for future patients. These actions may include, but not be limited to, the individual.

3b. Were the protocols/accepted practice workable and in routine use?

3c. Did the individual knowingly depart from these protocols?

YES TO ALL ↓

Recommendation
Action directed at the individual may not be appropriate; follow organisational guidance, which is likely to include senior HR advice on what degree of mitigation applies. The patient safety incident investigation should indicate the wider actions needed to improve safety for future patients.

Q4. Substitution test

4a. Are there indications that other individuals from the same peer group, with comparable experience and qualifications, would behave in the same way in similar circumstances?

4b. Was the individual missed out when relevant training was provided to their peer group?

4c. Did more senior members of the team fail to provide supervision that normally should be provided?

YES TO ANY

Recommendation
Follow organisational guidance for appropriate management action. This could involve individual training, performance management, competency assessments, changes to role or increased supervision, and may require relevant regulatory bodies to be contacted, staff suspension and disciplinary processes. The patient safety incident investigation should indicate the wider actions needed to improve safety for future patients.

NO TO ALL →

YES

Q5. Mitigating circumstances

Were there any significant mitigating circumstances?

NO

2

2.5.3
REPORTING ADVERSE EVENTS

We encourage, as a matter of best practice, the reporting of suspected adverse drug reactions under the Yellow Card scheme. Following a discussion with the patient, it may also be appropriate to make a record in the patient's notes and to notify the prescriber.

Adverse events can be reported online via the MHRA website: www.gov.uk; alternatively, a tear-out paper copy is available at the back of the BNF. A Yellow Card mobile app is also available through which side effects to medicines can be reported. The app also enables users to receive news updates from the MHRA.

The following examples highlight the value of the Yellow Card Scheme and the importance of reporting suspected adverse events in this way:

- Warnings were added to the product information for varenicline after the MHRA received reports of suicidal ideation via the scheme and the Yellow Card

- Reporting of adverse reactions to rimonabant (which was formerly used to treat obesity) contributed to the drug being withdrawn as new evidence meant the risks were considered to outweigh any benefits.

If a suspected adverse drug reaction (SADR) is related to a veterinary medicine which has affected a human and/or an animal, refer to section 3.5.

COVID-19 YELLOW CARD REPORTING

A coronavirus yellow card reporting site coronavirus-yellowcard.mhra.gov.uk is dedicated to reporting any suspected side effects from medicines, vaccines and adverse incidents involving medical equipment (including ventilators or testing kits) relating to COVID-19 treatment. There is also a dedicated phone line to specifically report ventilators and respiratory support.

ERROR REPORTING STANDARDS

In collaboration with the Pharmacy Forum of Northern Ireland and the Association of Pharmacy Technicians UK, the RPS has published *Professional standards for the reporting, learning, sharing, taking action and review of incidents*. The standards are supplemented by an explanation of how pharmacy services protect patients, the link with patient safety, practical aspects and barriers to reporting, sharing, learning, taking action and review.

Diagram 6:
RPS error reporting standards

Standard 1 Open and honest	Be honest and open when things go wrong
Standard 2 Report	Report patient safety incidents to the appropriate local or national reporting programme
Standard 3 Learn	Investigate and learn from all incidents including those that cause harm and those that are 'no harm' or 'near miss'
Standard 4 Share	Share what you have learnt to make local or national systems of care
Standard 5 Act	Take action to change practice or improve local or national systems of care
Standard 6 Review	Review changes to practice

NATIONAL REPORTING AND LEARNING SYSTEM (NRLS)

From June 2012 the key functions for patient safety developed by the National Patient Safety Agency (NPSA) were transferred to the NHS Commissioning Board Special Health Authority – the National Reporting and Learning System (NRLS). The NPSA website continues to offer key information, guidance, tools and alerts. Healthcare organisations in England and Wales should report patient safety incidents to the NRLS (www.england.nhs.uk). The NRLS does not seek to collect identifiable information relating to staff and patients involved in an incident and so reporting is anonymous for the reporter, staff and patients.

In Scotland each NHS Board operates its own reporting system.

NEAR MISS ERRORS

Regular review of near miss errors (sometimes referred to as 'good catches') and action taken can prevent similar mistakes from happening in the future. The RPS has produced tools and guidance to help support clinical governance in pharmacy, and to promote an open culture of recording of near miss errors so that all pharmacy staff can reflect and learn from them. The *Near Miss Error Log and Near Miss Error Improvement Tool*, along with supporting guidance are available from the RPS.

FURTHER READING

Royal Pharmaceutical Society
Clinical governance.
www.rpharms.com

Royal Pharmaceutical Society
Leadership development framework and accompanying handbook.
www.rpharms.com

Royal Pharmaceutical Society
Near miss errors.
www.rpharms.com

Royal Pharmaceutical Society
Professional standards for the reporting, learning, sharing, taking action and review of incidents.
www.rpharms.com

Royal Pharmaceutical Society
Raising concerns.
www.rpharms.com

Care Quality Commission
Opening the door to change: NHS safety culture and the need for transformation. 2018.
www.cqc.org.uk

General Pharmaceutical Council
In practice: Guidance on raising concerns. 2017.
www.pharmacyregulation.org
(see MEP Appendix 5)

NHS Employers
Safety culture.
www.nhsemployers.org

NHS England
A just culture guide.
www.england.nhs.uk

2.5.4
RISK MANAGEMENT

Risk management is a topic covered extensively elsewhere (see 'Further reading') and whilst we don't want to duplicate existing resources, it's important here to acknowledge that managing risks and risk assessments are key to ensuring patient and employee safety.

Risk management in pharmacy practice is essential as part of effective governance. Indeed, all pharmacy professionals are required to 'assess the risks in the care they provide and do everything they can to keep these risks as low as possible' (see GPhC Standards for Pharmacy Professionals www.pharmacyregulation.org or Appendix 1).

The GPhC describes risk management in the context of registered pharmacies as:

- Having the necessary systems, processes and skilled staff in place to minimise the likelihood of providing poor quality care

- Having mechanisms to learn from situations where, despite having those systems something has gone wrong

- Identifying and minimising the potential for harm or adverse health outcomes if something goes wrong as a result of a pharmacy's activities and services

Risk assessments do not have to be complex or done in a formal way. Every time you cross the road, you conduct a risk assessment ("Is it safe? Can I reduce the risk by waiting, or by using a pelican/zebra crossing?"). Likewise, every time you exercise your professional judgement and decide to do this instead of that, you have probably conducted a very fast risk assessment without realising it.

Although you can do a risk assessment in your head, at the time you need it, for some situations – for instance, hazards where the risk of harm is great, or frequent, or applies to several people – it is better to do a formal risk assessment and write down what you find. A risk assessment is often apart of a Standard Operating Procedure, when it is important that everyone follows the same procedure to avoid or reduce the risk of a particular adverse outcome occurring.

When making a risk assessment factors to consider include:

- Hazards – this could be a substance or a process that could cause harm such as handling cytotoxic medicines; mixing up medicines packed in similar looking packages or with similar names; temperature control of medicines, storage areas, etc.

- The risk. This is how likely harm is to take place. Is it very likely indeed (e.g. mixing up two similarly-packaged medicines with similar names placed side-by-side on the shelf) or not likely (e.g. harm coming to staff when handling blister-packed cytotoxic medicines)?

- The degree of harm likely. Is the harm likely to be only minor, or severe? Is it short-lasting or permanent?

- Who may be harmed – e.g. employees / self-employed, service users, patients, customers, visitors, etc

- Any preventative measures to reduce or eliminate the risk – e.g. colour coding systems; protective equipment. It is important to remember that you do not always need to eliminate a risk, just reduce it to a reasonable level. Sometimes trying to eliminate risk entirely does more harm than good, as it might prevent you doing an important task.

- Record the outcome – e.g. in standard operating procedures

- Monitor and review – was the hazard avoided? Could the risk be reduced further? Did the procedure work the way you hoped, or does it need to be adjusted? Has an incident occurred?

FURTHER READING

General Pharmaceutical Council
Standards for Pharmacy Professionals
www.pharmacyregulation.org

General Pharmaceutical Council
Focus on Risk Management in Pharmacy
www.pharmacyregulation.org

Health and Safety Executive
Managing Risks and Risk assessment at work
www.hse.gov.uk

NHS England
Suggested Guidance for Community Pharmacy Teams: Coronavirus (COVID-19) Risk Assessment (June 2020)
www.england.nhs.uk

Health and Safety Executive
Sample risk assessment template (HSE):
www.hse.gov.uk

Pharmaceutical Journal
How to deal with Risks in your Practice
www.pharmaceutical-journal.com

Pharmaceutical Journal
Reducing Risk and managing dispensing errors
www.pharmaceutical-journal.com

2.5.5
HANDLING DISPENSING ERRORS

Professionalism and a culture of candour are vital for patient safety, this is why it is important that pharmacists report, learn, share, act and review instances when there has been dispensing errors or near misses. Pharmacists report various reasons why they find it difficult to report and learn from mistakes. It is estimated that 20% of under reporting is because of fear of prosecution.

Whether you are the person who made the error or another member of the pharmacy team, once you become aware, you need to promptly take all reasonable steps to let the patient know and to make things right, unless the circumstances mean it is not necessary or appropriate to. Keeping records can also help to justify your decision.

1   Take steps to let the patient know promptly

2   Make things right (this may involve contacting the prescriber)

3   Offer an apology

4   Let colleagues involved in the error know.

Use the steps from the RPS error reporting standards illustrated in Diagram 7 below:

Diagram 7:
RSLAR wheel

RSLAR wheel reproduced with the permission of the Community Pharmacy Patient Safety Group.

LEGAL DEFENCES

Legislation introducing a legal defence to prevent the automatic criminalisation of inadvertent dispensing errors *The Pharmacy (Preparation and Dispensing Errors – Registered Pharmacies) Order 2018* came into force on the 16th April 2018. It is hoped this will reduce the risk of prosecution in the profession, leading to a professional increase in the reporting of dispensing errors, the learning from which could prevent the same error occurring in the future. The sharing and review of data from dispensing error reporting will result in improvements to patient safety across the healthcare system.

The legal defence against criminal prosecution can be used when the error has been:

1   Dispensed in a registered pharmacy, **and**

2   Dispensed by or under the supervision of a registered pharmacist, **and**

3   Supplied against a prescription, PGD or direction from a prescriber, **and**

4   Promptly notified to the patient once the pharmacy team are aware of the error

FURTHER READING

Royal Pharmaceutical Society
Near miss errors.
www.rpharms.com

Royal Pharmaceutical Society
Professional standards for the reporting, learning, sharing, taking action and review of incidents.
www.rpharms.com

General Pharmaceutical Council
Joint statement on professional duty of candour.
www.pharmacyregulation.org

General Pharmaceutical Council
Standards for pharmacy professionals.
(See Standard 8.) 2017.
www.pharmacyregulation.org
(see MEP Appendix 1)

NHS England
NHS Patient Safety Strategy
www.england.nhs.uk

Pharmacy (Preparation and Dispensing Errors – Registered Pharmacies) Order 2018
www.legislation.gov.uk

2

SAFEGUARDING

PROTECTING CHILDREN AND YOUNG PEOPLE

You have a professional, legal and moral duty to protect children from abuse or neglect and to work with other organisations and authorities to safeguard children. The following points (Table 1) may help with recognising signs of abuse or neglect; however, the list is not exhaustive and a series of minor factors could also be indicative of child abuse or neglect:

If child abuse is suspected, you should follow local child protection procedures where these are available. If not, the process outlined in Diagram 8 may be useful.

Where you consider the nature of the child abuse to be an emergency then the police should be contacted.

Otherwise make a decision on next steps such as referring to local Social Services where appropriate or taking further advice. You should feel comfortable with sharing concerns and suspicions of abuse, even where these are not proven facts with Social Services.

You should not attempt to investigate suspicions or allegations of abuse directly.

You should make appropriate records of concerns and suspicions, decisions taken, and reasons whether or not further action was taken on a particular occasion.

Table 1:
Children and young adults – signs of abuse or neglect

Children and young adults – signs of abuse or neglect	
Physical abuse	Unusual/unexplained injuries, injuries in inaccessible places, bite marks, scalds, fingertip bruising, fractures, repeated injuries, age of injuries inconsistent with account given by adult, injuries blamed on siblings
Neglect	Poor growth and weight. Poor hygiene, dirty and messy. Inappropriate food or drink
Emotional abuse	Evidence of self-harm/self mutilation, behavioural problems, inappropriate verbal abuse, fear of adults or a certain adult
Sexual abuse	Indication of sexually transmitted disease, evidence of sexual activity or relationship that is inappropriate to the child's age or competence
Additional signs	Parent/carer delays seeking medical treatment or advice and/or reluctant to allow treatment, detachment from the child, lacks concern at the severity or extent of injury, reluctant to give information, aggressive towards child or children

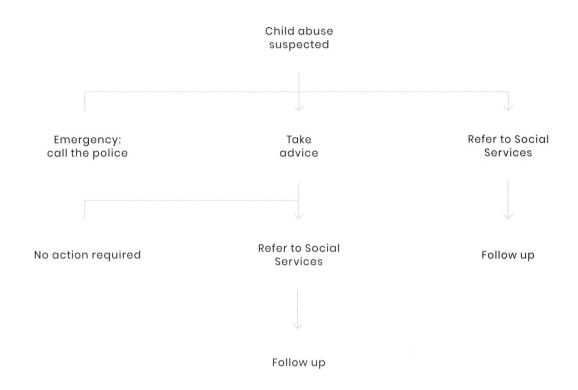

SEXUAL ACTIVITY IN CHILDREN

Children under the age of 13 are legally too young to consent to any sexual activity. Instances should be treated seriously with a presumption that the case should be reported to Social Services, unless there are exceptional circumstances backed by documented reasons for not sharing information.

Sexual activity with children under the age of 16 is also an offence but may be consensual. The law is not intended to prosecute mutually agreed sexual activity between young people of a similar age, unless it involves abuse or exploitation.

You can provide contraception (e.g. on prescription or under PGD) or sexual health advice to a child or young person under 16 as long as, in England and Wales, the Fraser criteria are met, i.e. that:

- They have sufficient maturity and intelligence to understand the nature and implications of the proposed treatment
- They cannot be persuaded to tell her parents or to allow the practitioner to tell them
- They are very likely to begin or continue having sexual intercourse with or without contraceptive treatment

- Their physical or mental health is likely to suffer unless they receive the advice or treatment
- The advice or treatment is in the young person's best interests.

In Scotland, the Age of Legal Capacity Act applies similar criteria.

The general duty of patient confidentiality still applies, so consent should be sought whenever possible prior to disclosing patient information.

This duty is not absolute and information may be shared if you judge on a case-by-case basis that sharing is in the child's best interest (e.g. to prevent harm to the child or where the child's welfare overrides the need to keep information confidential).

Remember that it is possible to seek advice from experts without disclosing identifiable details of a child and breaking patient confidentiality – and that where there is a decision to share information, this should be proportionate.

FURTHER READING

Royal Pharmaceutical Society
Protecting children and young people.
www.rpharms.com

Children's Society
Safeguarding children, young people and adults at risk of abuse: Policy and Procedure.
www.childrenssociety.org.uk

General Pharmaceutical Council
Female genital mutilation: Mandatory duty for pharmacy professionals to report.
www.pharmacyregulation.org

NHS England
Safeguarding.
www.england.nhs.uk

PROTECTING VULNERABLE ADULTS

You have a professional, social and moral duty to protect vulnerable adults from abuse or neglect and to work with other organisations and authorities to safeguard vulnerable adults.

The vulnerable adult's wishes should be taken into account at all times as a key issue is patient consent. Vulnerable adults are persons who are over the age of 18 and are at a greater risk of abuse or neglect.

Note that any person, including those who do not fall within the groups below, could be a vulnerable adult. There are various types of abuse or neglect and while the following lists may be helpful but are not exhaustive. The presence of one or more of these signs may not necessarily be caused by abuse or neglect.

They may fall into one of the following groups:

- Suffers from mental or physical disability
- Has learning difficulties
- Is frail or elderly
- Is in an abusive relationship
- Is a substance misuser.

Possible signs of abuse or neglect in vulnerable adults are shown in Table 2.

Local procedures may be available from your employer, the NHS trust, Health Board or local council, and you should follow these procedures where available when abuse or neglect is suspected.

The process outlined in Diagram 9 may also be useful.

Table 2:
Vulnerable adults – signs of abuse or neglect

Vulnerable adults – signs of abuse or neglect	
Physical abuse	Injuries which are unusual or unexplained. Bite marks, scalds, fingertip bruising, fractures. Repeated injury
Neglect	Failure to thrive – evidence of malnourishment. Poor hygiene, dirty and messy
Emotional abuse	Evidence of self-harm/self-mutilation. Inappropriate verbal abuse. Fear of certain people
Sexual abuse	Indication of sexually transmitted disease. Repeated requests for emergency hormonal contraception
Financial abuse	Sudden changes to their finances, e.g. getting into debt. Inappropriate, exploitative or excessive control over the finances of the vulnerable adult
Additional signs	Delays seeking medical treatment or advice and/ or reluctant to allow treatment of the vulnerable adult. Detachment from the vulnerable adult. Lacks concern at the severity or extent of injury or other signs. Is reluctant to give information. Aggressive towards the vulnerable adult.

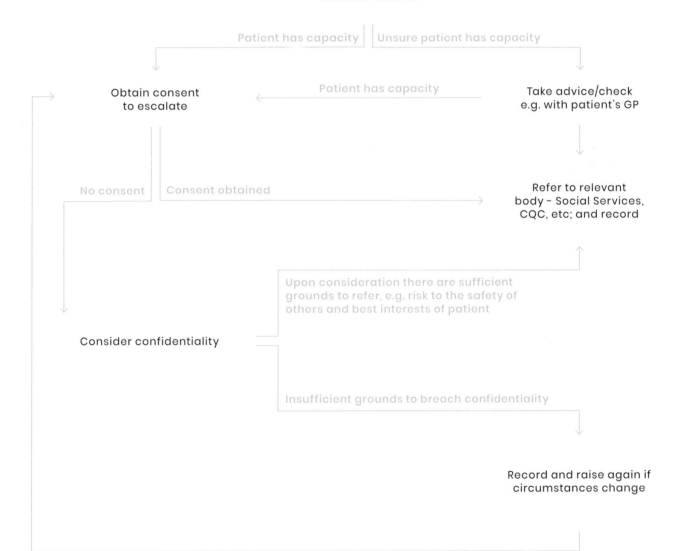

Abuse or neglect of
a vulnerable adult suspected

In an emergency situation - take immediate action to ensure the safety
of the individual or others (e.g. contact police or emergency services)

Consider consent

Patient has capacity | Unsure patient has capacity

Obtain consent
to escalate

Patient has capacity

Take advice/check
e.g. with patient's GP

No consent | Consent obtained

Refer to relevant
body - Social Services,
CQC, etc; and record

Upon consideration there are sufficient
grounds to refer, e.g. risk to the safety of
others and best interests of patient

Consider confidentiality

Insufficient grounds to breach confidentiality

Record and raise again if
circumstances change

A vulnerable adult's wishes should be taken into account at all times. Obtain consent from the patient before disclosing confidential information about them. However, if there are overriding circumstances requiring you to take immediate action to ensure the safety of the individual or others the need for referral, even if they do not give consent, should be considered. If you are unsure of someone's mental capacity to provide consent seek additional advice, e.g. from their GP.

You should not attempt to investigate suspicions or allegations of abuse directly or to discuss concerns with the alleged perpetrator of the abuse or neglect.

You should make appropriate records of concerns and suspicions, decisions taken and reasons whether or not further action was taken on a particular occasion.

FURTHER READING

Royal Pharmaceutical Society
Protecting vulnerable adults.
www.rpharms.com

Care Information Scotland
Adult support and protection.
www.careinfoscotland.scot

Department of Health and Social Care
Mental Health Act 1983: Code of practice. 2015.
www.gov.uk

NHS England
Abuse and neglect of vulnerable adults.
www.nhs.uk

NHS Wales
Welsh Government - Mental Health Act 1983: Code of Practice for Wales Review
www.gov.wales

Office of the Public Guardian
Safeguarding policy.
www.gov.uk

Public Health Wales
National Safeguarding team (NHS Wales): safeguarding adults.
www.phw.nhs.wales

2.6
Pharmaceutical Care

2.6.1
DEVELOPMENT OF PHARMACEUTICAL CARE

Pharmaceutical care was defined by Hepler and Strand in 1990 as "the responsible provision of drug therapy for the purpose of achieving definite outcomes that improve a patient's quality of life". Since the 1990's the definition has developed further and rather than being focussed on processes, systems, now focusses on patient outcomes. The Primary Care Network Europe (PCNE) defines it as "the pharmacist's contribution in the care of individuals in order to optimise medicines and improve health outcomes". This definition recognises that pharmaceutical care is done as part of a multi-disciplinary team and empowers the patient, through shared decision making, to make the most of their medicines.

Pharmaceutical care is an essential part of many of the regular day-to-day activities of pharmacists. Diagram 10 illustrates how improved patient outcomes drive the various aspects of pharmaceutical care.

PRINCIPLES OF PHARMACEUTICAL CARE

Pharmaceutical care is a person-centred philosophy and practice that aims to optimise the benefits of drug therapy and minimise the risk of drug therapy to patients by providing the framework for pharmacists to apply their knowledge and skills. The pharmacist will assess the pharmaceutical needs of patients and take responsibility for meeting those needs in collaboration with other health and social care professionals.

Key components are:

- The patient assessment to identify unmet pharmaceutical care needs and issues

- The development of a pharmaceutical care plan to document the needs identified

- To agree patient outcomes, the actions required or taken and the follow-up required.

Pharmaceutical care is embedded within undergraduate and postgraduate education, the community pharmacy contractual framework and clinical pharmacy services including pharmacist prescribing.

In practice, the assessment will identify any pharmaceutical care issues with concordance and sets out to establish within the available information:

- If the drug therapy and dose is appropriate for the condition in this patient

- If any additional therapy (drug and non-pharmacological) is required

- If the drug therapy and dose is safe

- If the person is suffering from any avoidable side effects

- If the drug therapy, dose and non-pharmacological therapy are effective and achieving a defined desired outcome.

It is a holistic philosophy and practice that will also identify and address the following needs: public health, educational, medicines management, non-pharmacological management and changes in clinical need.

NATIONAL POLICY

Pharmaceutical care has become the cornerstone of national policy and practice in each of the home countries. Links are provided below for information on the national priorities; but bear in mind, the principles of pharmaceutical care are equally valid in all the home countries regardless of the terminology used.

ENGLAND

NHS England
Medicines optimisation hub.
www.england.nhs.uk

SCOTLAND

Community Pharmacy Scotland
Medicines Care and Review Service.
www.cps.scot

Scottish Government
Achieving excellence in pharmaceutical care: A strategy for Scotland, Aug 2017.
www.gov.scot

WALES

Welsh Pharmaceutical Committee
Pharmacy: Delivering a healthier Wales. 2019.
www.rpharms.com

Royal Pharmaceutical Society
Your care, your medicines: Pharmacy at the heart of patient-centred care.
www.rpharms.com

2.6.3
MEDICINES OPTIMISATION

Medicines optimisation looks at how people use medicines and acknowledges that the way people use medicines over time may change. It may involve stopping some medicines as well as starting others and considers opportunities for lifestyle changes and non-medical therapies to reduce the need for medicines. Ultimately, medicines optimisation can help encourage people to take ownership of their treatment.

The goal is to help patients to:

- Improve their outcomes
- Take their medicines correctly
- Improve adherence
- Avoid taking unnecessary medicines
- Reduce wastage of medicines
- Improve medicines and patient safety.

FOUR PRINCIPLES OF MEDICINES OPTIMISATION

There are four principles of medicines optimisation. To ensure a patient-centred approach these principles are measured and monitored to ensure improved patient outcomes. (See Diagram 11 below.)

Diagram 11:
Four principles of medicines optimisation

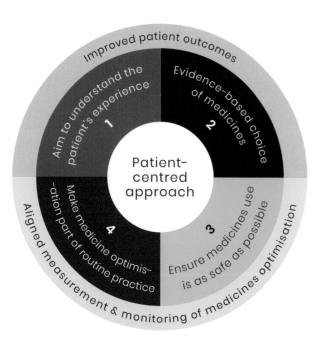

PRINCIPLE 1: AIM TO UNDERSTAND THE PATIENT'S EXPERIENCE

To ensure the best possible outcomes from medicines, there is an ongoing, open dialogue with the patient and/or their carer about the patient's choice and experience of using medicines to manage their condition; recognising that the patient's experience may change over time even if the medicines do not.

PRINCIPLE 2: EVIDENCE-BASED CHOICE OF MEDICINES

Ensure that the most appropriate choice of clinically and cost-effective medicines (informed by the best available evidence base) are made which can best meet the needs of the patient.

PRINCIPLE 3: ENSURE MEDICINES USE IS AS SAFE AS POSSIBLE

The safe use of medicines is the responsibility of all professionals, healthcare organisations and patients, and should be discussed with patients and/or their carers. Safety covers all aspects of medicines usage, including unwanted effects, interactions, safe processes and systems, and effective communication between professionals.

PRINCIPLE 4: MAKE MEDICINES OPTIMISATION PART OF ROUTINE PRACTICE

Health professionals routinely discuss with each other and with patients and/or their carers how to get the best outcomes from medicines throughout the patient's care.

FURTHER READING

Royal Pharmaceutical Society
Helping patients to make the most of medicines.
www.rpharms.com

Royal Pharmaceutical Society
Medicines optimisation hub.
www.rpharms.com

Hepler CD, Strand LM
Opportunities and responsibilities in pharmaceutical care.
American Journal of Hospital Pharmacy.
March 1990, Volume 47, p533-543.
www.ncbi.nlm.nih.gov/pubmed/2316538

National Institute for Health and Care Excellence
Medicines optimisation: the safe and effective use of medicines to enable the best possible outcomes.
NICE guideline. 2015.
www.nice.org.uk

NHS England
Medicines optimisation.
www.england.nhs.uk

2.6.4
MEDICINES RECONCILIATION

Medicines reconciliation is the process of identifying an accurate list of a patient's current medicines (including over-the-counter and complementary medicines) and carrying out a comparison of these with the current list in use, recognising any discrepancies, and documenting any changes. It also takes into account the current health of the patient and any active or long-standing issues. The result is a complete list of medicines that is then accurately communicated. The pharmacist who is carrying out medicines reconciliation should ensure that any discrepancies are resolved by highlighting these and working with relevant members of the multidisciplinary team. The pharmacist should also keep the patient informed.

Medicines reconciliation should take place whenever patients are transferred from one care setting to another, when they are admitted to hospital, transferred between wards and on discharge. The way that the process is carried out will vary between care settings.

Accurate medicines reconciliation prevents medication errors and provides a foundation for assessing the appropriateness of a patient's current medicines and directing future treatment choices to ensure that the patient receive the best care. The process also allows other pharmaceutical issues such as poor adherence or non-adherence to be identified.

SOURCES OF INFORMATION

Sources of information that may be used when carrying out medicines reconciliation include:

- Patient or patient's representative
- Patient's medicines
- Repeat prescriptions
- GP referral letters
- The patient's GP surgery
- Hospital discharge summaries or outpatient appointment notes
- Community pharmacy patient medication records
- Care home records
- Drug treatment centre records
- Other healthcare professionals and specialist clinics

- Patient medical records where available (e.g. in prisons or the Emergency Care Summary (Scotland), Summary Care Record (England), or Welsh GP Record (see also section 2.6.5).

ARE THE SOURCES YOU USE UP-TO-DATE?

Aim to use the most complete, reliable and up-to-date source(s) of information.

CROSS-CHECK ADHERENCE

Medication histories should be cross-checked against different sources and confirmed with the patient or patient's representative. The medicines they are actually taking, and how they are taking them, may differ from written documentation (e.g. the prescribing record held by the patient's GP).

NON-DAILY MEDICINES

Remember to ask patients whether they take any medicines 'when required' (e.g. reliever inhalers), or on certain days of the week. Also remember to ask about the sorts of formulations that might be forgotten (e.g. nasal sprays, eye or ear drops, ointments, depot injections, patches, etc.). Patients may also need prompting to remember medicines such as oral contraceptives and hormone replacement therapy.

HISTORICAL MEDICINES

The medication history should not be restricted to current therapies but should include any recently stopped or changed medicines.

SELF-SELECTED MEDICINES

Include any medicinal product that the patient is taking – whether prescribed or not – and do not restrict the medication history to medicines obtained on prescription. Over-the-counter (OTC) medicines, herbal products, vitamins, dietary supplements, recreational drugs (e.g. alcohol and tobacco) and remedies purchased over the internet should also be included.

General tips for obtaining a medication history

- Explain to the patient why the history is being taken
- Use a balance of open-ended questions (e.g. what, how, why, when) with closed questions (i.e. those requiring yes/no answers)
- Avoid jargon – keep it simple
- Clarify vague responses with further questioning or by using other sources of information
- Keep the patient at ease

For each medicine, the following should be determined:

- Generic name of the drug
- Brand name of the drug, where appropriate (for example, where bioavailability variations between brands can have clinical consequences, such as lithium therapy)
- Strength of the medicine taken
- Dose – both the prescribed dose and the actual dose the patient is taking (NB: This may best be described to the patient as a quantity of tablets rather than as milligrams of active ingredient)
- Formulation used (e.g. phenytoin – 100mg as a liquid does not deliver the same dose as a 100mg tablet)
- Route of administration
- Frequency of administration – this should include the time of administration for certain medicines (e.g. levodopa)
- Length of therapy, if appropriate (e.g. for antibiotics)
- Administration device and brand for injectables (e.g. insulin)
- Day or date of administration for medicines taken on specific days of the week or month.

CLINICAL CHECK

One of the key skills of a pharmacist is to perform a clinical assessment or clinical check before medicines are prescribed, supplied or administered. Clinical checks involve identifying potential pharmacotherapeutic problems by gathering and evaluating all relevant information, including patient characteristics, disease states, medication regimen and, where possible, laboratory results.

The purpose of the clinical check is to ensure the medicine supplied is both safe and effective for use by a particular patient in relation to the risk and benefit to the patient.

Importantly, it is not a mere dose and interaction check, or a simple tick box exercise but rather a complex skill which often requires interaction with patients and healthcare professionals. A clinical check is underpinned by knowledge of human pathophysiology as well as medicines (pharmacokinetics, pharmacology, pharmaceutics, pharmacognosy) coupled with clinical experience and the rational application of professional judgement. It is a key part of clinical pharmacy contributing to patient safety and public health.

By using a structured, logical approach to a clinical check, you can balance the risks and benefits of a prescribed medicine regimen and, in doing so, improve the medicine's safety and effectiveness.

OBTAINING INFORMATION

The sources for obtaining information, and the level of detail available, will vary depending on the pharmacy setting. It may not always be practical to obtain all the information needed and sometimes, decisions will need to be made on limited information. You should consider the level of risk when deciding if further information is required from one or more additional sources.

In primary care, you may be able to obtain information from:

- The prescription
- The patient, patient's representative or carer
- The patient's GP or other healthcare professionals involved in the patient's care

- The patient's medication record
- Other patient medical records where available (e.g. in Scotland – access to the Emergency Care Summary; access to the Summary Care Record where available; in a prison – access to medical records).

In secondary care, additional sources of information available would include other healthcare professionals involved in the patient's care (e.g. dieticians, microbiologists and physiotherapists), medical and nursing care notes, additional ward charts and laboratory results.

UNDERTAKING A CLINICAL CHECK

The areas that you need to consider when undertaking a clinical check include:

- Patient characteristics
- Medication regimen
- How treatment will be administered and monitored

Further information on these areas can be seen overleaf.

In addition to the points discussed below in undertaking a clinical check, there are other issues relating to the safe and effective use of medicines which pharmacists should consider. These include, but are not limited to:

- Antimicrobial stewardship.
- Appropriate opioid prescribing.
- Review and deprescribing of medicines which are no longer appropriate or required.
- Participation in local medicines safety initiatives.

Patient characteristics	Patient type	Establish whether the patient falls into a group where treatment is contraindicated or cautioned. Specific groups of patients to be aware of include: • Children • Women who are pregnant or breastfeeding • The elderly • Certain ethnic groups – a patient's ethnic origin can affect the choice of medicine or dose (e.g. the initial and maximum dose of rosuvastatin is lower for patients of Asian origin) • For some medicines, the gender of the patient should be considered. For example, finasteride is contraindicated for women.
	Co-morbidities	Patient co-morbidities, such as renal or hepatic impairment or heart failure, can exclude the use of a particular treatment or necessitate dose adjustments.
	Patient intolerances and preferences	Other patient factors that can affect the choice of treatment include known medication adverse events (e.g. allergies), dietary intolerances (e.g. to lactose containing products), patient preferences (e.g. vegan patients may refuse products of porcine origin), religious beliefs, and patients' knowledge and understanding of medicines and why they are being taken (patient beliefs about medicines).
Medication regimen factors	Indication	Ascertain the indication for treatment to check whether the medicine prescribed is appropriate for the indication and compatible with recommended guidelines.
	Changes in regular treatment	Where there are changes in regular therapy (e.g. strength or dose), you should confirm that these are deliberate and not an error.
	Dose, frequency and strength	You should check that the dose, frequency and strength of the prescribed medicine are appropriate – having considered the patient's age, renal and hepatic function, weight (and surface area where appropriate), co-morbidities, concomitant drug treatments and lifestyle pattern.
	Formulation	Check that, for the formulation prescribed, the dose and frequency are appropriate.
	Drug compatibility	Regular and new therapies should be evaluated for any clinically significant interactions, duplications and antagonistic activity.
	Monitoring requirements	For medication or conditions that require monitoring, you should check for the latest test results and ascertain whether any dose adjustments are required.
Administration and monitoring	Route of administration	Check whether the prescribed route of administration is suitable for the patient and whether a preparation is available for the route prescribed. Also, check for compatibility issues that may arise from administering via that route (e.g. due to co-administration of food or other medicines). For example, phenytoin can interact with enteral feeds so administration via an enteral feeding tube would need to be managed accordingly.
	Aids to administration	Check whether any aids are required to support administration. For example, spacer devices, eye drop devices, Braille or large type or pictogram labels, additional information sheets or verbal information and multi-compartment compliance aids (MCAs).

RECORDING

Record keeping is important for continuity of care, evidence of the benefit of pharmacy input and improving patient care. You should make a record of significant clinical checks, and interventions made. This should include details of discussions and agreed decisions with other healthcare professionals. Depending upon the circumstances it may be appropriate to make this record in the patient's medical record, an intervention record book, handover record book or prescription register.

FURTHER READING

Royal Pharmaceutical Society
Clinical documentation for pharmacists.
www.rpharms.com

Royal Pharmaceutical Society
Improving patient outcomes through MCA.
www.rpharms.com

Royal Pharmaceutical Society
Professional guidance on the administration of medicines in healthcare settings. 2019.
www.rpharms.com

Royal Pharmaceutical Society
(Various titles re pharmacy practice and clinical aspects of pharmacy).
www.rpharms.com

General Pharmaceutical Council
Guidance on consent. 2018.
www.pharmacyregulation.org
(see MEP Appendix 4)

National Institute for Health and Care Excellence
Medicines optimisation: The safe and effective use of medicines to enable the best possible outcomes.
www.nice.org.uk

2.6.6
MEDICATION REVIEW

NICE has defined a structured medication review as 'a critical examination of a person's medicines with the objective of reaching an agreement with the person about treatment, optimising the impact of medicines, minimising the number of medication related problems and reducing waste.'

There are numerous support tools for good medication review but many of the medication review tools share common principles such as:

- Seeking the person's (and/or their carer's) perspective of their medicines and how they will take them

- Identification of the aims of the drug therapy (from a clinical perspective and from the person's perspective)

- Assessment of whether the medicines are essential or not

- Assessment of the person's level of adherence to the medicines

- Assessment of the effectiveness (both clinical and cost effectiveness) of the medicines

- Assessment of the safety of the medicines, and

- Decision and actions regarding stopping or continuing the medicines.

2

Triggers for a structured medication review

Proactive	Reactive	Reactive	Reactive
Polypharmacy data tool or similar identifies person as being potentially 'at risk' or as being 'at risk from harm' from multiple medicines.	Crisis or incident such as admission to hospital should be explored to see if polypharmacy is a contributory factor. Consider also if carer becomes poorly then medication issues may become acute for the person they care for.	Person highlights concern about the growing number of medicines they are being asked to take.	Health care professional or healthcare worker highlights concern about the growing number of medicines a person is trying to manage.

Holistic, structured medication review should aim to:

- Identify and discuss the person's goals
- Identify and discuss any adherence issues
- Identify and assess medicines with potential risks to cause harm
- Identify and assess the use of any unnecessary medicines
- Agree with the person the actions to be taken regarding medicines, including stopping
- Share any decisions with the person, their carers, healthcare professionals, pharmacist
- Review and adjust as needed or refer if required

Healthcare professionals to ensure they are skilled in good consultations and share decision making

Adapted from: Patient-centred management of polypharmacy: a decision process for practice: ejhp.bmj.com/content/23/2/113.full

POLYPHARMACY

Polypharmacy is a term used to describe the situation when people are taking a number of medicines. More people are taking more medicines than ever, and this trend is likely to continue as people are now living longer with multiple conditions. For example:

- A person may be taking medicines that are no longer suitable or the best available for them
- The benefit of a particular medicine is lower than its possible harm
- Sometimes taking a combination of medicines has the potential to harm, or actually cause harm
- The practicalities of using the medicines are no longer manageable or are causing harm or distress.

Sometimes however, polypharmacy is necessary – stopping medicines, or deprescribing, is not always appropriate. The evidence base to support prescribers in stopping medicines safely is small and peoples' attitudes to medicines being stopped can be a challenge to healthcare professionals.

The RPS has published guidance on polypharmacy for pharmacists and all healthcare organisations involved with medicines. It provides a summary of the scale and complexity of the issue of polypharmacy. It outlines how healthcare professionals, patients and carers can find solutions when polypharmacy causes problems for patients and points to useful resources that can help. It recommends that all healthcare organisations have systems in place to ensure people taking multiple medicines (especially those taking 10 or more) can be identified and highlighted as requiring a comprehensive medication review with a pharmacist.

The benefits of such reviews include:

- A reduction in problematic polypharmacy
- Improved health
- Patients more likely to take their medicines
- Fewer wasted medicines.

FURTHER READING

Royal Pharmaceutical Society
Medicines adherence.
www.rpharms.com

Royal Pharmaceutical Society
Polypharmacy: Getting our medicines right.
www.rpharms.com

Care Quality Commission
Medicines reconciliation and medication review.
www.cqc.org.uk

NHS Scotland
Polypharmacy: Manage medicines.
managemeds.scot.nhs.uk

National Institute for Health and Care Excellence
Medicines adherence: Involving patients in decisions about prescribed medicines and supporting adherence. Clinical guideline. 2009 (reviewed 2019).
www.nice.org.uk

PrescQIPP
Ensuring appropriate polypharmacy: A practical guide to deprescribing. 2017.
www.prescqipp.info

Specialist Pharmacy Service.
English Deprescribing Network. 2019.
www.sps.nhs.uk

Specialist Pharmacy Service.
Polypharmacy, oligopharmacy and deprescribing: resources to support local delivery. 2017.
www.sps.nhs.uk

2

PATIENT CONSULTATIONS

A pharmacist consultation is any discussion of a professional nature between a pharmacist and a patient and is an essential part of providing patient-centred care in practice. Patients should be encouraged to engage in the consultation to ensure that it is a two-way discussion where they can share their views and be involved in decision-making around their treatment.

The Consultation Skills Assessment (also known as the Medication Related Consultation Framework) can be used to support the development of your consultation behaviours and skills. This tool provides a structured approach to reviewing a patient's medicines to identify any problems they may have, including how the patient adheres to their treatment. This tool is useful for pharmacists completing training programmes - further information can be found in the Credentialing area on the RPS website: www.rpharms.com

Pharmacists are more commonly conducting remote consultations (i.e. over the phone or via video). The Pharmaceutical Journal article titled "Remote consultations: how pharmacy teams can practise them safely" www.pharmaceutical-journal.com provides you with relevant information, advice and best practice principles for a patient centred approach when undertaking remote video consultations.

HELPING PATIENTS TO UNDERSTAND THEIR MEDICINES

A key role of pharmacists is ensuring that patients understand their medicines, the role that they play in maintaining their wellbeing and to empower patients to use these safely and effectively to get the most from their treatment. Providing information for patients on their medicines involves being able to build a rapport with the patient, having good communication skills, empathy, being able to put the patient at ease and being able to confer an understanding and belief that the health of the patient is important to the pharmacist. Involving and engaging the patient in this process is essential in ensuring that the pharmacist-patient relationship is concordant.

OPPORTUNITIES FOR HELPING PATIENTS UNDERSTAND THEIR MEDICINES

Consultations should not be limited to when a supply of newly prescribed medicines is made, and almost any interaction with the patient can be used as an opportunity to help them understand their medicines. A simple question asking, "How are you getting on with your medicines?" can often be a successful engaging starting point.

Illustrative examples of opportunities include:

- Point of sale for over-the-counter medicines
- Any medication reviews
- Diagnostic testing and screening
- Patient group directions
- Minor ailment schemes
- Whilst taking medication history
- During a hospital stay
- Point of discharge
- Outpatient clinics
- When a change has been made to a current medicine
- When there is a change of packaging e.g. a different generic supplier is used
- Point of a supply of a regular prescription.

ADVICE FOR SUCCESSFUL PATIENT CONSULTATIONS

Try to understand the level of existing knowledge, understanding and concerns the patient has regarding their medicines. Consider any misunderstandings which could be a barrier to adherence. Explore what the patient has already been told about their medicines, whether there are any concerns and what the patient's expectations are.

Ensure you are familiar with the medicines you will be providing counselling on and any additional information that is relevant to those medicines. If in doubt, take time to review and re-familiarise yourself with the medicine. For example – look out for interactions with other medicines, food, or supplements, or medicines with common or significant side effects, complex administration regimens, special storage requirements, or narrow therapeutic index. Check standard references (e.g. BNF or national guidelines for additional patient and carer advice).

Aim for a structured approach and tailor the language and level of detail used to the patient. The format that is appropriate will depend upon both patient characteristics and the medicines that are taken. As an illustration, the patient may be knowledgeable about their medicines and condition, for example as a result of caring for a family member with the same condition.

Where appropriate use different methods of communication to support your discussions such as pictograms and medication cards.

Respect patient privacy and ensure that confidentiality is protected.

Ensure that the process is two-way and interactive, not simply a list of facts about medicines. There should be opportunities for questions and discussion.

As a minimum, you should consider discussing the following points:

- What is the medicine and why has it been prescribed? How does it impact upon the medical condition and how does it alleviate the symptoms? e.g. This is a blood pressure medicine which should lower your blood pressure to normal levels which will help prevent further complications

- How and when to take the medicine

- How much to take and what to expect, e.g. antibiotics need to be taken regularly and the course completed even after symptoms subside

- What to do if the patient misses a dose

- What are the likely side effects and how to manage them

- If applicable, any lifestyle or dietary changes that need to be made or that can affect the treatment

- Additional information relating to storage requirements, expiry dates, disposal and monitoring requirements can also be included where appropriate

- Check patient understanding by asking them to describe back to you the key information you have provided.

FURTHER READING

Royal Pharmaceutical Society
Counselling people on the use of medicines.
www.rpharms.com

Royal Pharmaceutical Society
Medication history.
www.rpharms.com

Healthcare Improvement Scotland
Medicines reconciliation care bundle. 2015.
www.ihub.scot

National Institute for Health and Care Excellence
Medicines optimisation: Quality standard. 2016.
www.nice.org.uk

National Institute for Health and Care Excellence
Medicines optimisation: The safe and effective use of medicines to enable the best possible outcomes. NICE guideline. 2015.
www.nice.org.uk

2.7
Sustainability

Pharmacists are the experts in medicines and their safe and effective use. Medicines have three major impacts on the environment: the chemical effects of the Active Pharmaceutical Ingredients (APIs), the large carbon footprint involved in manufacture and distribution, and pharmaceutical waste.

We know that medicines account for about 25% of carbon emissions within the NHS, so pharmacists have a professional responsibility to ensure more sustainable use of medicines and to decrease the carbon footprint and environmental risk of all pharmaceutical care.

The RPS has developed the following four policies on Sustainability to help pharmacists and their teams to reduce the impact of medicines and the services they provide on the climate:

1   Improving prescribing and medicines use

2   Tackling medicines waste

3   Preventing ill health

4   Infrastructure and ways of working

Detailed information on these policies and actions to take can be viewed on the RPS website www.rpharms.com (search for "RPS Sustainability Policies").

FURTHER READING

Pharmaceutical Group of the European Union (PGEU)
Best Practice Paper on Green and Sustainable Pharmacy in Europe.
www.pgeu.eu

NHS England
Delivering a "Net Zero" National Health Service.
www.england.nhs.uk

Carbon Trust
NHS Wales Decarbonisation Strategic Delivery Plan 2021-2030.
www.gov.wales

Underpinning knowledge – legislation and professional issues

An awareness of pharmacy legislation, professional standards and good practice helps pharmacists exercise their professional judgement. To ensure that the medicine prescribed or supplied is appropriate for the patient, as well as simply ensuring that prescriptions are dispensed accurately.

The Human Medicines Regulations 2012 consolidated most of the legislation regulating the authorisation, sale and supply of medicinal products for human use, made under the Medicines Act 1968. It is important to understand that the Medicines Act 1968 has not been replaced fully and that certain parts are still active. Further information on the Human Medicines Regulations 2012 and the consolidation can be found in Dale and Appelbe's Pharmacy and Medicines Law (12th Edition).

The Veterinary Medicines Regulations 2013 covers the prescribing and supply for animals. Further information on the Veterinary Medicines Regulations can be found in Chapter 12 of Dale and Appelbe's Pharmacy and Medicines Law (12th Edition) and the Veterinary Medicines Directorate (VMD) website at www.gov.uk

The Programme Board for Rebalancing Medicines Legislation and Pharmacy Regulation reviews relevant pharmacy legislation and regulation to ensure it provides safety for users of pharmacy services. It facilitates a systematic approach to quality in pharmacy, allowing innovation and development of pharmacy practice, whilst reducing the burden of unnecessary and inflexible regulations. The Programme will build on and propose amendments to legislation as required, to deliver a modern approach to regulation which maintains patient and public safety, whilst supporting professional and quality systems development, including learning from dispensing errors made in registered pharmacies.

Further information and updates on the Rebalancing Medicines Legislation and Pharmacy Regulation Programme Board can be found on the UK government website at www.gov.uk

The MEP is not intended to be a complete repository of pharmacy legislation and aims instead to provide a practical resource, professional guide and digest to the most relevant aspects of pharmacy legislation.

3.1
Classification of medicines

3.1.1	General sale medicines
3.1.2	Pharmacy (P) medicines
3.1.3	Prescription-only medicines (POM)
3.1.4	Reclassified medicines

There are three classes of medicinal products for humans under the Human Medicines Regulations 2012 and several classes of veterinary medicinal products under the Veterinary Medicines Regulations. An understanding of these and associated professional issues is important to pharmacists as medicines should not be considered normal items of commerce, and the final decision on sale or supply is one determined by the professional judgement of the pharmacist.

Pharmacists are empowered to refuse to sell or supply ANY medicines, if the sale or supply is contrary to the pharmacist's clinical judgement.

3.1.1
GENERAL SALE MEDICINES

General sale medicines, also known as 'General Sales List' (GSL) medicines, are those that can be made available as 'self-selection' items for sale in registered pharmacies. They can also be sold in other retail outlets that can 'close so as to exclude the public'.

Within a pharmacy, GSL medicines can only be sold when a pharmacist has assumed the role of responsible pharmacist; however, the pharmacist may be physically absent for a limited period of time while remaining responsible, thus permitting sales of general sale medicines during this absence (see Chapter 4).

3.1.2
PHARMACY (P) MEDICINES

A pharmacy medicine is a medicinal product that can be sold from a registered pharmacy premises by a pharmacist or a person acting under the supervision of a pharmacist. Pharmacy medicines must not be accessible to the public by self-selection.

Together with GSL medicines, P medicines are collectively known as over-the-counter (OTC) or non-prescription medicines. The sale of some of these medicines is associated with additional legal and professional considerations; the most common issues are explained in section 3.2.

FURTHER READING

Royal Pharmaceutical Society
Interim statement of Professional Standard: Supply of Over the Counter (OTC) medicines.
www.rpharms.com

3.1.3
PRESCRIPTION-ONLY MEDICINES (POM)

A prescription-only medicine (POM) is a medicine that is generally subject to the restriction of requiring a prescription written by an appropriate practitioner.

An appropriate practitioner includes the following:

- doctors
- dentists
- supplementary prescribers
- nurse independent prescribers
- pharmacist independent prescribers
- EEA and Swiss approved health professionals (see section 3.3.5)
- community practitioner nurse prescribers
- optometrist independent prescribers (not for Controlled Drugs, or parenteral medicines)
- paramedic independent prescribers
- physiotherapist independent prescribers
- podiatrist independent prescribers
- therapeutic radiographer independent prescribers (for certain medicines see section 3.3.14)

There are exemptions to requiring a prescription in some circumstances (see section 3.3.10). Further details about the legal and professional issues associated with POMs are discussed in section 3.3. Some medicines can be classified under more than one category and this can depend upon formulation, strength, quantity, indication or marketing authorisation.

FURTHER READING

Wingfield J, Pitchford K, editors
Dale and Appelbe's Pharmacy and Medicines Law. 12th edition. 2021. London; Pharmaceutical Press.
www.pharmpress.com

3.1.4
RECLASSIFIED MEDICINES

More medicines are being reclassified from POM to P providing pharmacists with a larger range of medicines to select from to treat patients. It is important that pharmacists and pharmacy support staff involved in the sale of medicines are appropriately trained to support patients with the medicines that they need.

FURTHER READING

Guidance for the following reclassified medicines are available from the RPS website www.rpharms.com:

- Amorolfine nail lacquer
- Anti-malarials
- Chloramphenicol eye drops and eye ointment
- Desogestrel
- Emergency contraceptives
- Mometasone 0.05% nasal spray
- Oral lidocaine-containing products for teething in children
- Orlistat
- Proton pump inhibitors
- Sildenafil
- Sumatriptan
- Tamsulosin
- Tranexamic acid

3.2
Professional and legal issues: pharmacy medicines

3.2.1   Pseudoephedrine and ephedrine

3.2.2   Oral emergency contraception

3.2.3   Paracetamol and aspirin

3.2.4   Codeine and dihydrocodeine

3.2.1
PSEUDOEPHEDRINE AND EPHEDRINE

Pseudoephedrine and ephedrine are widely used decongestant pharmacy medicines. However, due to their potential for misuse in the illicit production of methylamphetamine (crystal meth) – a class A Controlled Drug – there are legal restrictions on the quantities that can be sold or supplied without prescription.

- It is unlawful to supply a product or combination of products that contain more than 720mg of pseudoephedrine OR 180mg of ephedrine at any one time, without a prescription (Regulation 237 of *Human Medicines Regulations 2012*)

- It is unlawful to sell or supply any pseudoephedrine product at the same time as an ephedrine product without a prescription (Regulation 237 of *Human Medicines Regulations 2012*).

Sales or supplies of pseudoephedrine or ephedrine should either be made personally by the pharmacist or by pharmacy staff who have been trained and are competent to deal with pseudoephedrine and ephedrine issues, and who know when it is necessary to refer to the pharmacist.

Even when a request is made for a lawful quantity, the sale or supply can be refused where there are reasonable grounds for suspecting misuse.

A person purchasing pseudoephedrine and ephedrine for illicit purposes may not be a 'user' of methylamphetamine and, therefore, may not conform to stereotypes. They may be of any gender and of any age or background.

SIGNS OF POSSIBLE MISUSE

The following signs in combination can be useful for identifying when a request is more likely to be suspicious:

- **Lack of symptoms**
  Not suffering from cough, cold or flu symptoms, or unable to describe these in the patient if buying for someone else

- **Rehearsed answers**
  Gives answers that appear to be rehearsed or scripted

- **Impatient or aggressive**
  In a rush or hurrying to complete the transaction

- **Opportunistic**
  Waiting for busy periods in the shop or until less experienced staff are available

- **Specific products**
  Wants certain brands that contain only pseudoephedrine or ephedrine

- **Paraphernalia**
  Wishes also to purchase other items which can be used to manufacture methylamphetamine (e.g. lithium batteries, chemicals such as acetone)

- **Quantities**
  Requests large quantities

- **Frequency**
  Makes frequent requests

Suspicions can be reported to your local GPhC inspector, local Controlled Drugs liaison police officer or accountable officer.

FURTHER READING

Royal Pharmaceutical Society
Pseudoephedrine and Ephedrine: look, listen and report.
www.rpharms.com

3

3.2.2
ORAL EMERGENCY CONTRACEPTION

There are three methods of emergency contraception:

- copper intrauterine device (Cu-IUD)
- oral ulipristal acetate
- oral levonorgestrel.

The pharmacist should be involved in providing advice on all methods of emergency contraception, assessing suitability, and approving sales or signposting to alternative providers.

Guidance on the choice of emergency contraception, including decision-making algorithims are available from the Faculty of Sexual and Reproductive Healthcare www.fsrh.org/home.

ORAL EMERGENCY CONTRACEPTIVES AS PHARMACY MEDICINES

Levonorgestrel 1500 microgram tablet and ulipristal acetate 30mg tablet are licensed as pharmacy medicines for emergency hormonal contraception (EHC). Levonorgestrel is licensed for women aged 16 years or over for emergency contraception within 72 hours of unprotected sexual intercourse or failure of a contraceptive method. Ulipristal acetate is licensed for emergency contraception within 120 hours (five days) of unprotected sexual intercourse or failure of a contraceptive method.

ADVANCE SUPPLY OF ORAL EMERGENCY CONTRACEPTION

Pharmacists can provide an advance supply of oral emergency contraception (i.e. prior to unprotected sexual intercourse or in case of failure of a contraceptive method) to a patient requesting it at a pharmacy. The patient should be assessed to ensure that they are competent, they intend to use the medicine appropriately and it is clinically appropriate.

RELIGIOUS OR MORAL BELIEFS

The GPhC have published regulatory guidance on the provision of pharmacy services affected by religious or moral beliefs.

If your religious or moral beliefs impact on your willingness to supply oral emergency contraception, inform your employer, your locum agency and colleagues you will be working with, as soon as possible.

The *GPhC practice guidance on religion, personal values and moral beliefs* describes the factors to consider if a patient requests a supply of oral emergency contraception and the questions you should ask yourself so you can ensure patient-centred care. Referral is an option but may not always be possible. The GPhC have outlined factors to consider when deciding whether a referral is appropriate.

Employers and pharmacy professionals need to work together to consider a broad range of situations.

VULNERABLE ADULTS AND CHILDREN

Be aware that, in some circumstances, requests for oral emergency contraception could be linked to abuse (non-consensual intercourse) of children or vulnerable adults. The Department of Health has published a document called *Responding to domestic abuse: A handbook for health professionals*, which provides practical advice on dealing with domestic abuse, keeping records, confidentiality and sharing information.

The Department for Education has published a guidance document called *Working together to safeguard children*, which includes sections for health professionals and on referral.

The supply of ulipristal acetate to patients under the age of 16 years is not contraindicated by the manufacturer. However, pharmacists may wish to consider the following additional factors:

- Children under the age of 13 are legally too young to consent to any sexual activity. Instances should be treated seriously with a presumption that the case should be reported to social services, unless there are exceptional circumstances backed by documented reasons for not sharing information.

- Sexual activity with children under the age of 16 is also an offence but may be consensual. The law is not intended to prosecute mutually agreed sexual activity between young people of a similar age, unless it involves abuse or exploitation.

- Pharmacists can provide contraception or sexual health advice to a child under the age of 16 (see section 2.5.5 for information on meeting the Fraser Criteria) and the general duty of patient confidentiality applies, so where there is a decision to share information, consent should be sought whenever possible prior to disclosing patient information. This duty is not absolute and information may be shared if you judge on a case-by-case basis that sharing is in the child's best interest (e.g. to prevent harm to the child or where the child's welfare overrides the need to keep information confidential). Remember that it is possible to seek advice from experts without disclosing identifiable details of a child and breaking patient confidentiality – and that where there is a decision to share information, this should be proportionate.

OTHER MECHANISMS FOR SUPPLY

There are various mechanisms for the supply of oral emergency contraception and it may be appropriate to refer to other service providers rather than make a sale, in some circumstances (e.g. where a sale would be outside of the terms of the marketing authorisation). Other providers include family planning clinics, general practice clinics and providers of PGDs for oral emergency contraception and genitourinary medicine (GUM) clinics.

The RPS guide *Oral Emergency Contraceptive as Pharmacy Medicines* can be used to obtain relevant information to determine whether supply is appropriate or not. The guidance also includes advice that can be given to a patient after a supply has been made. See also section 3.3.10

FURTHER READING

Royal Pharmaceutical Society
Oral emergency contraceptive as pharmacy medicines.
www.rpharms.com

Royal Pharmaceutical Society
Protecting children and young people.
www.rpharms.com

Department for Education
Working together to safeguard children. 2018
www.gov.uk

Department of Health
Responding to domestic abuse: A resource for health professionals. 2017.
www.gov.uk

Faculty of Sexual and Reproductive Healthcare
Various resources available.
www.fsrh.org

Family Planning Association
Various resources available.
www.fpa.org.uk

General Pharmaceutical Council
Guidance on consent. 2018.
www.pharmacyregulation.org
(see MEP Appendix 4)

General Pharmaceutical Council
Guidance on patient confidentiality. 2018.
www.pharmacyregulation.org
(see MEP Appendix 3)

General Pharmaceutical Council
Guidance on religion, personal values and beliefs. 2017.
www.pharmacyregulation.org

National Institute for Health and Care Excellence
Contraceptive services for under 25s: Public health guideline. 2014.
www.nice.org.uk

National Institute for Health and Care Excellence
Domestic violence and abuse: Multi-agency working. Public health guideline. 2014.
www.nice.org.uk

Scottish Government
National Guidance for Child Protection in Scotland: Guidance for Health Professionals in Scotland.
www.gov.scot

3

3.2.3
PARACETAMOL AND ASPIRIN

Paracetamol and aspirin are medicinal products that are available in a range of formulations, strengths and packaged quantities. They have marketing authorisations as POM, P and general sale medicines – depending upon pack size and formulation. Table 3 illustrates the quantities of paracetamol and aspirin that can be sold legally.

Table 3:
Paracetamol and Aspirin – OTC legal restrictions

	Legal restriction	Additional note
Paracetamol	Not more than 100 non effervescent* tablets or capsules can be sold to a person at any one time. Since most OTC pack sizes are for 16 or 32 dose units, this means that, in practice, 96 is the maximum number that can be sold.	There are no legal limits on the quantity of over-the-counter effervescent* tablets, powders, granules or liquids that can be sold to a person at any one time. Use professional judgement to decide the appropriate quantity to supply and what limits to impose.
Aspirin	Not more than 100 non-effervescent* tablets or capsules can be sold to a person at any one time. Since most OTC pack sizes are for 16 or 32 dose units, this means that, in practice, 96 is the maximum number that can be sold.	There are no legal limits on the quantities of over-the-counter effervescent* tablets or powders that can be sold to a person at any one time. Use professional judgement to decide the appropriate quantity to supply and what limits to impose.

NB: The definition of effervescent for the purposes of the restrictions above is provided by medicines legislation. Soluble or dispersible formulations as defined by the British Pharmacopoeia may not meet the definition of effervescent in medicines legislation. Where in doubt, quantities of soluble or dispersible formulations sold should be restricted as non-effervescent preparations.

3.2.4
CODEINE AND DIHYDROCODEINE

There are tighter controls and warnings on packaging of OTC solid dose medicines (e.g. tablets and capsules) containing codeine or dihydrocodeine. These were introduced to minimise the risk of overuse and addiction to these medicines. The changes include:

• **Indications**
Indications for solid dose OTC codeine and dihydrocodeine products are now restricted to the short-term treatment of acute, moderate pain that is not relieved by paracetamol, ibuprofen or aspirin alone. All other previous indications, including cold, flu, cough, sore throats and minor pain have been removed.

• **Pack sizes**
Any pack containing more than 32 dose units (including effervescent formulations) is a POM.

• **Patient information leaflet and labels**
The warning 'Can cause addiction. For three days use only' must be positioned in a prominent clear position on the front of the pack. In addition, both the PIL and packaging must state the indication and that the medicine can cause addiction or headache if used continuously for more than three days. The PIL must also contain information about the warning signs of addiction.

We support these tighter controls and recommend that only one pack of OTC medication containing codeine or dihydrocodeine should be sold, if appropriate, as sale of more than one pack would undermine the reduction in pack size and POM restriction on packs containing more than 32 dose units.

3.3
Professional and legal issues: prescription-only medicines

3.3.1
GENERAL PRESCRIPTION REQUIREMENTS

The sale, supply and administration of prescription-only medicines (POMs) are restricted by the Human Medicines Regulations 2012. A pharmacist is able to sell or supply a POM under the authority of a prescription from an appropriate practitioner (for example, a doctor, dentist, supplementary prescriber, independent prescriber or community practitioner nurse, etc), or via an exemption (see section 3.3.9 and 3.3.10). A full list of different types of appropriate practitioner, prescribing restrictions and checking registration can be found in section 3.3.14 and 3.3.15. Information on requirements for prescriptions issued by prescribers registered in an EEA country or Switzerland can be found in section 3.3.5.

NB: The additional prescription requirements for Controlled Drugs are discussed in section 3.6.7.

It is important to note the prescribing of POMs is restricted by the Human Medicines Regulations 2012 (and Controlled Drugs legislation) and the specific prescriber's regulatory and professional body . See Table 6 (section 3.3.14) for information on different types or prescribers and their prescribing restrictions.

Several pieces of information must be present for a prescription to be legal (Regulation 217 and 218 Human Medicines Regulations 2012). These are specified in Diagram 13.

3

Diagram 13: Prescription requirements

Pharmacy Stamp	Age **7 AGE** D.o.B.	Title, Forename, Surname & Address: **5 PATIENT NAME** **6 PATIENT ADDRESS**
Please don't stamp over age box		
Number of days' treatment NB Ensure dose is stated		NHS Number:
Endorsements		

Signature of Prescriber

1 SIGNATURE OF PRESCRIBER

Date

3 DATE

For dispenser No. of Prescns. on form

4 PARTICULARS OF PRESCRIBER
2 ADDRESS OF PRESCRIBER

NHS

1 **Signature**
Prescriptions need to be signed in ink by an appropriate practitioner (see sections 3.1.3 and 3.3.14) in his or her own name. An 'advanced electronic signature' can be used to authorise an electronic prescription (see Advanced Electronic Signature)

2 **Address of prescriber**
Prescriptions must include the address of the appropriate practitioner

3 **Date**
A prescription is valid for up to six months from the appropriate date (for prescriptions for Schedules 2, 3 or 4 Controlled Drugs, see section 3.6.7). For an NHS prescription, the appropriate date is the later of either the date on which the prescription was signed or a date indicated by the appropriate practitioner as the date before which it should not be dispensed. For private prescriptions, the appropriate date will always be the date on which it was signed

4 **Particulars of prescriber**
Prescriptions require particulars that indicate the type of appropriate practitioner

5 **Name of the patient**

6 **Address of the patient**

7 **Age of the patient** (If under 12 years)

HOMECARE PRESCRIPTIONS

The details shown in Diagram 13 would also apply to homecare prescriptions. Some homecare service providers however, may also require additional information e.g. GMC number of prescribing doctor.

RPS Professional Standards for homecare services and the supporting handbook for providing these services in England and Wales can be accessed at www.rpharms.com.

The Homecare Medicines "Towards a Vision for the Future" (Hackett Report), November 2011 can be viewed at www.gov.uk, this report made a list of recommendations to improve the financial and clinical governance arrangements for patients receiving medicines via the homecare route.

NOTE

- **Indelible**
  Prescriptions need to be written in indelible ink – they may be computer generated or typed.

- **Private prescriptions**
  Diagram 13 shows the image of an NHS prescription; however, the same requirements apply to private prescriptions.

- **Carbon copies**
  It is permissible to issue carbon copies of NHS prescriptions as long as they are signed in ink.

ADVANCED ELECTRONIC SIGNATURE

An advanced electronic signature is a signature that is linked uniquely to the signatory, capable of identifying the signatory and created using means over which the signatory can maintain sole control (Regulation 219(5) Human Medicines Regulations 2012). The RPS is unable to confirm whether or not individual systems are able to issue advanced electronic signatures. Suitable assurances should be obtained from the system manufacturer and business indemnity providers.

Electronic prescriptions are normally sent to the pharmacy by the prescribing organisation. Copies of 'electronic prescriptions' on an email or on a patient's phone in their online account do not normally meet the requirements of an advanced electronic signature.

ELECTRONIC PRESCRIPTIONS

Detailed information on existing electronic prescription systems is available from the following websites:

NHS Digital
Electronic Prescription Service (EPS)
www.digital.nhs.uk

Pharmaceutical Services Negotiating Committee (PSNC)
Electronic Prescription Service (EPS)
www.psnc.org.uk

NHS Education for Scotland
Electronic Transfer of Prescriptions (ETP) Implementation Pack to Support eAMS
www.communitypharmacy.scot.nhs.uk

NHS England
Electronic Repeat Dispensing Guidance. 2015.
www.england.nhs.uk

NOTE

Electronic prescriptions must still meet the general prescription requirements (see 3.3.1). A copy of a prescription in an online account, does not constitute a legitimate electronic prescription even if it is emailed to the pharmacist.

DISPENSING A PRESCRIPTION IN WELSH LANGUAGE

Medicines legislation describes the requirements which need to be on a legally valid prescription. Language is not specified. There is currently no law or act that specifies that prescriptions in Wales have to be bilingual.

If the pharmacist is not a Welsh speaker and can't understand the prescription, the RPS advice is to put patient safety first.

The pharmacist is responsible for finding the best way to help the patient. If the pharmacist is presented with a prescription they do not fully understand, this might be through translation services or informal networks. Some local health boards use LanguageLine.

In the interests of patient safety, the RPS Welsh Pharmacy Board recommends that medicines should be labelled in english to ensure that if a patient is seen by a non-welsh speaker these important instructions are understood.

FURTHER READING

Royal Pharmaceutical Society
Use of the Welsh language in pharmacy.
www.rpharms.com

PRESCRIPTIONS FROM THE CROWN DEPENDENCIES (JERSEY,GUERNSEY AND ISLE OF MAN)

Pharmacists may be presented with prescriptions written by prescribers from the Crown Dependencies (Jersey, Guernsey and Isle of Man).

You should be satisfied that all prescription requirements (Diagram 13, section 3.3.1) are present for the prescription to be legally valid. Please note: Prescriptions for Schedule 2 and 3 CDs, the prescriber's address must be within the UK (see Diagram 18, section 3.6.7).

A report published by the GMC *GMC regulation in Crown Dependencies and other overseas territories* www.gmc-uk.org advises the following: "*Crown Dependencies such as the Channel Islands and Isle of Man are not part of the UK. We have nevertheless established agreements with those territories to facilitate the revalidation of doctors within their jurisdiction using local system.*" Therefore, doctors from Crown Dependencies are expected to be registered with GMC.

3

Details on checking registration of healthcare professionals can be found in section 3.3.15.

Requests for emergency supply from a patient or prescriber should be considered on a case by case basis considering the legal requirements as detailed in section 3.3.10 and using your professional judgement in the best interests of the patient.

PRESCRIPTION FORMS

Details of prescription forms which are allowed and not allowed on the NHS in England and Wales is available on PSNC website at www.psnc.org.uk (search for 'Is this prescription form valid'). For Scotland contact Community Pharmacy Scotland www.cps.scot for information.

REPEATABLE PRESCRIPTIONS

Repeatable prescriptions are private prescriptions which contain a direction that they can be dispensed more than once e.g. "repeat x 5".

They are commonly used in the community, hospital (where a prescriber can issue a private prescription in a private hospital or NHS hospital providing private services) and the homecare setting.

This section relates to repeatable prescriptions where a prescriber has added a direction for a prescription to be repeated. Repeatable prescriptions are commonly found on private prescriptions; FP10, WP10, and GP10 type NHS prescriptions are not used in this way. For information about veterinary prescriptions see section 3.5.

Repeatable prescriptions can be repeated as indicated by the prescriber.

If a number is not stated, they can only be repeated once (dispensed twice) unless the prescription is for an oral contraceptive in which case it can be repeated five times (dispensed six times in total)

- Prescriptions for Schedule 2 and 3 CDs are not repeatable; however, those for Schedule 4 and 5 are repeatable

- The first dispensing for a POM or Schedule 5 CD must be made within six months of the appropriate date, following which there is no legal time limit for the remaining repeats

- If the prescription is for a Schedule 4 CD, the first dispensing must be made within 28 days of the appropriate date, following which there is no time limit for remaining repeats

While there is no time limit for remaining repeats, pharmacists should use professional judgement, taking into consideration clinical factors, to determine whether further repeat dispensing is appropriate. The patient can choose to have repeats dispensed from different pharmacies and can retain the prescription. To maintain an audit trail mark on the prescription the name and address of the pharmacy from where supply has been made and the date of supply.

Prisons and other residential custodial secure environments in England provide NHS healthcare and pharmacy services to detained people. FP10 forms are not used for routine prescribing as a customised prescription form, generated by the clinical IT system, is used instead, however these are still considered a NHS prescription. FP10s are available in these settings but are only used to access urgent medicines (e.g. out of hours) or are supplied to a released person to access medicines that couldn't be supplied to them on release. Therefore the NHS repeat dispensing scheme using FP10s or EPS cannot be used. Further information about how medicines are handled in secure environments can be found in the *RPS Professional Standards Optimising Medicines in Secure Environments* www.rpharms.com.

The word 'repeat' is also used in various contexts in relation to prescribing and dispensing:

- **Repeat slips**
  These are not prescriptions, themselves, but a list of medications which patients can use to reorder their regular medication.

- **Instalment prescriptions**
  These provide for a single prescription for a CD to be dispensed in several instalments (see section 3.6.7).

- **NHS repeat dispensing service**
  Where the prescriber authorises a prescription with a specified number of 'batch' issues that may be dispensed at specified intervals from a pharmacy (England and Wales only).

VALIDITY OF OWINGS ON PRESCRIPTIONS

Table 4 : Validity of owings on NHS and private prescriptions

Medicine	Validity of owings
POMs and CDs Schedule 5 (For POMS on Pregnancy Prevention Programme (PPP) (e.g. Sodium Valproate and Oral Retinoids) see *below)	Six months from the appropriate date (see 'Date' in Diagram 13, section 3.3.1)
P and General Sale Medicines	Six months from the appropriate date (see 'Date' in Diagram 13, section 3.3.1)**
Schedule 2 , 3 and 4 CDs	28 days after the appropriate date (see 'Date' in Diagram 18, section 3.6.7)

* Supply of owing can exceed 7 days from when the prescription is written only if the pharmacist follows the PPP checklist to ensure there is no risk of pregnancy (see section 3.3.11).

** Please note this is a professional requirement.

Medicines must be supplied within a certain period from the appropriate date (i.e. the date on which the prescription was signed by the prescriber or the date indicated as being the start date), therefore any owed medicines should be supplied within this validity period.

Table 4 summarises the validity of owings on NHS and private prescriptions (please note that this table does not cover repeatable prescriptions, NHS repeat dispensing prescriptions in England and Wales or CDs instalment prescriptions).

RECORD KEEPING

Private prescriptions for a POM must be retained for two years from the date of the sale or supply or for repeatable prescriptions from the date of the last sale or supply. Private prescriptions for Schedule 2 and 3 CDs must be submitted to the relevant NHS agency (for further information see section 3.6.7). Records must be made in the POM register (written or electronically), which should be retained for two years from the date of the last entry in the register. The record must include:

- **Supply date**
  The date on which the medicine was sold or supplied

- **Prescription date**
  The date on the prescription

- **Medicine details**
  The name, quantity, formulation and strength of medicine supplied (where not apparent from the name)

- **Prescriber details**
  The name and address of the practitioner

- **Patient details**
  The name and address of the patient.

The record should be made on the day the sale or supply takes place or if that is not practical, on the next day following.

Prescriptions for oral contraceptives are exempt from record keeping; as are prescriptions for Schedule 2 CDs where a separate CD register record has to be made (see section 3.6.11).

Appendix 2 of the Records Management Code of Practice 2021 guide provides detail on how long records should be retained, either due to their ongoing administrative value or as a result of statutory requirement www.nhsx.nhs.uk

INCOMPLETE PRESCRIPTIONS

Although details of the medicinal product, such as name strength, form, quantity and dose are not legal requirements for POM prescriptions, they are important to identify which medicine to supply, how much to supply and at what dose. They are also important from a pricing and remuneration perspective.

Information on endorsing incomplete prescriptions is available from:

- **England**
  Pharmaceutical Services Negotiating Committee (PSNC)
  www.psnc.org.uk

- **Scotland**

  Community Pharmacy Scotland

  www.cps.scot

- **Wales**

  Community Pharmacy Wales

  www.cpwales.org.uk

FURTHER READING

Royal Pharmaceutical Society

Supporting people to manage their repeat medicines

www.rpharms.com

PRESCRIPTIONS FOR DISCHARGED PRISONERS

ENGLAND

FP10 prescriptions are not allowed for patients while they are in prison (unless authorised by the Prison Trust). However, those who are about to be discharged from prison without the usual methods for ensuring continuity of supply of their medicines (e.g. those released unexpectedly from court, those who fail to obtain a take-out supply of their medicines or those who fail to obtain a same or next day prescribing appointment with a drug treatment agency) can be given an FP10 or FP10[MDA] prescription to take to their community pharmacy.

These FP10 forms have the name and address of the prison printed on them and the patient is exempt from payment by virtue of having HMP in the address.

For more information see the NHS Business Services Authority website www.nhsbsa.nhs.uk

FALSIFIED MEDICINES DIRECTIVE (FMD)

The 'safety features' elements of the Falsified Medicines Directive (FMD) legislation and delegated regulation no longer apply in GB.

The Government are looking at alternative options. For further details and information see the UK FMD Working Group for Community Pharmacy: fmdsource.co.uk or check our website for the latest information.

3.3.2
DENTAL PRESCRIPTIONS

Dentists can legally write prescriptions for any POM. The General Dental Council advises that dentists should restrict their prescribing to areas in which they are competent and generally only prescribe medicines that have uses in dentistry.

When prescribing on an NHS dental prescription, dentists are restricted to the medicines listed in the Dental Prescribers' Formulary (Part 8a of the Drug Tariff for Scotland or Part XVIIa of the Drug Tariff for England and Wales). The dental formulary is also reproduced within the British National Formulary. See also section 3.3.14.

3.3.3
FAXED PRESCRIPTIONS

A fax of a prescription does not fall within the definition of a legally valid prescription within human medicines legislation because it is not written in indelible ink and has not been signed in ink by an appropriate practitioner.

Supplying medicines against a fax is associated with considerable risks:

1 Uncertainty that the supply has been made in accordance with a legally valid prescription

2 Risks of poor reproduction

3 Risks of non-receipt of the original prescription and therefore inability to demonstrate that a supply had been made in accordance with a prescription

4 Risks that the original prescription is subsequently amended by the prescriber in which case the supply would not have been made in accordance with the prescription

5 Risks the fax is sent to multiple pharmacies and duplicate supplies are made.

6 Risks that the prescription is not genuine

7 Risks that the system of sending and receiving of the fax is not secure

Alternative mechanisms for the supply of medicines in an emergency exist for pharmacists working in registered pharmacies and can achieve a similar outcome in many scenarios with a better risk profile. Where this option can be used, it should be used.

Electronic prescriptions are also recognised in Human Medicines Regulations 2012 and where a system is being developed should be considered as an option.

Pharmacists considering supplying medicines against a fax should make an informed decision and take steps to safeguard patient safety, and where possible mitigate the risks identified above. Where appropriate, you should consider making a record of the decision-making process and your reasons leading to a particular course of action. The supply of Schedule 2 and 3 CDs without possession of a lawful prescription could be prosecuted as a criminal offence.

NOTE

These same principles apply to copies of an emailed private prescription printed out or presented on a patient's mobile telephone.

FURTHER READING

Department of Health and Social Care
Health and social care secretary bans fax machines in NHS.
www.gov.uk

NHS England
Practice guidance: Removal of facsimile (fax) machines from general practice.
www.england.nhs.uk

3.3.4
FORGED PRESCRIPTIONS

Although it can be difficult to detect a forged prescription, every pharmacist should be alert to the possibility that any prescription could be a forgery.

The following checklist may be useful to help detect fraudulent prescriptions and prompt further investigation:

- Is a large or excessive quantity prescribed and is this appropriate for the medicine and condition being treated?
- Is the prescriber known?
- Is the patient known?
- Has the title 'Dr' been inserted before the signature?
- Is the behaviour of the patient indicative? (e.g. nervous, agitated, aggressive, etc.)
- Is the medicine known to be commonly misused?

Further investigation may be necessary. The following are appropriate actions to take:

1 Scrutinise the signature carefully – possibly checking against a known genuine prescription from the same prescriber

2 Confirm details with the prescriber (e.g. whether or not a prescription has been issued, the original intention of the prescriber and whether or not there has been an alteration)

3 Use contact details for the prescriber that are obtained from a source other than the suspicious prescription (e.g. directory enquiries)

REPORTING CONCERNS
Depending upon the nature of the fraudulent prescription, use your professional judgement to assess whether or not it is a matter that requires referral to the police, NHS Counter Fraud Services (for NHS prescriptions only) or whether the matter can be resolved by discussions with the patient and prescriber.

3

3.3.5
PRESCRIPTIONS FROM THE EEA OR SWITZERLAND

Prescriptions and repeatable prescriptions issued by an approved health professional in an approved country are legally recognised in the UK. Emergency supplies for patients of these healthcare professionals are also permitted.

APPROVED HEALTH PROFESSIONAL

Approved health professionals include doctors and dentists as well as other professions with prescribing rights i.e. chiropodists or podiatrists, nurses (including community nurses), optometrists, paramedics, pharmacists, physiotherapists and therapeutic radiographers.

APPROVED COUNTRIES

Approved countries comprise EEA countries and Switzerland:

Austria, Belgium, Bulgaria, Croatia, Cyprus, Czech Republic, Denmark, Estonia, Finland, France, Germany, Greece, Hungary, Iceland, Republic of Ireland, Italy, Latvia, Liechtenstein, Lithuania, Luxembourg, Malta, The Netherlands, Norway, Poland, Portugal, Romania, Slovakia, Slovenia, Spain, Sweden, Switzerland.

If the prescription originates from a country or prescriber not on the approved list the prescription is not valid and you should use your professional judgement (e.g. refer to local GP), in finding the best way to help the patient.

PRESCRIPTION REQUIREMENTS

It is important to remember that as well as meeting the legal prescription requirements outlined here for dispensing a prescription from an EEA prescriber you need to also be satisfied the medicine(s) supplied is clinically appropriate for the patient.

The GPhC have updated "Guidance for registered pharmacies providing pharmacy services at a distance, including on the internet" March 2022 www.pharmacyregulation.org and expect all pharmacy professionals to follow the guidance to provide pharmacy services safely and effectively at a distance (including on the internet).

The following details are required on a prescription from an approved health professional from an approved country:

- **Patient details**
  Patient's full first name(s), surname and date of birth

- **Prescriber details**
  Prescriber's full first name(s), surname, professional qualifications, direct contact details including email address and telephone or fax number (with international prefix), work address (including the country they work in)

- **Prescribed medicine details**
  Name of the medicine (brand name where appropriate), pharmaceutical form, quantity, strength and dosage details

- **Prescriber signature**

- **Date of issue**
  Prescriptions are valid for up to six months from the appropriate date (prescriptions for Schedule 4 CDs 28 days). For prescriptions from these countries the appropriate date is the date on which the prescription was signed.

PLEASE NOTE

Even if the prescription requirements have been written in a foreign language the prescription is still legally acceptable. However, you will need to have enough information to enable the safe supply of medicines considering patient care and wellbeing.

CHECKING THE REGISTRATION STATUS OF APPROVED HEALTH PROFESSIONALS

An international database of prescribers does not exist and, indeed, not all of the approved countries have a register of practitioners or online registers in English. Therefore, it may not always be possible to check the registration of approved health professionals.

Up-to-date contact details for EEA competent authorities to check registration details of doctors and dentists can be obtained from:

- **Doctors**
  General Medical Council (GMC)
  www.gmc-uk.org

- **Dentists**
  General Dental Council (GDC)
  www.gdc-uk.org
  (search for 'List of EEA competent authorities')

You can search regulated professions and competent authorities in the approved countries on the European Commission website (ec.europa.eu/info/index_en).

IF YOU ARE UNABLE TO CONFIRM REGISTRATION STATUS

If it is not possible to confirm the registration status of the approved health professional after taking all reasonable steps to do so, then it may still be possible to make a safe and legal supply in the interests of patient care. It would be beneficial to keep a record of the details of any interventions and steps taken. This would require checking (and being satisfied) that prescription requirements are fulfilled, questioning the patient and careful use of professional judgement. A due diligence defence exists for EEA prescriptions. However, only a court could decide, ultimately on a case-by-case basis, whether due diligence has been exercised.

MEDICINES NOT AVAILABLE

Schedule 1, 2 and 3 CDs and medicinal products without a marketing authorisation valid in the UK are not permitted. Consider referral to an appropriate UK-registered prescriber if such items are required.

EMERGENCY SUPPLY

Emergency supplies at the request of a patient, or at the request of an approved health professional, are legally possible. Follow the usual emergency supply process (see section 3.3.10) and remember that where the request originates from an approved health professional then a prescription needs to be received within 72 hours.

Schedule 1, 2 and 3 CDs (including phenobarbital) or unlicensed products cannot be supplied in an emergency to a patient of an approved health professional.

REFERRAL

It is important to bear in mind that the details outlined above are enabling – it is not obligatory to dispense a prescription from an approved country if presented with one.

You should however, always use your professional judgement when handling prescriptions or emergency supply requests from approved health professionals from approved countries.

If you are not satisfied that a prescription is clinically appropriate or legally valid and an emergency supply is not appropriate, then it may be appropriate to refer the patient to a prescriber based in the UK as an alternative.

3

FURTHER READING

RPS
Prescriptions from the European Economic Area and Switzerland
www.rpharms.com

RPS
Brexit Hub
www.rpharms.com

General Pharmaceutical Council
Letter on Patient safety concerns relating to online prescribing services (August 2021)
www.pharmacyregulation.org

General Pharmaceutical Council
Guidance for registered pharmacies providing pharmacy services at a distance, including on the internet. March 2022
www.pharmacyregulation.org

GOV.UK
Prescriptions issued in the EEA and Switzerland: guidance for pharmacists
www.gov.uk

3.3.6
MILITARY PRESCRIPTIONS

Military primary healthcare medical centres are broadly similar to dispensing doctors practices in the NHS, where the doctor in charge delegates the dispensing function to a suitably trained individual. However, only large medical centres have retained their in-house dispensary. The remaining, smaller medical centres have outsourced the dispensing process to designated community pharmacies under a Ministry of Defence (MOD) contract. Community pharmacies not covered by the contract will not routinely handle military prescriptions.

Military prescriptions are written on a military form FMed 296, see Diagram 14.

Pharmacies with a dispensing contract with the MOD will usually invoice the MOD directly.

Diagram 14: Example of an FMed 296 prescription

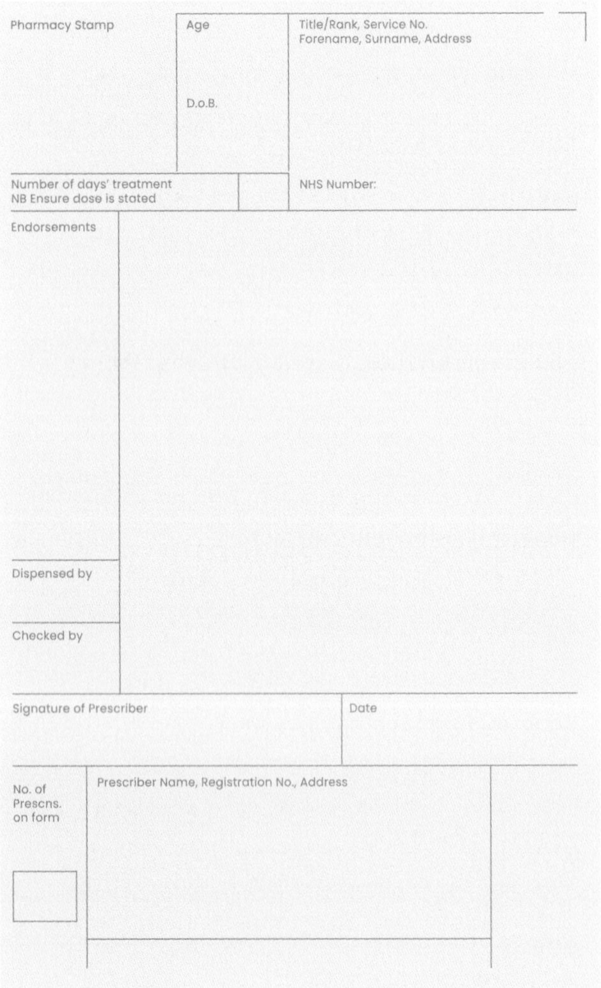
Pharmacy Stamp
Age
Title/Rank, Service No.
Forename, Surname, Address
D.o.B.
Number of days' treatment
NB Ensure dose is stated
NHS Number:
Endorsements
Dispensed by
Checked by
Signature of Prescriber
Date
No. of Prescns. on form
Prescriber Name, Registration No., Address

In the unusual event that an FMed 296 is presented to a non-contracted pharmacy, then the prescription should be treated as a private prescription. In these circumstances, non-contracted pharmacies are not to invoice the MOD directly but are to charge the patient the appropriate fee. It is then up to the individual patient to recover any costs incurred from their military unit (please note: this practice should only be used in exceptional circumstances). Similarly, any military personnel that presents an NHS or other private prescription (including using an FMed 296 as a private prescription) should pay the appropriate fee and request a receipt to reclaim any costs, if eligible. This is unless, of course, for an NHS prescription they fall into an NHS exemption category and present an exemption certificate.

Prescriptions for Schedule 2 and 3 CDs should be written on pink FP10PCD forms (or equivalent in Devolved Administrations) which prescribers obtain from their regional Defence Primary Health Care headquarters supplied by NHS England and NHS Scotland. A Schedule 2 or 3 CD written on an MOD FMed296 form cannot be legally dispensed by community pharmacies.

If there is any doubt to the validity of the FMed 296, normal procedures should be employed (see section 3.3.4). Particular attention should be paid in the following circumstances:

- **Handwritten FMed 296**
  The majority of FMed 296 prescriptions will be computer generated. It is highly unusual to see handwritten prescriptions, especially for MOD accountable drugs (these include Schedule 3, 4 and 5 CDs, codeine, sedatives and medicines for erectile dysfunction).
- **British Forces Post Office (BFPO) address stamp**
  Prescriptions with a BFPO address stamp have been generated abroad and are normally not seen in the UK. If there is any doubt, pharmacists are advised to check the registration status of the doctor, dentist or independent prescriber (see section 3.3.15).

3.3.7
LABELLING OF DISPENSED MEDICINAL PRODUCTS

It is a legal requirement for the following to appear on dispensed medicinal products:

- Name of the patient
- Name and address of the supplying pharmacy
- Date of dispensing
- Name of the medicine
- Directions for use
- Precautions relating to the use of the medicine: "(e.g. For external use only)".

The RPS recommends the following also appears on the dispensing label:

- 'Keep out of the reach and sight of children'
- 'Use this medicine only on your skin' where applicable.

NB: In secure environments it is strongly recommended that the prisoner number is also included on the label as a definitive patient identifier.

Additional information can be added to the dispensing label if the pharmacist considers it to be necessary.

Outer container
Whilst it is lawful to label the outer container, we advise that the labelling recommendations of the National Patient Safety Agency are followed. These guidelines raise the issue that the outer container may be discarded and, therefore, the labelling information could be lost, so the actual container (e.g. inhaler or tube of cream) should be labelled rather than the outer container.

Optimisation of labelling
Subject to the professional skill and judgement of a pharmacist, if he/she is of the opinion that the directions for use, name or common name of the medicine, or precautions, relating to the use of the medicine, are not appropriate on the prescription, they can substitute these with appropriate particulars of a similar kind when producing the dispensing label without contacting the prescriber.

It would be good practice to make a record to maintain a clinical audit trail underpinning patient care. It is important to understand that the above is enabling and not mandatory. The options to contact the prescriber or refer the patient to the prescriber remain available and should be used where this is appropriate in the opinion of the pharmacist having exercised professional skill and judgement.

Full details can be viewed in *Optimising Dispensing Labels and Medicines Use* on the RPS website at www.rpharms.com

ASSEMBLY AND PRE-PACKING MEDICINES
The assembly or pre-packing of medicines by the pharmacy to be supplied to a separate legal entity (e.g. for a NHS Trust to supply a different NHS Trust or an out of hours medical practice) requires the appropriate licence from the MHRA (i.e. Manufacturer's/importer's licence (MIA) or Manufacturer 'specials' licence (MS)). The MHRA can be contacted for further details on the licence and any additional requirements (www.gov.uk).

For activities that include over-labelling for supply, the RPS also advise you contact the MHRA for further details.

LABELLING OF MEDICINES BROKEN DOWN FROM BULK CONTAINERS FOR DISPENSING
Pharmacists are able to break down bulk containers into smaller quantities more appropriate for dispensing against prescriptions which have already been received and are being dispensed or in anticipation of these prescriptions.

For the latter case medicines must be labelled with the:

- Name of the medicine
- Quantity of the medicine in the container
- Quantitative particulars of the medicine (i.e. the ingredients)
- Handling and storage requirements where appropriate
- Expiry date
- Batch reference number (e.g. LOT number or BN).

The medicines which have been broken down from bulk need to be labelled with usual labelling requirements upon dispensing.

If both of the above (Assembly and pre-packing medicines and Labelling of medicines broken down from bulk containers for dispensing) do not apply to you, you should contact the MHRA for further information.

FURTHER READING

Royal Pharmaceutical Society
*Professional guidance on the safe
and secure handling of medicines.*
www.rpharms.com

**Medicines and Healthcare products
Regulatory Agency**
*Additional warning statements for inclusion on the
label and/or in the leaflet of certain medicines.* 2014.
www.gov.uk

**Medicines and Healthcare products
Regulatory Agency**
*Best practice guidance on the labelling and
packaging of medicines.* 2014.
www.gov.uk

Specialist Pharmacy Service
*Advice on labelling of P medications to be supplied
under a Patient Group Direction (PGD).*
www.sps.nhs.uk

Specialist Pharmacy Service
*Labelling requirements for Prescription Only
Medicines (POM) supplied under a Patient Group
Direction.*
www.sps.nhs.uk

3.3.8
ADMINISTRATION

In healthcare settings organisational policies define who can administer medicines, or the appropriate delegation of the administration of medicines, within that setting.

(Please note: The organisation should have a policy for self administration of medicines. Patients maintain responsibility for the administration of some or all of their medicines, during a stay in the healthcare setting, unless a risk assessment indicates otherwise.)

Registered healthcare professionals who administer medicines, or when appropriate delegate the administration of medicines, are accountable for their actions, non-actions and omissions, and exercise professionalism and professional judgement at all times. They would be expected to meet their own professional and regulatory standards and guidance. Non registered healthcare professionals are appropriately trained, assessed as competent and meet relevant organisational guidance on medicines administration.

Before administration, the person administering the medicine must have an overall understanding of the medicine being administered and seeks advice if necessary from a prescriber or a pharmacy professional.

Wherever possible, the actions of prescribing, dispensing/supply and administration are performed by separate healthcare professionals. Exceptionally, where clinical circumstances make it necessary and in the interests of the patient, the same healthcare professional can be responsible for the prescribing and supply/administration of medicines. Where this occurs, an audit trail, documents and processes are in place to limit errors.

Parenteral POMs can only be administered to another person in accordance with the directions of an appropriate practitioner or by an appropriate practitioner. There is an exemption allowing administration for saving life in an emergency and a list of parenteral medicines authorised for this purpose can be found in Schedule 19 of The Human Medicines Regulations 2012 (www.legislation.gov.uk)

Examples include administering naloxone as emergency first aid for a drug-related overdose (see section 3.3.10); or administering adrenaline for the emergency treatment of anaphylaxis.

Further exemptions apply to the administration of smallpox vaccine or administration linked to medical exposure (including radioactive medicines).

Specific classes of persons, such as midwives, paramedics and others can also administer POMs under certain conditions. Details are available in Schedule 17 of the Human Medicines Regulations 2012 (as amended). Certain healthcare professionals can also administer medicines in accordance with a Patient Group Direction (see section 3.3.10).

Medicines that are not POMs may be administered according to a locally agreed homely remedy protocol.

FURTHER READING

Royal Pharmaceutical Society
Professional guidance on the administration of medicines in healthcare settings. 2019.
www.rpharms.com

Royal Pharmaceutical Society
Professional guidance on the safe and secure handling of medicines.
www.rpharms.com

All Wales Medicines Strategy Group
All Wales policy for medicines administration, recording, review, storage and disposal. 2015.
www.awmsg.org

Care Quality Commission
Administering medicines in care homes.
www.cqc.org.uk

Department of Health and Social Care
Administration of medicines in care homes (with nursing) for older people by care assistants.
www.gov.uk

Department for Education
Supporting pupils at school with medical conditions.
www.gov.uk

Health Education England
Administration of medicines by nursing associates: advisory guidance.
www.hee.nhs.uk

Medicines and Healthcare products Regulatory Agency
Rules for the sale, supply and administration of medicines for specific healthcare professionals.
www.gov.uk

National Institute for Health and Care Excellence
Managing medicines for adults receiving social care in the community. NICE guidance. 2017.
www.nice.org.uk

National Institute for Health and Care Excellence
Medicines management in care homes: Social care guideline. 2014.
www.nice.org.uk

National Education Union
Administering medicines.
www.neu.org.uk

Regional Medicines Optimisation Committee (Midland and East)
Homely Remedies: Position Statement. 2018
www.sps.nhs.uk

Royal College of Nursing
Health care support workers administering inactivated influenza, shingles and pneumococcal vaccines for adults and live attenuated influenza vaccine for children.
www.rcn.org.uk

COVERT ADMINISTRATION OF MEDICINES

'Covert administration' is the term used when medicines are administered in a disguised format without the knowledge or consent of the person receiving them, for example, in food or in a drink. Medicines are administered covertly only to people who actively refuse their medication and who are considered to lack mental capacity in accordance with an agreed management plan. Where deemed necessary, covert administration of medicines takes place within the context of existing legal and best practice frameworks. Organisational policies and procedures in place covering covert administration should be followed.

Pharmacists who are asked to sign covert administration documentation should check carefully what they are being asked to sign off as this may indicate they have performed a clinical medication review, and provided advice on how medicines should be administered or what to do if a patient consumes only part of their food or drink.

FURTHER READING

Royal Pharmaceutical Society
Professional guidance on the administration of medicines in healthcare settings. 2019.
www.rpharms.com

Royal Pharmaceutical Society
Professional guidance on the safe and secure handling of medicines.
www.rpharms.com

3

Mental Welfare Commission for Scotland
Covert Medication. **2017.**
www.mwcscot.org.uk

National Institute for Health and Care Excellence
Managing medicines for adults receiving social care in the community. NICE guidance. 2017.
www.nice.org.uk

National Institute for Health and Care Excellence
Medicines management in care homes: Social care guideline. 2014.
www.nice.org.uk

National Institute for Health and Care Excellence
Medicines management in care homes: Quality Statement 6 – Covert administration. 2015.
www.nice.org.uk

Office of the Public Guardian
Mental Capacity Act Code of Practice. 2007.
www.gov.uk

PrescQIPP
Best practice guidance in covert administration of medicines. 2015.
www.prescqipp.info

UKMi
What legal and pharmaceutical issues should be considered when administering medicines covertly? 2017.
www.sps.nhs.uk

ADMINISTRATION OF ADRENALINE IN AN EMERGENCY

Adrenaline is a POM and is given intramuscularly for the treatment of anaphylaxis. Brands of adrenaline intramuscular injections in your pharmacy may include Epipen®, Emerade® and Jext®.

Where a pharmacist is expected to recognise and treat an anaphylactic reaction as part of their usual clinical role (for example, if they are offering a vaccination service), they must have access to an anaphylaxis pack (as outlined in the Immunisation against infection disease [the Green Book]) and have received the required training in the recognition of anaphylaxis and administration of adrenaline. The anaphylaxis pack will include ampoules of adrenaline and syringes and needles or prefilled syringes which should be used in preference to auto injectors such as those listed above.

ADMINISTRATION OF ADRENALINE

Regulation 238 of the Human Medicines Regulations 2012 allows adrenaline to be administered by anyone for the purpose of saving life in an emergency.

Therefore pharmacists using their professional and clinical judgement can administer adrenaline in an emergency to persons presenting with symptoms of anaphylaxis. Detailed information on Anaphylaxis signs and symptoms can be found in the RPS pharmacy guide "Adrenaline auto-injectors (AAI)" at www.rpharms.com

If a pharmacist administers adrenaline they must also ensure that an ambulance is called by dialling 999 and reporting that there is a case of suspected anaphylaxis.

FURTHER READING

National Institute for Health and Care Excellence
Anaphylaxis: assessment and referral after emergency treatment. Clinical guideline. 2011.
www.nice.org.uk

Public Health England
Immunisation against infectious disease: the green book
www.gov.uk

Resuscitation Council (UK)
Emergency treatment of anaphylactic reactions: Guidelines for healthcare providers.
www.resus.org.uk

3.3.9
PATIENT SPECIFIC DIRECTIONS AND ADMINISTRATION, SALE AND SUPPLY IN HOSPITALS AND OTHER SETTINGS

The Human Medicines Regulations 2012 provides a range of exemptions to the restrictions on the sale, supply and administration of medicines.

A number of these exemptions are collectively described as patient specific directions (PSDs).

Legislation does not specifically define a PSD. However, it is generally accepted to mean a written instruction from a doctor, dentist or non-medical prescriber for a medicine to be supplied or administered to a named patient after the prescriber has assessed that patient on an individual basis.

Some organisations may limit who is authorised to supply and/or administer medicines under a PSD within their local medicines policies and governance arrangements. Any trained and competent health professional would be suitable. PSDs relate to a specific named patient but do not need to comply with the requirements specified for a prescription.

In a hospital ward, written PSDs are encountered on inpatient charts as directions to administer. While the law does not stipulate what should be included in a PSD, sufficient information must be available for the person administering the specified medicine to do so safely. In addition a PSD, if sufficiently clear, may also be a direction to make a sale or supply.

Typically the directions within an inpatient chart are copied onto an order form for the pharmacy to prepare discharge ('take home') medicines. The pharmacist in this instance is not prescribing, and the supply is made under the authority of the original written direction to supply. This process should be carried out or counter-checked by a pharmacist. This order form does not replace a discharge letter; however, it can form part of the discharge letter.

For the purpose of administration (rather than supply) it is also possible for the directions of an appropriate practitioner to be verbal or telephoned. This is because not all of the exemptions specify that the authorisation to administer a medicine needs to be in writing. Nevertheless, a written authorisation should be used wherever possible and any applicable standards that require the authorisation to be in writing should be adhered to. For example, in England, the Care Quality Commission fundamental standards, and the standards of any relevant healthcare professionals involved in administration (e.g. nurses) will be applicable.

Some hospitals have formulated policies to permit, in an emergency, the administration of medicines following a telephoned or verbal request from an appropriate practitioner – usually involving two nurses checking one another.

Some hospitals have also formulated policies for the supply and/or administration of POMs (and P or general sale medicines) to ensure that medicines are handled safely, securely and appropriately. Such policies should be carefully considered and agreed by medical, nursing and pharmacy staff to ensure that patients are not put at risk. The policy should be cross-referenced against standards set by any applicable body, including regulatory and professional bodies of relevant healthcare professionals involved in the process. If in doubt, the Department of Health should be consulted for hospitals in England (along with the hospital's legal advisors). Hospitals in Scotland should contact the Scottish Executive, while hospitals in Wales should contact the Department of Health and Social Services.

FURTHER READING

Royal Pharmaceutical Society
Professional guidance on the administration of medicines in healthcare settings. 2019.
www.rpharms.com

Royal Pharmaceutical Society
Professional guidance on the safe and secure handling of medicines.
www.rpharms.com

British Medical Association
Patient group directions and patient specific directions in general practice. 2016.
www.bma.org.uk

Care Quality Commission
Various resources available.
www.cqc.org.uk

NHS Education for Scotland
Various resources available.
www.nes.scot.nhs.uk

Specialist Pharmacy Service
Medicine matters: A guide to mechanisms for the prescribing, supply and administration of medicines (in England). 2018.
www.sps.nhs.uk

Specialist Pharmacy Service
Various resources available.
www.sps.nhs.uk

3.3.10
EXEMPTIONS: SALE AND SUPPLY WITHOUT A PRESCRIPTION

There are several exemptions that allow POMs to be sold or supplied without a prescription.

Pharmacists are likely to be involved in many of these mechanisms and need to be aware of:

- Patient group directions (PGDs)
- Patient specific directions (PSDs) (see section 3.3.9)
- Emergency supplies
- Optometrist or podiatrist signed patient orders
- Supply of salbutamol inhalers to schools
- Supply of adrenaline autoinjectors to schools
- Supply of naloxone by individuals providing recognised drug treatment services

PATIENT GROUP DIRECTIONS (PGDS)

A PGD is a written direction that allows the supply and/or administration of a specified medicine or medicines, by named authorised health professionals, to a well-defined group of patients requiring treatment for a specific condition.

It is important that pharmacists involved with PGDs understand the scope and limitations of PGDs as well as the wider context into which they fit to ensure safe, effective services for patients.

The supply and administration of medicines under a PGD should only be reserved for those limited situations where this offers an advantage for patient care, without compromising patient safety.

A PGD should only be developed after careful consideration of all the potential methods of supply and/or administration of medicines, including prescribing, by medical or nonmedical prescribers.

Pharmacists can supply, offer to supply and administer diamorphine or morphine under a PGD for the immediate, necessary treatment of sick or injured persons.

LABELLING OF PGDS

Prescription only medicines supplied under a PGD should be labelled in the same way as if supplied against a prescription.

FURTHER READING

Medicines and Healthcare products Regulatory Agency
Patient group directions: Who can use them. 2017.
www.gov.uk

National Institute for Health and Care Excellence
Patient group directions: Medicines practice guidelines (including a PGD template). 2013.
www.nice.org.uk

Specialist Pharmacy Services
Medicines matters: A guide to mechanisms for the prescribing, supply and administration of medicines (in England).
www.sps.nhs.uk

Specialist Pharmacy Services
What are the legal requirements for labelling a Prescription Only Medicines (POM) issued via a PGD before supply to the patient?
www.sps.nhs.uk

Specialist Pharmacy Services
When and how can dentists supply medicines?
www.sps.nhs.uk

EMERGENCY SUPPLY

In an emergency a pharmacist working in a registered pharmacy can supply POMs to a patient (humans not animals) without a prescription on the request of a 'relevant prescriber' or a patient (conditions apply, see below).

Each request should be considered on a case-by-case basis, using professional judgement in the best interests of the patient.

A 'relevant prescriber' includes:

- A doctor
- A dentist
- A supplementary prescriber
- A nurse independent prescriber
- A pharmacist independent prescriber
- A community practitioner nurse prescriber
- A physiotherapist independent prescriber
- A podiatrist independent prescriber
- A therapeutic radiographer independent prescriber
- An optometrist independent prescriber
- An EEA or Swiss health professional (see section 3.3.5)
- A paramedic independent prescriber

Healthcare professionals from countries outside of the EEA or Switzerland are not recognised as "relevant prescribers" in the United Kingdom.

EMERGENCY SUPPLY AT THE REQUEST OF A PRESCRIBER

The conditions for an emergency supply at the request of a prescriber are:

Relevant prescriber
The pharmacist is satisfied that the request is from one of the prescribers stated above

Emergency
The pharmacist is satisfied that a prescription cannot be provided immediately due to an emergency (e.g. patient cannot collect the prescription from the prescriber, the prescriber is unable to drop off prescription at the pharmacy and patient urgently needs the medicine(s), etc.)

Prescription within 72 hours
The prescriber agrees to provide a written prescription within 72 hours

Directions
The medicine is supplied in accordance with the direction given by the prescriber

Not for CDs, except phenobarbital
Schedule 1, 2 or 3 CDs cannot be supplied in an emergency whether requested by UK, EEA or Swiss health professionals. Phenobarbital (also known as phenobarbitone or phenobarbitone sodium) is the exception and can be authorised by UK doctor, dentist, nurse or pharmacist independent prescriber or supplementary prescriber in an emergency for the treatment of epilepsy.

Record kept
An entry must be made into the POM register on the day of the supply (or, if impractical, on the following day). The entry needs to include:

- The date the POM was supplied
- The name (including strength and form where appropriate) and quantity of medicine supplied
- The name and address of the prescriber requesting the emergency supply
- The name and address of the patient for whom the POM was required
- The date on the prescription (this can be added to the entry when the prescription is received by the pharmacy)
- The date on which the prescription is received (this should be added to the entry when the prescription is received in the pharmacy)

Labelling
Usual labelling requirements apply (see section 3.3.7).

EMERGENCY SUPPLY AT THE REQUEST OF A PATIENT

The conditions for an emergency supply at the request of a patient are:

Interview
Regulation 225 Human Medicines Regulations 2012 requires a pharmacist to interview the patient. The RPS recognises that in some circumstances this might not be possible, for example if the patient is a child, or being cared for, etc. In these circumstances the RPS advises pharmacists to use their professional judgement and consider the best interest of the patient

3

Immediate need

The pharmacist must be satisfied that there is an immediate need for the POM and that it is not practical for the patient to obtain a prescription without undue delay

Legislation does not prevent a pharmacist from making an emergency supply when a doctor's surgery is open. As with any request for an emergency supply, pharmacists must consider the best interests of the patient. Where a pharmacist believes that it would be impracticable in the circumstances for a patient to obtain a prescription without undue delay they may decide that an emergency supply is necessary. Automatically referring patients who are away from home and have forgotten or run out of their medication to the nearest local surgery to register as a temporary resident may not always be the most appropriate course of action.

Previous treatment

The POM requested must previously have been used as a treatment and prescribed by a UK, EEA or Swiss health professional listed above.

NB: The time interval from when the medicine was last prescribed to when it is requested as an emergency supply would need to be considered and you should use your professional judgement to decide whether a supply or referral to a prescriber is appropriate

Dose

The pharmacist must be satisfied of knowing the dose that the patient needs to take (e.g. refer to the PMR, electronic health record, prescription repeat slip, labelled medicine box, etc.).

Not for CDs, except phenobarbital

Phenobarbital can be supplied to patients of UK-registered prescribers for the purpose of treating epilepsy. Medicinal products cannot be supplied if they consist of or contain any other Schedule 1, 2 or 3 CDs or the substances listed below: ammonium bromide, calcium bromide, calcium bromidolactobionate, embutramide, fencamfamin hydrochloride, fluanisone, hexobarbitone, hexobarbitone sodium, hydrobromic acid, meclofenoxate hydrochloride, methohexitone sodium, pemoline, piracetam, potassium bromide, prolintane hydrochloride, sodium bromide, strychnine hydrochloride, tacrine hydrochloride, thiopentone sodium

(NB: Requests made by a patient of an EEA or Swiss health professional cannot be supplied if they are for medicines that do not have a marketing authorisation valid in the UK – see section 3.3.5)

Length of treatment

If the emergency supply is for a CD (i.e. phenobarbital or Schedule 4 or 5 CD), the maximum quantity that can be supplied is for five days' treatment. For any other POM, no more than 30 days can be supplied except in the following circumstances:

- If the POM is an insulin, an ointment, a cream, or an inhaler for asthma (i.e. the packs cannot be broken), the smallest pack available in the pharmacy should be supplied

- If the POM is an oral contraceptive, a full treatment cycle should be supplied

If the POM is an antibiotic in liquid form for oral administration, the smallest quantity that will provide a full course of treatment should be supplied. (NB: Pharmacists should also consider whether it is appropriate to supply less than the maximum quantity allowed in legislation. Professional judgement should be used to supply a reasonable quantity that is clinically appropriate and lasts until the patient is able to see a prescriber to obtain a further supply).

Records kept

An entry must be made in the POM register on the day of the supply (or, if impractical, on the following day). The entry needs to include:

- The date the POM was supplied

- The name (including strength and form where appropriate) and quantity of medicine supplied

- The name and address of the patient for whom the POM was supplied

- Information on the nature of the emergency, such as why the patient needs the POM and why a prescription cannot be obtained, etc.

Labelling

In addition to standard labelling requirements, the words 'Emergency supply' need to be added to the dispensing label.

OTHER POINTS TO CONSIDER WHEN FACED WITH REQUESTS FOR AN EMERGENCY SUPPLY

Pharmacists should be mindful of patients abusing emergency supplies (for example, where a patient medication record shows that a patient has requested a medicine as an emergency supply on several occasions). It is possible to make an emergency supply even during surgery opening hours; trying to obtain a prescription can sometimes cause undue delay in treatment and, potentially, harm to the patient. If patients are away from home and have run out of their medicines, referring them to the nearest surgery to register as a temporary patient may not always be appropriate. An emergency supply can be made provided the conditions above are met.

REFUSAL TO SUPPLY

If a pharmacist decides not to make an emergency supply after gathering and considering the information discussed in this guidance, the patient should be advised on how to obtain a prescription for the medicine or appropriate medical care. This could involve referral to for example, a doctor, NHS 111, NHS walk-in centre or to an Accident and Emergency department.

A record could be made of why request was refused for audit purposes.

COMMUNITY PHARMACY CONSULTATION SERVICE (CPCS) - ENGLAND

In England, an NHS Advanced Service, enables NHS 111, urgent care settings and 999 providers to refer patients to a community pharmacy for an emergency supply of regular medicines under the NHS.

UNSCHEDULED CARE - SCOTLAND

In Scotland, a national PGD allows participating pharmacies and pharmacists to supply medicines for the urgent provision of current repeat medicines, appliances and ACBS (borderline) items.

Emergency supply remains an option for patients who are not eligible for treatment under the national PGD.

FURTHER READING

Royal Pharmaceutical Society
Electronic Health Record (includes Using electronic health records professionally).
www.rpharms.com

Royal Pharmaceutical Society
Emergency supply.
www.rpharms.com

Royal Pharmaceutical Society
Professional judgement.
www.rpharms.com

Royal Pharmaceutical Society
Summary care records – England.
www.rpharms.com

Community Pharmacy Scotland
Unscheduled care (CPUS).
www.cps.scot

NHS England
Advanced service specification - NHS community pharmacist consultation service.
www.england.nhs.uk

3

OPTOMETRIST OR PODIATRIST SIGNED PATIENT ORDERS

Optometrists and podiatrists cannot authorise supplies of POMs by writing prescriptions unless they are additionally qualified as independent or supplementary prescribers.

However, pharmacists working in a registered pharmacy can supply certain POMs directly to patients in accordance with a signed patient order from any registered optometrist or podiatrist.

The medicine requested must be one which can be legally sold or supplied by the optometrist or podiatrist rather than one which they can only administer. See MHRA website for list.

Please note: Optometrists who have undertaken additional training and are accredited by the GOC as 'additional supply optometrists' can issue signed patient orders for an extended range of medicines.

The signed patient order is not a prescription; therefore the usual prescription requirements would not be needed. However, you should be satisfied the optometrist or the podiatrist has provided sufficient advice to enable the patient to use the medicine safely and effectively.

If the supply is made, the pharmacist should ensure that the medicine is labelled accordingly as a dispensed medicinal product (see section 3.3.7), a patient information leaflet is supplied to the patient and an appropriate record is made in the POM register.

Any additional information or advice that enables the patient to use the medicine safely and effectively should also be provided if it has not already been provided by the optometrist or podiatrist. Details on how to check the registration of the optometrist or podiatrist can be found in section 3.3.15.

FURTHER READING

Royal Pharmaceutical Society
Supply of medicines to podiatrists.
www.rpharms.com

College of Optometrists
Use and supply of drugs or medicines in optometric practice.
www.college-optometrists.org

Medicines and Healthcare products Regulatory Agency
Rules for the sale, supply and administration of medicines for specific healthcare professionals. 2014.
www.gov.uk

SUPPLY OF MEDICINES TO SCHOOLS

Schools can obtain supplies of adrenaline auto-injectors (AAIs) and/or salbutamol inhalers from a pharmacy on a signed order. These can then be administered in an emergency, by persons trained to administer them, to pupils previously prescribed such medication and where parental consent has been received.

Table 5: Supplying adrenaline auto-injectors and salbutamol inhalers to schools

		Additional information
What information should be included on the signed order	The signed order should contain: • Name of the school • Product details (including spacer if relevant) • Strength (if relevant) • Purpose for which the product is required • Total quantity required • Signature of the principal or head teacher Ideally, appropriately headed paper should be used; however, this is not a legislative requirement.	Different brands of AAIs and salbutamol are available, and each brand may have different instructions for administration. See individual Summary of Product Characteristics (SPC) for up to date product details. **Note:** The Department of Health advises schools to hold an appropriate quantity of a single brand of AAI device to avoid confusion in administration and training. The decision as to how many brands the school can purchase will depend on local circumstances and is left to the discretion of the school.
How many can be ordered?	The number that can be obtained by individual schools is not specified in legislation. Schools can purchase salbutamol inhalers and/or AAIs from pharmacies provided it is for small quantities, on an occasional basis and not for profit.	Pharmacists should exercise their professional judgement when responding to requests from schools. Factors to consider include: • School size and number of sites it is comprised of • Number of children known to be affected • Past experiences e.g. of children not having access to an AAI or inhaler

3

What records need to be kept in the pharmacy?	The signed order needs to be retained for two years from the date of supply or an entry made into the POM register. Even when the signed order is retained, it is good practice to make a record in POM register for audit purposes.	In line with normal record keeping requirement an entry in the POM register would include: • Date the POM was supplied • Name, quantity and where it is not apparent formulation and strength of POM supplied • Name and address, trade, business or profession of the person to whom the medicine was supplied • Purpose for which it was sold or supplied.
Where can I find details of a school including head teacher/principal details?	There is no centralised database containing details of schools and head teachers across Great Britain.	Possible sources of information would include: • Department for Education's register of educational establishments in England and Wales (www.get-information-schools.service.gov.uk) • Ofsted reports (www.reports.ofsted.gov.uk) • Information on the individual school's website.
What type of school can I supply?	All primary and secondary schools in the UK – including maintained schools, independent schools, pupil referral units and maintained nursery schools	
What additional advice can I provide?	• Explain how to use and store correctly • Advise on the most appropriate spacer device for the different age groups and how to use them correctly • Advise on correct storage, care and disposal • Advise importance of record keeping, regular date checking and when to replace	www.rightbreathe.com - shows you what's available and how to use using videos. Useful if pharmacists are showing schools how to use hcp.jext.co.uk/about-jext/video-demonstrations demonstration video www.emerade.com/instruction-video demo video www.epipen.co.uk/demonstrationvideo demo video

What guidance is available for schools?	England

England

Department of Health

Guidance on the use of emergency salbutamol inhalers in schools. 2014.

www.gov.uk

Department of Health

Guidance on the use of adrenaline auto-injectors in schools. 2017.

www.gov.uk

Wales

Welsh Government

Use of emergency adrenaline auto-injectors in schools. 2017.

www.gov.wales

Welsh Government

Use of emergency salbutamol inhalers in schools. 2017.

www.gov.wales

Scotland

Supporting children and young people with healthcare needs in schools: guidance. 2017.

www.gov.scot

Further reading

Royal Pharmaceutical Society

Supply of Salbutamol inhalers to schools

www.rpharms.com

Royal Pharmaceutical Society

Adrenaline auto - injectors (AAIs)

www.rpharms.com

Department for Education

Statutory framework for the early years foundation stage. 2017.

www.gov.uk

Department for Education

Supporting pupils at school with medical conditions. 2014.

www.gov.uk

Welsh Government

Supporting learners with healthcare needs. 2017.

www.gov.wales

3

SUPPLY OF NALOXONE BY INDIVIDUALS EMPLOYED OR ENGAGED IN THE PROVISION OF RECOGNISED DRUG TREATMENT SERVICES

Deaths in the UK involving heroin and/or morphine have significantly increased in recent years. Naloxone is an opioid /opiate antagonist which can completely or partially reverse the central nervous system depression, especially respiratory depression, caused by natural or synthetic opioids and is licensed for the treatment of suspected acute opioid overdose.

Following legislative changes in October 2015, naloxone falls into a unique category. Naloxone remains a POM but the Human Medicines (Amendment) (No.3) Regulations 2015 allow staff engaged or employed in "lawful drug treatment services" to obtain naloxone from a wholesaler and make direct supplies to patients without a prescription, patient group direction (PGD) or patient specific direction (PSD). From February 2019 this included nasal naloxone. Lawful drug treatment services is defined as:

"Persons employed or engaged in the provision of drug treatment services provided by, on behalf of or under arrangements made by one of the following bodies:

(a) an NHS body

(b) a local authority

(c) Public Health England, or

(d) Public Health Agency".

This definition extends to commissioned services providing needle and syringe programmes (including those provided by pharmacies) and pharmacies providing drug treatment services (includes instalment and supervised dispensing of Opioid Substitute Therapies (OST)).

Anyone can administer naloxone for the purpose of saving a life (Schedule 19 of the Human Medicines Regulations 2012) and there is evidence for the effectiveness of training family members or peers in how to administer the drug. The 2015 amendments widen the groups of people who are eligible to receive supplies of naloxone. This has been extended to cover people likely to witness an overdose and includes family members, peers and staff in regular contact with drug users where naloxone may be required for example.

A number of naloxone products are licensed for use in reversing acute opioid overdose.

A pharmacy may be commissioned to participate in a local take home naloxone scheme.

Please note: This is a service that can continue to be provided by appropriately trained staff in the absence of the RP.

FURTHER READING

Department of Health and Social Care. Clinical Guidelines on Drug Misuse and Dependence Update 2017 Independent Expert Working Group *Drug misuse and dependence: UK guidelines on clinical management.* 2017. www.gov.uk

Department of Health and Social Care, Medicines and Healthcare products Regulatory Agency (MHRA) and Public Health England. *Widening the availability of naloxone.* 2019. www.gov.uk

Specialist Pharmacy Service *What naloxone doses should be used in adults to reverse urgently the effects opioids?* www.sps.nhs.uk

3.3.11
PREGNANCY PREVENTION PROGRAMMES

Certain medicines, e.g. oral retinoids, valproate, thalidomide, lenalidomide and pomalidomide, carry a high risk of causing foetal malformations and/or can increase the risk of spontaneous abortion when taken by women and girls.

Pregnancy Prevention Programmes (PPP) protect females of childbearing potential by minimising the risk of becoming pregnant while taking these medicines.

Pharmacists can help by ensuring that such medicines are not dispensed for women or girls who might be pregnant or are considering becoming pregnant unless they follow the manufacturer's Pregnancy Prevention Programme or the prescriber agrees there are compelling reasons that indicate there is no risk of pregnancy e.g. due to a hysterectomy.

Brief information on two PPP for medicines commonly dispensed in community pharmacy are provided below. Full details on all PPPs can be found in the manufacturer's 'Summary of Product Characteristics' and risk materials available at: www.medicines.org.uk. See also further reading for each medicine.

ORAL RETINOIDS PPP

Oral retinoids (including acitretin, alitretinoin and isotretinoin) are used for severe skin conditions. They are described in their Summary of Product Characteristics (SPCs) as 'a powerful human teratogen inducing a high frequency of severe and life-threatening birth defects' and therefore contraindicated in pregnant women and women of childbearing potential unless all of the conditions of the PPP are met.

The programme is a combination of education for healthcare professionals and patients, therapy management (including pregnancy testing before during and after treatment, contraception requirements) and distribution control.

Oral retinoids should only be initiated by or under the supervision of, a dermatologist, prescribing GP with an extended role in dermatology, or a specialist dermatology nurse, and under the conditions of the PPP. The prescriber must check that the patient complies with, understands and acknowledges the reasons for pregnancy prevention and agrees to monthly follow-up, contraceptive precautions and pregnancy testing.

SPECIAL DISTRIBUTION CONTROLS FOR FEMALES AT RISK OF PREGNANCY

1 **Prescription Validity**
   Under the PPP, prescriptions are valid only for seven days and ideally should be dispensed on the date the prescription is written. Prescriptions which are presented after seven days should be considered expired and the patient should be referred back to the prescriber for a new prescription. Pregnancy status may need to be reconfirmed by a further negative pregnancy test.

2 **Quantity**
   Check that the quantity is for a maximum of 30 days' supply. A quantity for more than 30 days can only be dispensed if the patient is confirmed by the prescriber as not being under the PPP.

Pharmacists should not accept repeat prescriptions, free sample distribution, or faxed prescriptions for oral retinoids. A telephone request should only be accepted if this is an emergency supply at the request of a PPP specialist prescriber together with confirmation that pregnancy status has been established as negative within the preceding seven days.

FURTHER READING

Royal Pharmaceutical Society
Oral retinoids and the Pregnancy Prevention Programme.
www.rpharms.com

Electronic Medicines Compendium
Full details of isotretinoin pregnancy prevention programmes are available on the 'Summary of Product Characteristics' for the oral retinoid preparations.
www.medicines.org.uk

Medicines and Healthcare products Regulatory Agency
Oral retinoid medicines: Revised and simplified pregnancy prevention education materials for healthcare professionals and women.
www.gov.uk

Medicines and Healthcare products Regulatory Agency
Oral retinoids: pregnancy prevention – Reminder of measures to minimise teratogenic risk.
www.gov.uk

3

VALPROATE PPP

Valproate is used to treat epilepsy, bipolar disorder and for preventing migraine (unlicensed). However, valproate can seriously harm an unborn child when taken during pregnancy and should not be taken by women and girls unless nothing else works and the person taking valproate is part of a pregnancy prevention programme (PPP).

WHAT PHARMACISTS SHOULD DO:

- Have a conversation with female patients of child-bearing age who are prescribed valproate to find out if they have had a review with their doctor, are aware of the risks and are on a PPP

- Those planning pregnancy should be advised to schedule an appointment with their prescriber to review treatment and to continue with contraception and valproate treatment in the meantime

- If there is an unplanned pregnancy whilst a patient is taking valproate medicines advise the patient NOT to stop their treatment and to arrange to see their prescriber urgently to review treatment

- Provide a patient card every time valproate is dispensed

- Dispense valproate preparations in original packs whenever possible. If dispensing in 'white boxes' ensure a patient information leaflet is provided and a valproate warning label/sticker added to the box

- Ensure the dispensing label does not cover the warning label/sticker

- Emphasize the importance of the need for an annual specialist review

- Report any suspected side effects to valproate medicines via the Yellow Card Scheme (see section 2.5.3 Reporting adverse events)

FURTHER READING

Royal Pharmaceutical Society
Valproate and the Pregnancy Prevention Programme.
www.rpharms.com

Electronic Medicines Compendium
Full details of valproate pregnancy prevention programmes are available on the 'Summary of Product Characteristics' for the valproate preparations.
www.medicines.org.uk

General Pharmaceutical Council
GPhC statement on supplying valproate safely to women and girls.
www.pharmacyregulation.org

Medical Royal Colleges
Guidance document on valproate use in women and girls of child bearing age. (endorsed by RPS).
www.rcpch.ac.uk

Medicines and Healthcare products Regulatory Agency
Drug Safety Update – Valproate medicines (Epilim, Depakote): Contraindicated in women and girls of childbearing potential unless conditions of Pregnancy Prevention Programme are met.
www.gov.uk

Medicines and Healthcare products Regulatory Agency
Valproate use by women and girls.
www.gov.uk

3.3.12
BIOSIMILAR MEDICINES

Advances in biotechnology have resulted in an increasing number of biological molecules and materials being used as medicines. This is a trend that is expected to continue, at least for the foreseeable future. A number of patents and periods of marketing exclusivity for biological medicines are expiring and biosimilar versions of the medicines are becoming more widely available e.g. insulin glargine. The introduction of biosimilars offers potential benefits in terms of cost savings for the NHS and increased access to treatments for patients. Biosimilars are not the same as a generic medicine and as a pharmacist you will need to be aware of the guidance around the use of biosimilars in order to ensure their safe and effective use.

WHAT IS A BIOLOGIC?

A biologic is a medicine made from a variety of natural sources that may be human, animal or microorganism in origin. Examples of a biologic include vaccines, blood and blood products, somatic cells, DNA, human cells and tissues and therapeutic proteins. In general, the first or original biologic on the market is termed the originator or reference product.

WHAT IS A BIOSIMILAR?

A biosimilar is a biologic medicine that is similar to an already licensed biologic medicine in terms of quality, safety and efficacy. A biosimilar is specifically developed and licensed to treat the same disease(s) as the original innovator product. A biosimilar can only be marketed after the patent protecting the originator product and any period of marketing exclusivity have expired.

WHY IS A BIOSIMILAR MEDICINE NOT A GENERIC MEDICINE?

Due to the complexity of structure and greater molecule size of biologics as well as their inherent heterogeneity resulting from their production methods, it is not possible to make an identical copy of the originator biologic. Biosimilars are licensed for use based on extensive data on quality, safety and efficacy compared to the originator product. It is not possible to characterise a biologic to the same extent as a small molecule drug, where an identical copy can be produced, known as a generic medicine.

IS IT POSSIBLE TO SWITCH BETWEEN AN ORIGINATOR BIOLOGIC AND A BIOSIMILAR?

Any decision to change the brand of a biologic used to treat a patient must only be made by a prescriber following discussions with the patient. It is recommended that, at the point of dispensing, the pharmacist confirms the patient has received the biologic they expect and that they are aware of how to store and use the medicine.

HOW WILL A BIOSIMILAR BE PRESCRIBED?

In contrast to generic products, all biosimilars will have their own unique brand name. The MHRA has recommended that all biologics should be prescribed by brand to avoid automatic substitution.

HOW ARE ADVERSE DRUG REACTIONS TO BIOSIMILARS REPORTED?

It is important that both the brand name and batch number of a biologic medicine are provided when reporting suspected adverse drug reactions to biologics to facilitate effective safety monitoring. To support patient safety, pharmacists should consider it good practice to record the brand name and batch number of any biologic medicine (including biosimilars) supplied to a patient.

FURTHER READING

Royal Pharmaceutical Society
Explaining biosimilar medicines.
www.rpharms.com

British Biosimilars Association
Various online resources available.
www.britishbiosimilars.co.uk

British National Formulary
www.medicinescomplete.com
or www.evidence.nhs.uk

European Medicines Agency
Various online resources available.
www.ema.europa.eu/en

Healthcare Improvement Scotland and NHS Scotland
Biosimilar medicines: A national prescribing framework. 2018.
www.healthcareimprovementscotland.org

International Federation of Pharmaceutical Manufacturers and Associations
Considerations for physicians on switching decisions regarding biosimilars. Joint position paper. 2017.
www.ifpma.org

Medicines and Healthcare products Regulatory Agency (MHRA)
Drug Safety Update – High strength, fixed combination and biosimilar insulin products: Minimising the risk of medication error. 2015.
www.gov.uk

Medicines and Healthcare products Regulatory Agency (MHRA)
What is a biosimilar medicine? 2015.
www.gov.uk

Medicines for Europe
Various online resources available.
www.medicinesforeurope.com

National Institute for Health and Care Excellence (NICE)
Biosimilar medicines. Key therapeutic topic. 2016.
www.nice.org.uk

NHS England
Biosimilar medicines.
www.england.nhs.uk

3.3.13 ADVANCED THERAPY MEDICINAL PRODUCTS (ATMPS)

An advanced therapy medicinal product (ATMP) is a biological medicinal product based on genes, tissues or cells which is either:

- a gene therapy medicinal product

- a somatic cell therapy medicinal product, or

- a tissue engineered product

In addition, some ATMPs may contain one or more medical devices as an integral part of the medicine, which are referred to as combined ATMPs. An example of this is cells embedded in a biodegradable matrix or scaffold.

Definitions of these can be found on the European Medicines Agency (EMA) website:
www.ema.europa.eu/en

The majority of ATMP use is in clinical trials; however, some are now available as licensed medicines e.g. talimogene laherparepvec for metastatic melanoma, and axicabtagene ciloleucel for large B cell lymphoma – the treatment being commonly known as CAR-T cell therapy.

As ATMPs are medicines they are subject to the same requirements as for other medicinal products. The Chief Pharmacist is responsible for their governance and management.

For more comprehensive information on ATMPs, including details of legislation and guidance as well as governance around the use, storage and handling of ATMPs see Further reading below.

FURTHER READING

National Pharmacy Clinical Trials Advisory Group
The role of pharmacy in the successful delivery of advanced therapy medicinal products: Information for Chief Pharmacists. 2017.
www.sps.nhs.uk

Pan UK Pharmacy Working Group for ATMPs
Gene therapy medicinal products: Governance and preparation requirements. 2019.
www.sps.nhs.uk

3.3.14
PRESCRIBER TYPES AND PRESCRIBING RESTRICTIONS

Doctors are by far the largest group of prescribers who, along with dentists and veterinary surgeons, are able to prescribe on registration. They have been joined over the years by independent and supplementary prescribers from a range of other healthcare professions who are able to prescribe within their scope of practice once they have completed an approved education programme.

All prescribers should recognise the limits of their own knowledge and skill and prescribe within their own competence and clinical expertise.

The prescribing restrictions for prescribers from each of the healthcare professions are summarised in Table 6.

Table 6 notes:

- When prescribing Schedule 2 and 3 Controlled Drugs (CD) the prescriber's address must be within the UK
- Schedule 1 CDs can only be prescribed under Home Office licence
- For further information on emergency supply see section 3.3.10

Table 6: Prescriber types and prescribing restrictions

Doctor	
Can prescribe Schedule 2 to 5 CDs?	Yes – a Home Office licence is required to prescribe cocaine, diamorphine or dipipanone for treating addiction
Can prescribe unlicensed and/or off-label medicines?	Yes
Can authorise an emergency supply for items which can be prescribed?	Yes – includes phenobarbital for epilepsy but no other Schedule 1, 2 or 3 CDs
Other information	To practise medicines in the UK, doctors are required to be registered with the GMC and hold a licence to practise

Dentist	
Can prescribe Schedule 2 to 5 CDs?	Yes – a Home Office licence is required to prescribe cocaine, diamorphine or dipipanone for treating addiction
Can prescribe unlicensed and/or off-label medicines?	Yes
Can authorise an emergency supply for items which can be prescribed?	Yes – includes phenobarbital for epilepsy but no other Schedule 1, 2 or 3 CDs
Other information	Dentists should restrict prescribing to treatment of dental conditions but legally can prescribe any medicine within their clinical expertise. NHS dental prescriptions are restricted to the medicines listed in the Dental Practitioners' Formulary (see BNF bnf.nice.org.uk). See also section 3.3.2.

3

Veterinary surgeon	
Can prescribe Schedule 2 to 5 CDs?	Yes Prescriptions for Schedule 2 and 3 CDs do not need to be on the standardised forms but must include the RCVS registration number of the prescriber
Can prescribe unlicensed and/or off-label medicines?	Yes Where the medicine is not licensed for the animal intended then it needs to be prescribed under the veterinary Cascade (see section 3.5.2)
Can authorise an emergency supply for items which can be prescribed?	No (emergency supply legislation applies to human use only)
Other information	For the treatment of animals only

Nurse/midwife independent prescriber	
Can prescribe Schedule 2 to 5 CDs?	Yes – but not cocaine, diamorphine or dipipanone for treating addiction
Can prescribe unlicensed and/or off-label medicines?	Yes Unlicensed medicines are excluded from the Nurse Prescribers' Formulary in Scottish Drug Tariff and therefore are not reimbursed on NHS prescriptions in Scotland
Can authorise an emergency supply for items which can be prescribed?	Yes – includes phenobarbital for epilepsy but no other Schedule 1, 2 or 3 CDs

Optometrist independent prescriber	
Can prescribe Schedule 2 to 5 CDs?	No
Can prescribe unlicensed and/or off-label medicines?	Only 'off-label' medicines (i.e. using a licensed medicine outside of its approved use)
Can authorise an emergency supply for items which can be prescribed?	Yes
Other information	For treating conditions affecting the eye and surrounding tissue only; but not parenteral preparations

Paramedic independent prescriber (advanced paramedics)

Can prescribe Schedule 2 to 5 CDs?	No - at the time of writing proposed changes to legislation in relation to certain CDs were being considered by the Home Office
Can prescribe unlicensed and/or off-label medicines?	Only 'off-label' medicines (i.e. using a licensed medicine outside of its approved use)
Can authorise an emergency supply for items which can be prescribed?	Yes - but not Schedule 1, 2 or 3 CDs (including phenobarbital)

Pharmacist independent prescriber

Can prescribe Schedule 2 to 5 CDs?	Yes - but not cocaine, diamorphine or dipipanone for treating addiction
Can prescribe unlicensed and/or off-label medicines?	Yes
Can authorise an emergency supply for items which can be prescribed?	Yes - includes phenobarbital for epilepsy but no other Schedule 1, 2 or 3 CDs

Physiotherapist independent prescriber

Can prescribe Schedule 2 to 5 CDs?	Only the following CDs: For oral administration - diazepam, dihydrocodeine, lorazepam, morphine, oxycodone and temazepam For injection – morphine For transdermal administration - fentanyl
Can prescribe unlicensed and/or off-label medicines?	Only 'off-label' medicines (i.e. using a licensed medicine outside of its approved use)
Can authorise an emergency supply for items which can be prescribed?	Yes - but not Schedule 1, 2 or 3 CDs (including phenobarbital)

Podiatrist/chiropodist independent prescriber

Can prescribe Schedule 2 to 5 CDs?	Only the following CDs for oral administration - diazepam, dihydrocodeine, lorazepam and temazepam
Can prescribe unlicensed and/or off-label medicines?	Only 'off-label' medicines (i.e. using a licensed medicine outside of its approved use)
Can authorise an emergency supply for items which can be prescribed?	Yes - but not Schedule 1, 2 or 3 CDs (including phenobarbital)

Therapeutic radiographer independent prescriber

Can prescribe Schedule 2 to 5 CDs?	No At the time of writing proposed changes to legislation in relation to certain CDs were being considered by the Home Office
Can prescribe unlicensed and/or off-label medicines?	Only 'off-label' medicines (i.e. using a licensed medicine outside of its approved use)
Can authorise an emergency supply for items which can be prescribed?	Yes - but not Schedule 1, 2 or 3 CDs (including phenobarbital)

Supplementary prescriber: dietician, midwife, nurse, optometrist, paramedic, pharmacist, physiotherapist, podiatrist/chiropodist, radiographer (diagnostic/therapeutic)

Can prescribe Schedule 2 to 5 CDs?	Yes - but not cocaine, diamorphine or dipipanone for treating addiction
Can prescribe unlicensed and/or off-label medicines?	Yes
Can authorise an emergency supply for items which can be prescribed?	Yes - includes phenobarbital for epilepsy but no other Schedule 1, 2 or 3 CDs
Other information	Prescribing is restricted to areas of clinical competence and included within an agreed written clinical management plan (written and agreed with a prescriber and often the patient)

Community practitioner nurse prescriber

Can prescribe Schedule 2 to 5 CDs?	No
Can prescribe unlicensed and/or off-label medicines?	No – other than Nystatin off-label for neonates
Can authorise an emergency supply for items which can be prescribed?	Yes
Other information	Prescribing restricted to dressings, appliances and licensed medicines listed in the Nurse Prescribers' Formulary (see BNF)

EEA or Swiss registered approved health professional	
Can prescribe Schedule 2 to 5 CDs?	Schedule 4 and 5 CDs only
Can prescribe unlicensed and/or off-label medicines?	Only 'off-label' medicines (i.e. using a licensed medicine outside of its approved use)
Can authorise an emergency supply for items which can be prescribed?	Yes
Other information	Can only prescribe items which have a recognised marketing authorisation within the UK (see also section 3.3.5)

FURTHER READING

Royal Pharmaceutical Society
Competency framework for all prescribers.
www.rpharms.com

Royal Pharmaceutical Society
Independent prescriber guide.
www.rpharms.com

Pharmaceutical Press
British National Formulary: Non-medical prescribing.
bnf.nice.org.uk

Specialist Pharmacy Services
When and how can dentists supply medicines?
www.sps.nhs.uk

HUMAN MEDICINES REGULATIONS EXEMPTIONS

Some healthcare professionals can sell, supply and/or administer certain medicines under specific exemptions made under the Human Medicines Regulations 2012.

The healthcare practitioners covered by exemptions include:

- Midwives (see also section 3.6.6)
- Opthoptists
- Optometrists (see also section 3.3.10)
- Paramedics
- Podiatrists/chiropodists

Further information can be found in the Human Medicines Regulations 2012 (as amended) www.legislation.gov.uk or the MHRA website (*Guidance on Rules for the sale, supply and administration of medicines for specific healthcare professionals* www.gov.uk)

3

3.3.15
CHECKING REGISTRATION OF HEALTHCARE PROFESSIONALS

You may need to verify the registration status of pharmacists and other healthcare professionals as part of the due diligence process when checking whether a person can prescribe or whether they can be supplied by way of wholesaling.

Those healthcare professionals with additional independent and/or supplementary prescriber qualification are annotated in the relevant professional register and can be verified online. Contact details are provided in Table 7.

Table 7: Registration bodies for healthcare professionals

Profession	Registration body
Dentists	General Dental Council www.gdc-uk.org 020 7167 6000
Dieticians	Health and Care Professions Council www.hcpc-uk.org 0300 500 6184
Doctors	General Medical Council www.gmc-uk.org 0161 923 6602 To practise medicine in the UK doctors are required to be registered with the GMC and hold a licence to practise
Nurses / midwives	Nursing and Midwifery Council www.nmc.org.uk 020 7333 9333
Optometrists	General Optical Council www.optical.org 020 7580 3898
Orthoptists	Health and Care Professions Council www.hcpc-uk.org 0300 500 6184

Profession	Registration body
Paramedics	Health and Care Professions Council www.hcpc-uk.org 0300 500 6184
Pharmacists	General Pharmaceutical Council www.pharmacyregulation.org 020 3713 8000
Physiotherapists	Health and Care Professions Council www.hcpc-uk.org 0300 500 6184
Podiatrists / chiropodists	Health and Care Professions Council www.hcpc-uk.org 0300 500 6184
Radiographers	Health and Care Professions Council www.hcpc-uk.org 0300 500 6184
Veterinary surgeons	Royal College of Veterinary Surgeons www.rcvs.org.uk 020 7222 2001

3.3.16
PRESCRIBING AND DISPENSING BY THE SAME PERSON

The initial prescribing, and supply of medicines prescribed, should normally remain separate functions performed by separate healthcare professionals in order to protect patient safety.

Patient safety is improved by the opportunity for a second healthcare professional to check clinical appropriateness and to interact with the patient.

Where exceptionally it is in the interests of the patient for the same pharmacist prescriber to be responsible for prescribing, clinical check and supply of medicines on the same occasion, it would be good practice to: ensure processes are in place to limit errors (i.e. taking a break or implementing additional checks), maintain an audit trail, and to document reasons. Detailed guidance on points to consider in these exceptional circumstances can be found on the RPS website www.rpharms.com in the Independent prescriber guide for prescribers.

FURTHER READING

Royal Pharmaceutical Society
Independent prescriber guide.
www.rpharms.com

General Medical Council
Good practice in prescribing and managing medicines and devices.
www.gmc-uk.org

General Medical Council
Guidance on assessing the seriousness or concerns relating to self-prescribing, or prescribing to those in close personal relationships with doctors. 2016.
www.gmc-uk.org

3.3.17
DISPENSING SELF-PRESCRIBED PRESCRIPTIONS AND PRESCRIPTIONS FOR CLOSE FRIENDS AND FAMILY

Pharmacists are occasionally requested to dispense medicines that have been self-prescribed by a prescriber or have been prescribed for close family and friends of the prescriber.

Although a prescription (including one for CDs) in these circumstances may fulfil the usual legal requirements, pharmacists should consider the following before making a supply:

- It is generally considered poor practice to self-prescribe or to prescribe for persons for whom there is a close personal relationship

- The professional judgement of the prescriber may be impaired or influenced by the person they are prescribing for

- It may not be possible for a prescriber to conduct a proper clinical assessment on themselves or on close friends or family

- The regulatory body for doctors (General Medical Council) advises within the Good Medical Practice that doctors must wherever possible avoid prescribing for themselves or anyone with whom they have a close personal relationship

- The regulatory body for nurses (Nursing and Midwifery Council) advises within the document Standards of proficiency for nurse and midwife prescribers that nurses and midwives must not prescribe for themselves and, other than in exceptional circumstances, should not prescribe for anyone with whom they have a close personal or emotional relationship.

- The GPhC advises pharmacist prescribers that: 'Pharmacist prescribers must not prescribe for themselves or for anyone with whom they have a close personal relationship (such as family members, friends or colleagues), other than in exceptional circumstances.' See *In Practice: Guidance for pharmacist prescribers* www.pharmacyregulation.org

- The existence and content of any local trust, board or hospital policy covering self-prescribing

- The abuse potential of the drug being requested

- CDs should only be supplied in exceptional circumstances and details documented. Where appropriate, the supply or request may prompt referral to the local CD accountable officer.

In an emergency, after exercising professional judgement, a pharmacist may decide that it is appropriate to dispense a medicine that has been self-prescribed or prescribed for persons with whom the prescriber has a close personal relationship.

In the circumstance that refusing to supply is the most appropriate action, be prepared for the person requesting the supply to be disappointed. One strategy would be to clearly and calmly explain that in your professional judgement it would not be appropriate to supply the medicine.

In some circumstances where there is a risk of harm to patients or the public, there may be a duty to raise concerns to the appropriate body (e.g. General Medical Council).

See Appendix 5 for GPhC guidance on raising concerns. See also section 2.2.3: Pharmacist prescribing.

FURTHER READING

Royal Pharmaceutical Society
Independent prescriber guide.
www.rpharms.com
See case study on *Prescribing for yourself or close family and friends*

General Medical Council
Good practice in prescribing and managing medicines and devices.
www.gmc-uk.org

General Medical Council
Guidance on assessing the seriousness or concerns relating to self-prescribing, or prescribing to those in close personal relationships with doctors. 2016.
www.gmc-uk.org

3.4
Wholesaling

The Medicines and Healthcare products Regulatory Authority (MHRA) is the regulatory body with the responsibility for oversight and enforcement of the wholesale distribution of medicines.

3.4.1
WHOLESALER LICENCE REQUIREMENTS

Anyone trading medicines, other than to a patient, is required to:

- Hold a wholesaler licence – also known as a wholesale distribution authorisation (WDA)

- Comply with the Good Distribution Practice (GDP) standards, and pass regular GDP inspections

- Have a suitable experienced 'Responsible Person' named on the licence to ensure that medicines are procured, stored and distributed appropriately.

Trading medicines includes pharmacies who engage in the commercial trade of medicines e.g. to wholesalers, pharmacies, or other authorised or entitled to supply medicines.

Wholesale distribution authorisations (WDA) are specific to human medicines WDA(H) or veterinary medicines WDA(V) (see section 3.5.5. for further information on veterinary medicines wholesaling).

WDA EXEMPTIONS
Pharmacies supplying stock to another pharmacy within the same legal entity are not required to have a WDA.

Where however, a legal entity does hold a WDA, the pharmacy supplying the medicines for the purposes of wholesaling must be named on the WDA.

Additionally, registered pharmacies and hospitals supplying small quantities of medicines to healthcare professionals for treatment or onward supply to their patients, or to other community pharmacies or hospitals to meet a patient's individual needs are **not** required to hold a wholesale distribution authorisation provided:

- The transaction takes place on an occasional basis
- The quantity of medicines supplied is small
- The supply is made on a not for profit basis
- The supply is not for onward wholesale distribution.

Further information on exemptions for pharmacists can be found in the 'Guidance for pharmacists on the repeal of section 10(7) of the Medicines Act 1968': www.gov.uk

PLEASE NOTE

If you are making a supply outside of the scope of this regulatory statement you will probably be required to obtain a Wholesale Distribution Authorisation for Human use (WDA(H)). Further information about WDA(H) can be obtained from the MHRA: www.gov.uk.

3.4.2
WHOLESALING OF CONTROLLED DRUGS

The Home Office and MHRA have advised that if a WDA(H) is required, this also means that, if supplies include CDs in Schedules 2 to 5 in the Misuse of Drugs Regulations 2001, then it is likely that a corresponding Home Office CD licence is also needed by the pharmacy.

The document *Supplementary information on wholesale dealer and CD licences in the Health and Justice System in England* and the accompanying letter provide further information on this that is particularly relevant to pharmacists working in healthcare and secure environment settings. Please note that the requirements to hold WDA(H) and Home Office CD licences apply to all settings and not just those outlined in this document:

www.palliativedrugs.com

3.4.3
PERSONS AND ORGANISATIONS THAT CAN RECEIVE MEDICINES

The range of persons and organisations that can receive medicines by wholesale is controlled by legislation and may also be restricted to certain medicines for certain purposes. The full lists are extensive and beyond the scope of this document; however, Table 8 contains signposting information for persons who may commonly approach the pharmacy for medicines, for onward use:

Table 8: Persons who can be supplied with medicinal products

PERSONS

- Doctors
- Dentists
- Registered pharmacies
- Hospitals, clinics and independent medical agencies
- Midwives
- Chiropodists/Podiatrists
- Optometrists and Additional Supply Optometrists
- Paramedics
- Owner or Master of Ship
- Orthoptists
- First aid organisations
- Certified first aiders
- Working for National Lifeboat Institution
- Occupational health schemes
- Drug treatment services
- NHS Trusts

USEFUL REFERENCE SOURCES

Schedule 22 of the Human Medicines Regulations 2012 as amended contains an A to Z list of persons and organisations who can be supplied with medicines by wholesale.

This is available at www.legislation.gov.uk

Schedule 17 of the Human Medicines Regulations 2012 as amended contains information about various persons who have exemptions to sell, supply or administer certain medicines under specified conditions.

These persons can also obtain these medicines by wholesale. MHRA have published a summary of rules for the sale, supply and administration of medicines for specific healthcare professionals (www.gov.uk)

Maritime and Coastguard Agency: Ships Medical Stores www.gov.uk

3.4.4
SIGNED ORDERS AND RECORD KEEPING

When a POM is supplied from a registered pharmacy to healthcare professionals or organisations, an entry needs to be made in the POM register or the signed order/invoice needs to be retained for two years from the date of supply. Even where the signed order/invoice is retained, it is good practice to make a record in the POM register for audit purposes.

Schedule 17 of Human Medicines Regulations 2012 states which persons or organisations must provide a written signed order/invoice. For other persons or organisations where a requirement to have a signed order/invoice is not outlined in the legislation, we advise it is good practice to obtain a written signed order/invoice for maintaining an audit trail.

An entry in the POM register must include the:

- Date the POM was supplied

- Name, quantity and, where it is not apparent, formulation and strength of the POM supplied

- Name and address, trade, business or profession of the person to whom the medicine was supplied

- Purpose for which it was sold or supplied.

Legislation does not specify the details that need to be included on a signed order although local standard operating procedures (e.g. local NHS Trust policies or company SOPs) may require templates to be used. It would be advisable for the details required for a POM register entry (i.e. the list above) to be requested as a minimum for a signed order as this information would be required to complete the POM register.

See section 3.6.6 for details on the requisition requirements for CDs.

If you are making a supply to persons or organisations under a Wholesale Dealer's Licence you will be required to follow Good Distribution Practice (GDP) www.gov.uk

3.4.5
WHOLESALING AND MEDICINE SHORTAGES

Measures are in place to minimise medicines shortages by limiting those medicines which can be traded or exported.

The Department of Health and Social Care has published a paper titled *Trading Medicines for Human Use: Shortages and Supply Chain Obligations*; this document has been endorsed by the RPS. This paper sets out the key legal and ethical obligations on manufacturers, wholesalers, NHS Trusts, registered pharmacies and dispensing doctors in relation to the supply and trading of medicines. Recent increases in the export of medicines are a major contributor to supply problems and risk jeopardising patient care. The full paper can be viewed at www.gov.uk

In order to retain supplies for UK patients, the Medicines and Healthcare products Regulatory Agency (MHRA) publishes a list of medicines that cannot be parallel exported: www.gov.uk

MANAGING MEDICINES SHORTAGES IN THE PHARMACY

Best Practice Standards for Managing Medicines Shortages in NHS Hospitals are designed to provide advice to NHS hospitals in managing medicines shortages to minimise risk to patients. These standards can be viewed on the SPS website: www.sps.nhs.uk

Dealing with medicine shortages in community pharmacy - this RPS resource provides guidance for the pharmacy team in dealing with medicine shortages. Available on the RPS website: www.rpharms.com

Serious Shortage Protocols (SSPs) in England, Wales and Northern Ireland enable pharmacists to make amendments to prescriptions and supply an alternative medicine to those in short supply. SSPs are specific to each home country. Further information available from:

England

NHS Business Service Authority (NHS BSA)

www.nhsbsa.nhs.uk

Wales

Community Pharmacy Wales (CPW)

www.cpwales.org.uk

Scotland

Community Pharmacy Scotland (CPS)

www.cps.scot

FURTHER READING

Department of Health

Supplementary information on wholesale dealer and Controlled Drugs licences in the health and justice system in England and accompanying letter. 2014.

www.palliativedrugs.com

Medicines and Healthcare products Regulatory Agency

Licences to manufacture or wholesale medicines.

www.gov.uk

Medicines and Healthcare products Regulatory Agency

Rules and guidance for pharmaceutical distributors – The green guide. 2017. London; Pharmaceutical Press.

www.pharmpress.com

Medicines and Healthcare products Regulatory Agency

Rules and guidance for pharmaceutical manufacturers and distributors – The orange guide. 10th edition. 2017. London; Pharmaceutical Press.

www.pharmpress.com

Wingfield J, Pitchford K, editors

Dale and Appelbe's Pharmacy and Medicines Law. 12th edition. 2021. London; Pharmaceutical Press.

www.pharmpress.com

3

3.5 Veterinary medicines

Pharmacists working in registered premises are authorised to supply veterinary medicines for use in animals under certain circumstances (e.g. when there is a valid prescription) and, as with human medicines, are responsible for any medicines supplied. Pharmacists cannot diagnose conditions in animals and should refer to a veterinary surgeon when this is required. There are various classes of veterinary medicines, which are summarised in Table 9.

Table 9: Categories of veterinary medicines and their characteristic

CATEGORY	CHARACTERISTIC
NFA-VPS	A category of medicine for non-food animals that can be supplied by a veterinary surgeon, a pharmacist or a suitably qualified person. A written prescription is not required. These medicines should not be accessible by the public in a pharmacy.
POM-V	Prescription-only medicines that can only be prescribed by a veterinary surgeon and supplied by a veterinary surgeon or a pharmacist with a written prescription
POM-VPS	Prescription-only medicines that can be prescribed and supplied by a veterinary surgeon, a pharmacist or a suitably qualified person on an oral or written prescription. A written prescription is only required if the supplier is not the prescriber
AVM-GSL	An authorised veterinary medicine that is available on general sale
Exempt medicines under Schedule 6 of the veterinary medicines regulations – exemptions for small pet animals (SAES)	An unlicensed veterinary medicine that does not require a marketing authorisation because it meets criteria laid out in Schedule 6 of the Veterinary Medicines Regulations - Exemptions for small pet animals. Further details are available in Veterinary Medicines Guidance Exemption from authorisation for medicines for small pet animals (www.gov.uk)

CATEGORY

Unauthorised veterinary medicine

CHARACTERISTIC

An unlicensed medicine that does not have a marketing authorisation and is not eligible for exemption through the SAES. It can only be prescribed by a veterinary surgeon under the Cascade (see Diagram 16). This includes any human medicine used for animals

---

3.5.1
PRESCRIPTION REQUIREMENTS FOR POM-V, POM-VPS AND MEDICINES SUPPLIED UNDER THE VETERINARY CASCADE

The following must be present for a veterinary medicine prescription to be valid:

1   Name, address, telephone number, qualification and signature of the prescriber. Where Schedule 2 or 3 CDs have been prescribed, the Royal College of Veterinary Surgeons (RCVS) registration number of the prescriber must also be included.

2   Name and address of the owner.

3   Identification and species of the animal and its address (if different from the owner's address).

4   Date. prescriptions are valid for six months or shorter if indicated by the prescriber (the Veterinary Medicines Directorate (VMD) has confirmed in the case of repeatable prescriptions all supplies must be made within 6 months or shorter if indicated by prescriber). Prescriptions for Schedule 2, 3 and 4 CDs are valid for 28 days.

5   Name, quantity, dose and administration instructions of the required medicine *NB: The VMD advises that 'as directed' is not an acceptable administration instruction.*

6   Any necessary warnings and if relevant the withdrawal period (i.e. the time that must elapse between when an animal receives a medicine and when it can be used for food).

7   Where appropriate, a statement highlighting that the medicine is prescribed under the veterinary Cascade (e.g. 'prescribed under the Cascade' or other wording to the same effect).

8   If the prescription is repeatable, the number of times it can be repeated.

Note also: Where Schedule 2 or 3 CDs have been prescribed, a declaration that 'the item has been prescribed for an animal or herd under the care of the veterinarian' – usual CDs prescription requirements apply (see section 3.6.7).

Diagram 15: Veterinary prescription with Cascade wording

1   P.NIGHTINGALE
MRCVS PRACTICE NAME,
ADDRESS, TOWN, POSTCODE
TELEPHONE NUMBER

Endorsements

3   PRESCRIPTION FOR SPOT THE DOG

2   OWNED BY MRS R SWANN OF ADDRESS, TOWN, POSTCODE

5   SUPPLY PHENYTOIN SODIUM CAPSULES 100MG X 90
5 CAPSULES
3 TIMES A DAY WITH FOOD
6

8   REPEAT X4

7   PRESCRIBED UNDER THE VETERINARY CASCADE

Signature of Prescriber	Date
1 P.NIGHTINGALE	4 30TH MAY 2022

3

Table 10: Similarities and differences between veterinary and human Controlled Drug prescriptions

DIFFERENCES

- Standardised forms are not required for veterinary prescriptions; however, a statement that the medicines are 'prescribed for the treatment of an animal or herd under my care' is required for Schedule 2 and 3 CDs

- Standardised forms are required for human private prescriptions for Schedule 2 and 3 CDs (see section 3.6.7)

- Veterinary prescriptions should be retained for five years and not submitted to the relevant NHS agency. Original human private prescriptions for Schedule 2 and 3 CDs must be submitted to the relevant NHS agency (see section 3.6.7)

- For all CDs, it is considered good practice for only 28 days' worth of treatment to be prescribed on veterinary prescriptions unless in situations of long term ongoing medication (e.g. when treating epilepsy in dogs). For human prescriptions the maximum quantity of Schedule 2,3 or 4 CDs should not exceed 30 days. If more than 30 days is prescribed the prescriber should be able to justify the quantity requested (see section 3.6.7 under 'Total Quantity' for further detail)

- Veterinary prescriptions for Schedule 2 and 3 CDs must include the Royal College of Veterinary Surgeons (RCVS) registration number of the prescriber. Human private prescriptions for Schedule 2 and 3 CDs must include a prescriber identification number

SIMILARITIES

- Both are valid for 28 days from the appropriate date
- Usual CD prescription content requirements (e.g. Total quantity in words and figures, etc. – see section 3.6.7) apply to both

3.5.2
THE VETERINARY CASCADE

A veterinary medicine with a GB or UK marketing authorisation must be supplied where one exists and is clinically appropriate. It is unlawful to supply a human medicine against a veterinary prescription unless it is prescribed by a veterinary surgeon and specifically states that it is 'for administration under the Cascade', or other wording to this effect.

The Cascade is an exemption within the Veterinary Medicines Regulations and specifies that where a licensed veterinary product is not available, other medicines, in a strict order of preference, can be considered. (see Diagram 16).

Diagram 16: Veterinary Cascade

1. Supply a veterinary medicine with a GB or UK-wide marketing authorisation for the species and condition indicated

WHERE THIS IS NOT POSSIBLE

2. A veterinary medicine with a Northern Ireland (NI)* marketing authorisation for the species and condition indicated can be supplied

WHERE THIS IS NOT POSSIBLE

3. A GB, NI* or UK-wide veterinary medicine licensed for another species or different condition can be considered

WHERE THIS IS NOT POSSIBLE

4.a A GB, NI* or UK-wide licensed human medicine

OR

4.b A veterinary medicine authorised outside the UK* can be considered

WHERE THIS IS NOT POSSIBLE

5. An extemporaneous or a specially manufactured medicine can be considered

*For products not authorised in GB or UK-wide (including those licensed in NI only) a Special Import Certificate is required. Further information is available on the Veterinary Medicines Directorate website www.gov.uk

Prescriptions for veterinary medicines licensed for another species, or for another clinical condition in the same species, extemporaneously prepared medicines or human medicines cannot be supplied against a veterinary prescription unless the prescription specifically states that it is 'for administration under the Cascade', or other wording to this effect.

NB: Although the wording on the prescription is a legal requirement, it is important that it reflects the actual Cascade (i.e. if a prescription is written generically for an animal with the Cascade wording present but a licensed veterinary medicine exists, then the Cascade requires the licensed product to be supplied rather than a medicine only licensed for human use).

Further details of the Cascade and additional requirements for food producing animals is available on the VMD website www.gov.uk.

SALE OF UNAUTHORISED VETERINARY MEDICINES

It is unlawful to sell or supply unauthorised veterinary medicines (medicines not licensed as veterinary medicines), including human medicines such as GSL and P medicines, for an animal unless this takes place under the veterinary Cascade. This applies even if a veterinary surgeon asks the animal owner verbally to purchase an over-the-counter human product from a pharmacy.

SALE OF NFA-VPS AND POM-VPS MEDICINES

It is a legal requirement for pharmacists who supply NFA-VPS medicines or prescribe POM-VPS medicines to:

- Advise on how to use the product safely

- Advise on any applicable warnings and contraindications on the packaging or label

- Be satisfied that the recipient intends to use the medicine correctly and is competent to do so

- Prescribe or supply the minimum quantity required for treatment.

PHYSICAL PRESENCE OF A PHARMACIST

Unless a transaction has been individually authorised in advance by a pharmacist and the person handing out the medicine is judged to be competent, the physical presence of the pharmacist is required for POM-V, POM-VPS and NFA-VPS medicines to be supplied.

3

3.5.3
LABELLING OF DISPENSED VETERINARY MEDICINES

When a medicine is supplied by a pharmacy for use under the Cascade, the following details must appear on the dispensing label unless they already appear on the packaging and are not obscured by the dispensing label:

- Name of the prescribing veterinary surgeon
- Name and address of the animal owner
- Name and address of the pharmacy
- Identification and species of the animal
- Date of supply
- Expiry date of the product
- The name or description of the product or its active ingredients and content quantity
- Dosage and administration instructions
- If appropriate, special storage instructions
- Any necessary warnings for the user (e.g. relating to administration, disposal, target species, etc)
- Any applicable withdrawal period (i.e. the time between when an animal receives a medicine and when it can safely be used for food)
- The words: 'For animal treatment only'
- The words: 'Keep out of reach of children'.

Please note that the RPS recommends that the wording 'Keep out of the reach and sight of children' is included on the dispensing label. If the medicine is not prescribed under the Cascade, the Veterinary Medicines Regulations do not specify that a dispensing label is required if the medicines are dispensed in their original packaging. However, the RPS advises that it would be appropriate to generate a dispensing label for all veterinary medicines, particularly for individual animals (pets). Care should be taken so the dispensing labels do not obscure any information on the packaging.

3.5.4
RECORD KEEPING

It is a requirement to keep records of receipt and supply of POM-V and POM-VPS products showing:

- Name of the medicine
- Date of the receipt or supply
- Batch number
- Quantity
- Name and address of the supplier or recipient
- If there is a written prescription, record the name and address of the prescriber and keep a copy of the prescription
- Pharmacists can either keep all documents that show the required information or can make appropriate records in their private prescription book
- Records can be kept electronically
- Records and documents must be kept for at least five years
- Pharmacies that supply POM-V and POM-VPS medicines must undertake an annual audit.

ADVERSE REACTIONS TO VETERINARY MEDICINES

Pharmacists are increasingly supplying veterinary medicines and should be mindful to the possibility that veterinary medicines can cause adverse reactions in humans as well as in animals exposed to a veterinary medicine. Suspect adverse drug reactions (SADRs) in humans are often associated with a failure to read and/or adequately follow product guidance information. Examples include animal sprays and 'spot-ons' onto human skin. The adverse reaction scheme for veterinary medicines is the equivalent of the 'yellow card' scheme for human medicines. Both animal adverse reactions and human adverse reactions to veterinary medicinal products should be reported. Additionally report a suspected problem with a microchip. Details of the scheme and reporting forms are available at www.gov.uk.

3.5.5
WHOLESALING VETERINARY MEDICINES AND TEMPORARY SUPPLY SHORTAGES

VETERINARY MEDICINES

The VMD provides the following information in Veterinary Medicines Guidance Retail of Veterinary Medicines.

'*Only the manufacturer of a veterinary medicine or a holder of a wholesale dealer's authorisation (WDA) may routinely supply authorised retailers with veterinary medicines*'.

This guidance also states that '*An authorised retailer of veterinary medicines may supply products they are qualified to supply to another authorised retailer to relieve a temporary supply shortage, without a WDA. This exemption from the VMR is intended to prevent shortages of available medicines causing animal welfare problems. It is not intended to exempt wholesale supply from the need for a WDA.*'

Veterinary Medicines Directorate guidance *Retail of Veterinary Medicines* and *Veterinary Medicines Wholesale Dealer's Authorisation (WDA)* available at: www.gov.uk

3.5.6
SELLING VETERINARY MEDICINES ON THE INTERNET

Guidance on the legal requirement for selling veterinary medicines over the internet is available on the VMD website www.gov.uk .

The VMD accredits UK-based retailers of veterinary medicines who meet the Accredited Internet Retailer Scheme (AIRS). Further information on this can be found on the VMD website www.gov.uk.

FURTHER READING

Veterinary Medicines Directorate
Accredited internet retailer scheme (AIRS): List of accredited internet retailers.
www.vmd.defra.gov.uk

Veterinary Medicines Directorate
Guidance on prescribing or supplying veterinary medicines including requirements for registration and inspections of premises.
www.gov.uk

Veterinary Medicines Directorate
Marketing Authorisations Veterinary Information Service (MAVIS).
www.vmd.defra.gov.uk

Veterinary Medicines Directorate
Various additional online resources – including a database of veterinary medicinal products.
www.gov.uk

National Office of Animal Health (NOAH)
2021 NOAH Compendium
www.noahcompendium.co.uk

3

3.6
Controlled Drugs

CONTROLLED DRUGS RESOURCES

Accountable Officers Network Scotland
A guide to good practice in the management of Controlled Drugs in primary care – Scotland. 2014.
www.cps.scot

Care Quality Commission
Controlled Drugs governance self assessment tools (for primary care and secondary care).
www.cqc.org.uk

Care Quality Commission
The safer management of Controlled Drugs annual report.
www.cqc.org.uk

Department of Health. Clinical Guidelines on Drug Misuse and Dependence Update 2017 Independent Expert Working Group
Drug misuse and dependence: UK guidelines on clinical management. 2017.
www.gov.uk

Faculty of Pain Medicine
Opioids Aware: A resource for patients and healthcare professionals to support prescribing of opioid medicines for pain
www.rcoa.ac.uk

Home Office
Guidance for the safe custody of Controlled Drugs and drug precursors in transit. 2018.
www.gov.uk

Home Office
Security guidance for all existing or prospective Home Office Controlled Drug licensees and/or Precursor Chemical licensees and registrants. 2018.
www.gov.uk

National Institute for Health and Care Excellence
Controlled Drugs: safe use and management. NICE guideline. 2016.
www.nice.org.uk

National Institute for Health and Care Excellence
Managing medicines in care homes. Social care guideline. 2014
www.nice.org.uk

Wingfield J, Pitchford K, editors
Dale and Appelbe's Pharmacy and Medicines Law. 12th edition. 2021.
London; Pharmaceutical Press.
www.pharmpress.com

3.6.1
BACKGROUND

Legislation applicable to CDs and pharmacy include:

- The Misuse of Drugs Act 1971 as amended (herein referred to as 'the 1971 Act')

- The Misuse of Drugs Regulations 2001 as amended (herein referred to as 'the 2001 Regulations')

- The Misuse of Drugs (Safe Custody) Regulations 1973 as amended (herein referred to as 'Safe Custody Regulations')

- The Health Act 2006

- Controlled Drugs (Supervision of Management and Use) Regulations 2013 which affect England and Scotland.

The 1971 Act imposes prohibitions on the possession, supply, manufacture, import and export of CDs – except where permitted by the 2001 Regulations or under licence from the Secretary of State. The Safe Custody Regulations detail the storage and safe custody requirements for CDs.

The enforcement body for CDs offences is the Home Office, via the police.

The Health Act 2006 introduced the concept of an 'accountable officer' and requires healthcare organisations, and those providing services to healthcare organisations, to have standard operating procedures in place for using and managing CDs.

For registered pharmacies, the Responsible Pharmacist Regulations 2008 also require that a range of pharmacy procedures are established – including procedures for CDs (see Chapter 4).

Pharmacists should ensure that they are familiar with the standard operating procedures for managing CDs in their pharmacies and the steps that they should take should an incident or concern relating to CDs arise.

Legislation no longer details which specific CD SOPs should be in place. RPS *Professional Guidance on the Safe and Secure Handling of Medicines* however, requires that up-to-date organisational policies and procedures are in place covering the management of CDs such as (but not exclusively) the:

- Security, including access to CDs

- Ordering and receipt

- Record-keeping, including audit requirements

- Prescribing and clinical monitoring

- Administration, including any witness requirements

- Supply, including prompt access to ensure care is not compromised

- Denaturing and disposal, including any witness requirements

- Use and storage of patients' own CDs

- Transport (including transfer between care settings), including records

- Investigation and reporting of concerns.

GOSPORT REPORT

At least 450 patients are thought to have died after the administration of inappropriately high doses of opioids between 1988 and 2000 at Gosport War Memorial Hospital. In June 2018, the report of the Gosport Independent Panel into failures of care was published.

The report found no evidence that the pharmacists providing services to the hospital, or the Portsmouth Hospitals NHS trust drug and therapeutics committee which covered the Gosport War Memorial Hospital had challenged prescribing practices.

Whilst practice has improved and there are now professional standards for hospital pharmacy services, pharmacy teams are urged to continue to be medicine safety advocates for the public and support a culture of listening, speaking up and being heard.

Furrther information on the Gosport report can be viewed on the RPS website at www.rpharms.com.

ACCOUNTABLE OFFICERS

Accountable officers are responsible for supervising and managing the use of CDs in their organisation or setting. Their roles and responsibilities include:

- Oversight of the monitoring and auditing of the management, prescribing and use of CDs

- Ensuring that systems are in place for recording concerns and incidents involving CDs and the operation of these systems

- Attendance at Local Intelligence Network meetings

- Submission of occurrence reports which describe the details of any concerns the organisation has had regarding the management of CDs in a required time frame
- The appointment of authorised witnesses for the destruction of CDs

For those organisations not required to appoint a CDAO (e.g. general practice, dental clinic, community pharmacy) then an appointed 'Controlled Drugs lead' performs the same role.

Sources of further information on the duties of accountable officers are specified in Table 11.

Table 11: Sources of information on the duties of accountable officers

COUNTRY
England
SOURCE OF INFORMATION
NHS England has published guidance *The Controlled Drugs (Supervision of Management and Use Regulations 2013 NHS England Single Operating Model*: www.england.nhs.uk A register of accountable officers in England is published on the Care Quality Commission website: www.cqc.org.uk
COUNTRY
Scotland
SOURCE OF INFORMATION
Information on the role of accountable officers and a list of accountable officers in Scotland is available on the Healthcare Improvement Scotland website: www.healthcareimprovementscotland.org
COUNTRY
Wales
SOURCE OF INFORMATION
Information regarding the role of accountable officers in Wales and a list of accountable officers is available on the Healthcare Inspectorate Wales website: www.hiw.org.uk

3.6.2 CLASSIFICATION

The 2001 Regulations classify CDs into five Schedules according to the different levels of control attributed to each:

- Schedule 1 (CD Lic POM)
- Schedule 2 (CD POM)
- Schedule 3 (CD No Register POM)
- Schedule 4 (CD Benz POM and CD Anab POM)
- Schedule 5 (CD INV P and CD INV POM).

The BNF includes CD classification information for Schedule 1 to 4 medicines within the monograph.

SCHEDULE 1 (CD LIC POM)
Most Schedule 1 drugs have no therapeutic use and a licence is generally required for their production, possession or supply. Examples include hallucinogenic drugs (e.g. 'LSD'), ecstasy-type substances and raw opium.

SCHEDULE 2 (CD POM)
Pharmacists and other classes of person named in the 2001 Regulations have a general authority to prescribe, possess, supply and procure Schedule 2 CDs when acting in that capacity.

Schedule 2 includes opiates (e.g. diamorphine, morphine, methadone, oxycodone, pethidine), major stimulants (e.g. amfetamines), quinalbarbitone and ketamine.

SCHEDULE 3 (CD NO REGISTER POM)
Schedule 3 CDs include minor stimulants and other drugs (such as buprenorphine, temazepam, tramadol, midazolam, phenobarbital, gabapentin and pregabalin) that are less likely to be misused (and less harmful if misused) than those in Schedule 2.

SCHEDULE 4 (CD BENZ POM OR CD ANAB POM)
Schedule 4 is split into two parts:

- **Part I (CD Benz POM)**
  Contains most of the benzodiazepines (such as diazepam), non-benzodiazepine hypnotics (such as zopiclone), and Sativex (a cannabinoid oromucosal mouth spray)
- **Part II (CD Anab POM)**
  Contains most of the anabolic and androgenic steroids, together with clenbuterol (an adrenoceptor stimulant) and growth hormones.

SCHEDULE 5
(CD INV POM OR CD INV P)

Schedule 5 contains preparations of certain CDs (such as codeine, pholcodine and morphine) that are exempt from full control when present in medicinal products of specifically low strengths.

Table 12 summarises the various characteristics of CDs.

Table 12: Summary of various characteristics of CDs

	Sch 2	Sch 3	Sch 4 (Part I)	Sch 4 (Part II)	Sch 5
Designation	CD POM	CD No Reg POM	CD Benz POM	CD Anab POM	CD INV P or CD INV POM
Prescription requirements see section 3.6.7	Yes	Yes	No	No	No
Prescription valid for	28 days after appropriate date	28 days after appropriate date	28 days after appropriate date	28 days after appropriate date	6 months
Address of prescriber required to be within the UK	Yes	Yes	No	No	No
EEA and Swiss healthcare professionals can legally prescribe	No	No	Yes	Yes	Yes
Prescription is repeatable*	No	No	Yes	Yes	Yes
Emergency supply	No	No (except phenobarbital [also known as pheno-barbitone or pheno-barbitone sodium] for epilepsy by a UK-registered prescriber)	Yes	Yes	Yes
Requisition necessary	Yes	Yes	No	No	No
Requisition to be marked by the supplier	Yes	Yes	No	No	No
Invoices to be retained for two years**	No	Yes	No	No	Yes
Licence required to import or export	Yes	Yes	Yes	Yes (unless the substance is imported or exported by a person for self-administration)	No

*By 'repeatable' we mean the instance where the prescriber adds an instruction on the main prescription for the prescribed item to be repeated,e.g. repeat x 3. This does not refer to the prescription counterpart which is sometimes used as a patient repeat request to the prescriber. NHS prescriptions are not repeatable (see section 3.3.1 under repeatable prescriptions).

**NICE advise that organisations should consider retaining all CDs invoices for six years for the purpose of HM Revenue and Customs.

3.6.3
POSSESSION AND SUPPLY

Pharmacists, doctors and dentists, when acting in these capacities, are among those empowered by the 2001 Regulations under a general authority to possess, supply and procure Schedule 2, 3, 4 and 5 CDs.

Other mechanisms for the lawful possession of CDs include:

- **Home Office licence**
  Persons who have an applicable Home Office licence can possess and supply CDs in accordance with the terms of the licence (e.g. the RPS museum holds a Home Office licence to possess CDs for the purposes of the museum)

- **Home Office group authority**
  Persons who are covered by an applicable Home Office licence group authority can possess and supply CDs in accordance with the terms of the group authority (e.g. there is currently a group authority covering paramedics that allows them to possess and supply certain CDs)

- **Legislation: class of person**
  Other classes of person specified in the 2001 Regulations, provided they are acting in the capacity of the specified class (e.g. a postal operator or, for specified CDs, a registered practising midwife)

- **Legislation: class of drug**
  The 2001 Regulations indicate that possessing certain classes of CDs is lawful (e.g. Schedule 4 Part II drugs when contained in medicinal products and Schedule 5 drugs)

- **Patients**
  Persons who have been prescribed a CD by a doctor, supplementary prescriber, nurse independent prescriber, pharmacist independent prescriber, dentist or veterinary surgeon (for an animal).

A comprehensive analysis of the multiple classes of persons who, and organisations that, can possess and supply CDs is outside the scope of this document. However, this has been summarised in *Dale and Appelbe's, Pharmacy and Medicines Law* (12th edition. 2021) or can be found in the 2001 Regulations.

POSSESSION OF SCHEDULE 1 CONTROLLED DRUGS

A Home Office licence is required to possess Schedule 1 CDs; however, a pharmacist can take possession of such CDs for the purpose of destruction or to handover to a police officer.

Note that the Home Office has also advised that the possession of Schedule 1 CD by a pharmacist for the purpose of handing over to a licensed agency or laboratory may fall under the scope of the regulations. Before supplying in these circumstances you should take further advice from your organisation and/or accountable officer.

Some pharmacists, particularly those working within a hospital, may be asked to deal with substances removed from patients on admission, which may be Schedule 1 products. In such circumstances, you should refer to your organisation policy. The patient's confidentiality should normally be maintained and the police should be informed on the understanding that the source will not be identified. If, however, the quantity is so large that the drug could not be purely for personal use the pharmacist may decide that the greater interests of the public require identification of the source. Such a decision should not be taken without first considering discussing the situation with the other health professionals involved in the patient's care and taking advice from the pharmacist's professional indemnity insurer's legal adviser.

The patient should give authority for the drug to be removed and destroyed. If the patient refuses, the pharmacist may feel that he or she has no alternative other than to call in the police. Under no circumstances can a suspected illicit drug be handed back to a patient.

3.6.4
ADMINISTRATION OF CONTROLLED DRUGS

Schedule 1 CDs may only be administered, or prescribed under a Home Office licence. Schedule 2, 3 or 4 CDs can be administered to a patient by:

- A doctor, dentist, pharmacist independent prescriber or nurse independent prescriber acting in their own right
- A supplementary prescriber (including a pharmacist supplementary prescriber) acting in accordance with a clinical management plan
- A person acting in accordance with the directions of a prescriber entitled to prescribe CDs (including pharmacist independent prescribers).

Only medical prescribers who hold a special licence from the Home Secretary or Scottish Government's Chief Medical Officer can prescribe cocaine, diamorphine or dipipanone for treating addiction. This special licence is not required if treating organic disease or injury. Pharmacist independent prescribers, nurse independent prescribers and supplementary prescribers may not prescribe cocaine, diamorphine or dipipanone for treating addiction, but may prescribe these medicines for treating organic disease or injury.

NB: In healthcare environments, including secure environments, additional requirements and restrictions regarding who may administer or witness the administration of medicines may exist to satisfy medicines management, governance and patient safety considerations.

3.6.5
IMPORT, EXPORT AND TRAVELLERS

A licence is needed for a pharmacy to import or export Schedule 1, 2, 3 and 4 (Part I) CDs. A licence is needed for Schedule 4 (Part II) CDs, unless the substance is imported or exported by a person for self-administration. There are no restrictions on the import or export of Schedule 5 CDs (see Table 12). Pharmacists are often asked about arrangements for patients who are taking CDs abroad. The Home Office is the regulatory body in this instance and may require individuals to apply for personal licences in certain circumstances. Information can be found on the Home Office website (www.gov.uk) and *Drug misuse and dependence – UK guidelines on clinical management* (www.gov.uk)

TRAVELLERS

A personal licence is not required by the Home Office if a person travelling is carrying less than three months' supply of CDs. However, it is advised that a covering letter signed by the prescriber is obtained that confirms the name of the patient, travel plans, name of the prescribed CDs, total quantities and dose.

The patient should also check with the embassies or high commissions for the countries they will be travelling through to ensure that the import and export regulations in those countries are complied with.

It would be prudent for patients to check any additional requirements that their travel operator/ airline company may impose.

The patient may also want to refer to the NHS website *Can I take my medicines abroad* www.nhs.uk for further guidance.

3.6.6
OBTAINING CONTROLLED DRUGS – REQUISITION REQUIREMENTS FOR SCHEDULE 1, 2 AND 3 CONTROLLED DRUGS

On 30 November 2015, amendments to the Misuse of Drugs Regulations 2001 made the use of an approved form for the requisitioning of Schedule 2 and 3 CDs in the community mandatory. This applies to both requisitions for human and for veterinary use. Hospices and prisons are exempt from the requirement to use the approved form.

The introduction of an approved mandatory requisition form is a remaining Shipman Inquiry recommendation aimed at ensuring the purchase of all stocks of Schedule 2 and 3 CDs by healthcare professionals within the community can be monitored.

Details of the approved mandatory requisition form and where to obtain them can be seen in Table 13.

A summary of when an approved mandatory requisition form must be used is shown in Diagram 17.

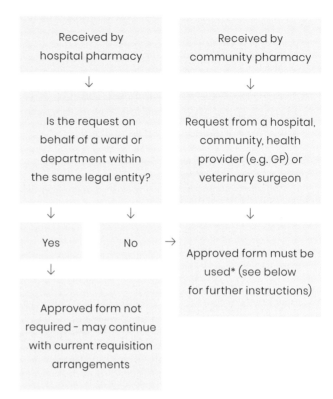

Diagram 17: Summary of when an approved mandatory requisition form must be used to request stock of Schedule 2 and 3 CDs

The handling of CDs in prisons requires specific processes. In England these are underpinned by the information currently found in the NPC document (UK Web Archive) *Safe Management and Use of Controlled Drugs in Prison Health in England*.

THE LEGAL REQUIREMENTS FOR A CONTROLLED DRUG REQUISITION ARE:

1   Signature of the recipient

2   Name of the recipient

3   Address of the recipient

4   Profession or occupation

5   Total quantity of drug

6   Purpose of the requisition

Table 13: Approved mandatory requisition forms

	England	Scotland	Wales
Type of form	FP10CDF	CDRF – for private supplies GP10A – for NHS supplies	WP10CDF
Where to obtain forms	Download from NHSBSA website (www.nhsbsa.nhs.uk)	Local NHS health board	Local NHS health board

In prisons in England, hospital-style requisition forms (instead of a standardised form) are usually used and are printed in a bound, book format – sequentially numbered with a carbon copy of each requisition to provide a robust audit trail. In Scotland, an approved internal ordering form from the supplying pharmacy is used.

HOSPITAL REQUISITIONS

Hospital pharmacy requisitions from a ward or department that are presented to a pharmacy that is a separate legal entity must also meet these requirements, including the use of an approved mandatory requisition form. The Home Office has advised that the person in charge or acting in charge of a hospital can issue a yearly 'bulk' or 'global' requisition on the approved mandatory form to the separate legal entity that supplies its wards or departments for the wards or departments to then draw on throughout the year using CDs requisition books with duplicate pages. The full Home Office guidance specific to this scenario can be accessed on the NHSBSA website (www.nhsbsa.nhs.uk). Where the person in charge, or acting in charge of a hospital issues and signs a requisition, this must also be signed by a doctor or dentist employed or engaged in that hospital.

PRACTICE ISSUES

- Supplies made against a faxed or photocopied requisition are not acceptable

- Legislation requires that a requisition in writing must be obtained by the supplier (i.e. the pharmacy) before delivery of any Schedule 2 or 3 CDs to the following recipients – practitioners, hospitals, care homes, ship and offshore installation personnel, senior registered nurses in charge of wards, theatres and other hospital departments. Some recipients (such as GPhC registered pharmacies) are not included in this legal requirement. However, the Home Office advises that supplies from one registered pharmacy to another registered pharmacy should only be made after receiving a written requisition on an approved requisition form

- In an emergency, a doctor or dentist can be supplied with a Schedule 2 or 3 CDs on the undertaking that a requisition will be supplied within the next 24 hours. Failure to do so would be an offence on the part of the doctor or dentist

- Where stock is collected by a messenger on behalf of a purchaser, a written authorisation must be provided to the supplying pharmacist that empowers the messenger to receive the medicines on behalf of the purchaser. The supplying pharmacist needs to be reasonably satisfied that the authorisation is genuine and must retain it for two years

- A licence would be required for any healthcare professional to possess Schedule 1 CDs; pharmacists are reminded that they are not able to requisition Schedule 1 CDs

- For further details on wholesale distribution see section 3.4.

3

PROCESSING REQUISITION FORMS (MARKING AND SENDING)

When a requisition for a Schedule 1, 2 or 3 CD is received, it is a legal requirement to:

- Mark the requisition indelibly with the supplier's name and address (i.e. the name of the pharmacy); where a pharmacy stamp is used this must be clear and legible
- Send the original requisition to the relevant NHS agency.

As a matter of good practice, pharmacies should retain a copy of the requisition for two years from the date of supply.

These processing requirements do not apply when the supply is made:

- By a person responsible for the dispensing and supply of medicines at a hospital, care home, hospice, prison or organisation providing ambulance services who must mark and retain the original requisition for two years
- By pharmaceutical manufacturers or wholesalers
- Against veterinary requisitions (the original requisition should be retained for five years).

MIDWIFE SUPPLY ORDERS

A registered midwife may use a midwife supply order to obtain the following CDs:

- Diamorphine
- Morphine
- Pethidine.

The order must contain the following:

- Name of the midwife
- Occupation of the midwife
- Name of the person to whom the CD is to be administered or supplied
- Purpose for which the CD is required
- Total quantity of the drug to be obtained
- Signature of an appropriate medical officer – a doctor authorised (in writing) by the local supervising authority or the person appointed by the supervising authority to exercise supervision over midwives within the area

For details on checking registration of nurses see section 3.3.15.

3.6.7
PRESCRIPTION REQUIREMENTS FOR SCHEDULE 2 AND 3 CONTROLLED DRUGS

The requirements that must be present for a prescription (both NHS and private) for Schedule 2 or 3 CDs to be valid are outlined in Diagram 13 (see section 3.3.1 for the usual prescription requirements which also apply). For private prescriptions see also Table 15 for information on the standardised forms that must be used.

Diagram 18: Controlled Drug prescription requirements for Schedule 2 or 3 CDs

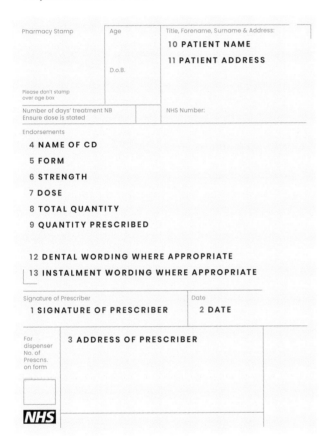

1 **Signature**

The prescription needs to be signed by the prescriber with their usual signature. The pharmacist should either recognise the signature (and believe it to be genuine) or take reasonable steps to satisfy themselves that it is genuine. The prescription may be signed by another prescriber other than the named prescriber and still be legally valid. However, the address of the prescriber needs to be applicable to the signatory for the prescription to be legally compliant. The CD register entry should record the details of the actual prescriber (the signatory) rather than the named prescriber. See Table 3.3.14 for prescriber types authorised to prescribe CDs. Advanced electronic signatures can be accepted for Schedule 2 and 3 CDs where the Electronic Prescribing Service (EPS) is used, see the pink box overleaf for further information.

2 **Date**

The prescription needs to include the date on which it was signed.

CD prescriptions are valid for 28 days after the 'appropriate date' on the prescription.

- The appropriate date is either the signature date or any other date indicated on the prescription (by the prescriber) as a date before which the drugs should not be supplied – whichever is later (see also under 'Instalment direction').

- The 28 day restriction includes prescriptions for Schedule 4 CDs and any owing balances (see section 3.3.1 for details on the validity of owings).

3 **Prescriber's address**

The address of the prescriber must be included on the prescription and must be within the UK.

4 **Name of CD**

It is good practice to write the name of the medicine in full as it appears in the manufacturer's summary of product characteristics. Although the name of the medicine is not specified as a requirement under the 2001 Regulations it needs to be on the prescription for obvious reasons.

5 **Form**

The formulation must be stated; the abbreviations 'tabs' and 'caps' are acceptable. It should be clear and unambiguous if the prescriber intends a supply of m/r , s/r etc.

6 Strength

The strength only needs to be written on the prescription if the medicine is available in more than one strength. To avoid ambiguity, where a prescription requests multiple strengths of a medicine, each strength should be prescribed separately (i.e. separate dose, total quantity, etc.).

7 Dose

The dose does not need to be in both words and figures; however, it must be clearly defined (see Table 14).

8 Total quantity

The total quantity must be written in both words and figures. For tablets, capsules, ampoules, etc. the quantity can be expressed as either

- the total number of dosage units required e.g. 10mg x 10 (ten);

- or the total quantity of drug as milligrams e.g. 100 (one-hundred) mg.

- The total quantity for liquid preparations should be the volume required e.g. 100 millilitres.

Both of the above are legal. The RPS advises where the CD is available as a dosage unit it is preferable to prescribe in dosage units, as this helps reduce the risk of arithmetic errors in prescribing or dispensing.

The total quantity of dosage units may be expressed either as the total number of dosage units e.g. 'sixty 10mg tablets' or as the multiplication of two numbers provided both components are written in words and figures, e.g. '10mg tablets, 2 packs of 30 tablets [two packs of thirty tablets]'. However, using pack sizes may introduce unnecessary complexity if products are supplied in different pack sizes, or the pack size prescribed is unavailable. Whichever form is used, the pharmacist must be satisfied that the total quantity is unambiguous.

The Home Office advise:

"If there are different strength tablets, the quantities for each strength must be listed in words and figures, either as:

- *'numbers of tablets' e.g. 7 (seven) x 8mg tabs, 14 (fourteen) x 2mg tabs or as:*

- *'milligrams' e.g. 56 (fifty-six) mg as 8mg tablets 28 (twenty-eight) mg as 2mg tablets*

For clarity, the name of the drug should also appear each time for each different strength so that there can be no ambiguity. If there is only one strength of tablets specified, the total can be provided simply in numbers of tablets or milligrams e.g. as: 112 (one hundred and twelve) mg, or 14 (fourteen) tablets."

For further information see *Drug misuse and dependence UK guidelines on clinical management*, update 2017, (www.gov.uk).

9 Quantity prescribed

The Department of Health and the Scottish Government have issued strong recommendations that the maximum quantity of Schedule 2, 3 or 4 CDs prescribed should not exceed 30 days. This is not a legal restriction but prescribers should be able to justify the quantity requested (on a clinical basis) if more than 30 days' supply is prescribed. There may be genuine circumstances for which medicines need to be prescribed in this way.

10 Name of patient

11 Address of patient

If the patient does not have a fixed address (e.g. because he or she is homeless or under a witness protection scheme), 'no fixed abode' or 'NFA' is acceptable. Use of a PO Box is not acceptable.

12 Dental prescriptions

Where the CD prescription is written by a dentist, the words 'for dental treatment only' must be present.

13 Instalment direction

Where the prescription is intended to be supplied in instalments a valid instalment direction is required. (For further information see 'Instalment direction for Schedule 2 or Controlled Drugs').

Additional requirements

When the CDs is supplied, it is a requirement to mark the prescription with the date of supply at the time the supply is made. The prescription needs to be written in indelible ink and can be computer generated.

Sugar free products

Pharmacists are reminded that sugar free and/or colour free products have a greater potential for abuse; therefore the RPS advise that these are only supplied when specifically prescribed.

Table 14: Examples of doses that are, and are not, legally acceptable (not exhaustive)

EXAMPLES OF DOSES THAT ARE NOT LEGALLY ACCEPTABLE

- As directed
- When required
- PRN
- As per chart
- Titration dose
- Weekly (this is just a frequency and not a dose)
- Decrease dose by 3.5ml every four days
- Twice a day

EXAMPLES OF DOSES THAT ARE LEGALLY ACCEPTABLE (NB: LEGAL ACCEPTABILITY DOES NOT AUTOMATICALLY INDICATE CLINICAL APPROPRIATENESS)

- One as directed
- Two when required
- One PRN
- Three ampoules to be given as directed (better still – three ampoules to be given over 24 hours as directed)
- One to two when required

CONTROLLED DRUGS ELECTRONIC PRESCRIPTIONS

Information on the national roll out in England of CDs in EPS can be viewed on the NHS Digital website www.digital.nhs.uk

The PSNC has published information on EPS and CDs including a *FAQ factsheet* and guidance on dispensing and supplying CDs via EPS www.psnc.org.uk

INSTALMENT DIRECTION FOR SCHEDULE 2 OR 3 CONTROLLED DRUGS

An instalment direction combines two pieces of information:

1 Amount of medicine to be supplied per instalment (this is in addition to the dose – see below)

2 Interval between each time the medicine can be supplied

Note: The Home Office has confirmed that an **instalment prescription must have both a dose**

and an instalment amount specified separately on the prescription.

The first instalment must be dispensed within 28 days of the appropriate date. The remainder of the instalments should be dispensed in accordance with the instructions (even if this runs beyond 28 days after the appropriate date).

- The appropriate date is either the signature date or any other date indicated on the prescription as a treatment start date before which the drugs should not be supplied – whichever is the later (see Date: Diagram 18).

- The prescription must be marked with the date of each supply.

HOME OFFICE APPROVED WORDING FOR INSTALMENT PRESCRIBING

The instalment direction is a legal requirement and needs to be complied with. However, because there are acknowledged practical difficulties with missed doses and dates when the pharmacy is closed (e.g. bank holidays), the Home Office has approved specific wording to be used that gives pharmacists a degree of flexibility when making a supply and to ensure patient care is not compromised, provided pharmacists are satisfied of the prescriber's intention.

HOME OFFICE APPROVED WORDING

1 Please dispense instalments due on pharmacy closed days on a prior suitable day.

2 If an instalment's collection day has been missed, please still dispense the amount due for any remaining day(s) of that instalment.

3 Consult the prescriber if three or more consecutive days of a prescription have been missed.

4 Supervise consumption on collection days.

5 Dispense daily doses in separate containers.

NB: If the prescriber selects instalment intervals that take bank holidays or other closure dates into account, it may not be necessary to include this wording.

NB: If you decide to supply against a prescription that uses wording not approved by the Home Office, it will not provide the same protection from enforcement when making the supply. In this instance, if practical, you should try to get the prescription amended by the prescriber to include the approved Home Office wording.

If the relevant approved wording is used, a pharmacist can:

- Supply the balance of an instalment if the interval date is missed (e.g. if three days' supply was directed to be supplied on day one but it was missed, it allows two days' supply to be issued on day two).

- Supply treatment prior to the start date on the prescription, if this is on a day the pharmacy is closed for example during bank holiday periods (e.g. if the start date is a bank holiday Monday and the pharmacy is closed, a supply can be made if the signature date is before the start date).

FURTHER READING

Department of Health. Clinical Guidelines on Drug Misuse and Dependence Update 2017 Independent Expert Working Group
Drug misuse and dependence: UK guidelines on clinical management. 2017.
www.gov.uk

Home Office
Home Office Circular 027/2015: Approved mandatory requisition form and Home Office approved wording. 2015.
www.gov.uk

MISSED DOSES

If you know a patient has missed three days' prescribed treatment (or the number of days defined by any local agreement with the prescriber), there is a risk that they will have lost tolerance to the drug and the usual dose may cause overdose. In the best interests of the patient, consider contacting the prescriber to discuss appropriate next steps.

TECHNICAL ERRORS

Where a prescription for a Schedule 2 or 3 CD contains a minor typographical error or spelling mistake, or where either the words or figures (but not both) of the total quantity has been omitted, a pharmacist can amend the prescription indelibly so that it becomes compliant with legislation.

The pharmacist needs to have exercised due diligence, be satisfied that the prescription is genuine and that the supply is in accordance with the intention of the prescriber. The prescription must also be marked to show that the amendments

are attributable to the pharmacist (e.g. name, date, signature and GPhC registration number, etc.).

Pharmacists cannot correct other amendments or omissions (e.g. missing date, incorrect dose, form or strength). These should be corrected by the original prescriber or, in an emergency, another prescriber authorised to prescribe CDs.

Amendments cannot be made by covering letter from the prescriber.

PRESCRIBING FOR TREATING ADDICTION

Only medical prescribers who hold a special licence from the Home Secretary or Scottish Government's Chief Medical Officer can prescribe cocaine, diamorphine or dipipanone for treating addiction. This special licence is not required if treating organic disease or injury. Pharmacist independent prescribers, nurse independent prescribers and supplementary prescribers may not prescribe cocaine, diamorphine or dipipanone for treating addiction, but may prescribe these medicines for treating organic disease or injury.

PRIVATE PRESCRIPTION REQUIREMENTS FOR SCHEDULE 2 AND 3 CONTROLLED DRUGS

1 STANDARDISED FORM

Private prescriptions for Schedule 2 or 3 CDs must be written on designated standardised forms. The forms that should be used are described in Table 15.

Private prescriptions that are not on the designated standardised form must not be accepted unless they are veterinary prescriptions. For a hospital pharmacy to lawfully supply a Schedule 2 or 3 CD against a private prescription issued outside that hospital (i.e. outside its legal entity), a standardised form must be used. Where the private prescription is issued and dispensed within the same legal entity, a standardised form is not required.

2 PRESCRIBER IDENTIFICATION NUMBER

A prescriber identification number must be included on standardised private prescriptions. This number is not the prescriber's professional registration number (i.e. the GMC number, GPhC number, etc.).
It is a number issued by the relevant NHS agency and the prescriber can obtain it from their local primary care organisation. In Scotland, a valid NHS prescriber code is used where available or new ones issued where necessary.

Table 15: Controlled Drugs private prescription forms

	England	Scotland	Wales
Type of form	FP10 PCD	PPCD(1)	WP10 PCD
Where to obtain forms	Local NHS England area team	Local NHS health board	Local NHS health board

3 SUBMISSION

Pharmacies must submit the original private prescription to the relevant NHS agency (NHS Business Services Authority or equivalent); for veterinary prescriptions see below. This requires an identifying code assigned to the pharmacy for this purpose by the local primary care organisation (an identifying code is not required for Scotland).

VETERINARY PRESCRIPTIONS

Veterinary prescriptions for CDs do not need to be written on standardised forms and do not need to be submitted to the relevant NHS agency. Forms must be retained for five years.

PRACTICE ISSUES: PRESCRIBING OTHER MEDICINES ON THE SAME PRIVATE PRESCRIPTION FORM AS CDS

Medicines that are not CDs should not be prescribed on the same form as a Schedule 2 or 3 CD. This is because the form needs to be sent to the relevant NHS agency so the pharmacist would be unable to comply with the requirement to keep private prescriptions for a POM for two years.

FURTHER READING

Public Health Scotland
Private prescribers of Controlled Drugs.
www.isdscotland.org

NHS Business Services Authority
Private CD prescribers.
www.nhsbsa.nhs.uk

3.6.8
COLLECTION OF DISPENSED CONTROLLED DRUGS

When a Schedule 2 CD is collected from a pharmacy, the pharmacist is legally required to determine whether the person collecting is a patient, patient's representative or healthcare professional.

Depending upon which type of person is collecting, the pharmacist needs to take appropriate action (see Table 16). See also section 3.6.11 for further information on record keeping requirements.

COLLECTION BY A REPRESENTATIVE OF A DRUG MISUSE PATIENT

If a drug misuser wants a representative to collect a dispensed CD on his or her behalf, pharmacists are advised to first obtain a letter from the drug misuser that authorises and names the representative. (This includes those detained in police custody who should supply a letter of authorisation to a police custody officer to present to the pharmacist.)

A separate letter should be obtained each time the drug misuser sends a representative to collect and the representative should bring identification. The pharmacist must be satisfied that the letter is genuine. It is also good practice to insist on seeing the patient in person at least once a week unless this is known not to be possible.

The record of supply in the CD register should include details of the representative.

If the directions on the prescription state that the dose must be supervised, the pharmacist should contact the prescriber before the medicine is supplied to the representative – since supervision will not be possible. It is legally acceptable to confirm verbally with the prescriber that they are happy with this arrangement since supervision, while important, is not a legal requirement under the 2001 Regulations. An appropriate record of this conversation should be made. It would not

Table 16: Actions required when a dispensed Schedule 2 Controlled Drug is collected

Person collecting	Action	Notes
Patient or patient's representative	Pharmacist may request evidence of that person's identity, unless already known to the pharmacist	The decision whether to supply or not is at the discretion of the supplying pharmacist – based on their professional judgement
*Healthcare professional acting in their professional capacity on behalf of the patient	Unless already known to the pharmacist, obtain: 1 Name of healthcare professional 2 Address of healthcare professional Also request evidence of identity	Where evidence of identity is not available, the pharmacist has discretion over whether to supply or not – based on their professional judgement

*In this scenario, 'healthcare professional' refers to any person authorised to collect a Schedule 2 CD medication on behalf of the person named on the prescription who is operating under a contract of employment in a health or social care occupation (for example a doctor, nurse or care worker).

be necessary to contact the prescriber if the person has been detained in police custody and the representative collecting the dose is a police custody officer or a custody healthcare professional. This is because the administration of any Schedule 2 or 3 CD in custody will be supervised by a healthcare professional. If the dose is usually supervised, but has been supplied, the pharmacist should consider annotating the prescription and patient medication records to advise others that the dose has not been supervised in the pharmacy.

PRACTICE ISSUES

- It is good practice for the person collecting a Schedule 2 or 3 CD to sign the space on the reverse of the prescription form that is specifically for this purpose. A supply can be made if this is not signed, subject to the professional judgement of the pharmacist

- Instalment prescriptions only need to be signed once

- A representative, including a delivery driver, can sign on behalf of a patient. However, a robust audit trail should be available to confirm successful delivery of the medicine to the patient.

3.6.9
SAFE CUSTODY

The Safe Custody Regulations refer to the physical security of certain Schedule 2 or 3 CDs. It requires that pharmacies, private hospitals and care homes keep relevant CDs in a 'locked safe, cabinet or room which is constructed as to prevent unauthorised access to the drugs'. For settings other than those listed above, these regulations are considered minimum standards for safe custody.

STRUCTURAL REQUIREMENTS OF SAFES, CABINETS AND ROOMS USED FOR STORING CONTROLLED DRUGS

The structural requirements and technical details with which CD safes, cabinets and rooms must comply are detailed in Schedule 2 of the Safe Custody Regulations. These requirements are of a technical nature requiring expertise and knowledge of construction. We do not endorse or approve individual (or brands of) CD cabinets. When purchasing a safe or cabinet, reassurance should be sought from the vendor or manufacturer that the product specifications comply with the requirements specified in the Safe Custody Regulations.

Alternatively, you must apply for an exemption certificate from the police, which certifies that the safe, cabinet or room provides an adequate degree of security for holding CDs. For further information, contact your local police station.

The Controlled Drugs that must be kept under safe custody are:

- Schedule 1 drugs
- Schedule 2 drugs except some liquid preparations and quinalbarbitone (secobarbital) Details of exempted Schedule 2 CDs are available from the Misuse of Drugs (Safe Custody) Regulations 1973 as amended
- Schedule 3 drugs unless exempted under the Misuse of Drugs (Safe Custody) Regulations 1973 as amended, where the full lists are available. Common **exemptions** include:
    - gabapentin
    - mazindol
    - meprobamate
    - midazolam
    - pentazocine
    - phentermine
    - phenobarbital
    - pregabalin
    - tramadol
- Common Schedule 3 CDs which require safe custody include temazepam and buprenorphine

SAFE CUSTODY REQUIREMENTS FOR SECURE ENVIRONMENTS AND SECONDARY CARE

Prison building regulations specify details of the robust nature required for all rooms that store CDs. For further information, see the Ministry of Justice's PSI 45/2010 *Prison Service Order for Integrated Drug Treatment System* (www.justice.gov.uk)

In prisons and hospitals, it is recommended that the CD cabinet should meet the 'Sold secure silver standard'. For further information, see:

Health Building Notes 14-02: Medicines storage in clinical areas www.england.nhs.uk

Health Building Notes 00-01 General design principles 14-01 Designing pharmacy and radiopharmacy facilities
www.gov.uk

Welsh Health Building Notes 00-01 General design principles 14-01 Designing pharmacy and radiopharmacy facilities
www.nwssp.nhs.wales

Some organisations may carry out a risk assessment which determines that CDs in Schedules 3, 4 and 5 should be handled in the same way as CDs in Schedule 2. This may result in CDs other than those that require safe custody by law, being stored in the CDs safe, cabinet or room. This should be included in the relevant policy documents and standard operating procedures. Regular monitoring and auditing arrangements should be considered for CDs in the lower schedules and amendments to policies and procedures made as appropriate and in response to local intelligence.

When CDs requiring safe custody are not kept in the CD cabinet, safe or room (e.g. during the dispensing process), they must be under the 'direct personal supervision' of a pharmacist.

Access to CDs (including handling of 'CD keys') should be documented within a policy. The policy should prevent unauthorised access and be able to identify who has had access to CDs (e.g. the electronic logs from a room or cabinet with electronic access or an audit trail for holders of the CD keys). In community pharmacies, it is common for the pharmacist to hold the CD keys.

A key log could be used to keep an audit trail of who has had access to the keys, including overnight storage in the pharmacy, the transfer of the keys from one pharmacist at the end of a shift to another pharmacist, etc. A template CD key log is available in the RPS guide *Safe custody of Controlled Drugs*: www.rpharms.com

3

PATIENT-RETURNED AND OUT-OF-DATE OR OBSOLETE CONTROLLED DRUGS

Safe custody applies to patient-returned, out-of-date and obsolete CDs until they can be destroyed (see section 3.6.10). To minimise the risk of supplying these to patients, this stock should be segregated from other pharmacy stock and be clearly marked (e.g. mark the stock as 'patient returns waiting to be destroyed' or 'out of date, waiting authorised witness to destroy', etc).

FURTHER READING

Royal Pharmaceutical Society
Professional guidance on the safe and secure handling of medicines.
www.rpharms.com

Royal Pharmaceutical Society
Safe custody of Controlled Drugs.
www.rpharms.com

Wingfield J, Pitchford K, editors
Dale and Appelbe's Pharmacy and Medicines Law.
12th edition. 2021. London; Pharmaceutical Press.
www.pharmpress.com

3.6.10
DESTRUCTION OF CONTROLLED DRUGS

Pharmacies are required to denature CDs prior to disposal. Usually, this process requires an appropriate licence but pharmacies can register an exemption without needing to obtain a licence.

In England and Wales, an exemption is issued by the Environment Agency and is known as the 'T28 exemption'. This allows pharmacies to sort and dispose of CDs and to comply with the 2001 Regulations by denaturing them prior to disposal. This exemption needs to be registered with the Environment Agency, which can be done on their website: www.gov.uk

In Scotland, the exemption is issued by the Scottish Environment Protection Agency (SEPA), which currently accepts that the denaturing of CDs forms part of the exempt activity of secure storage.

CONTROLLED DRUGS THAT NEED TO BE DENATURED BEFORE DISPOSAL

The Home Office has advised that all CDs in Schedules 2, 3 and 4 (Part 1) should be denatured and, therefore, rendered irretrievable before disposal.

PERSONS AUTHORISED TO WITNESS THE DENATURING OF CONTROLLED DRUGS

In some circumstances, the denaturing of CDs needs to be witnessed by an authorised person. Where there is a requirement to make a CD register entry, legislation also requires to have their destruction witnessed. Typically, the destruction of pharmacy stock of Schedule 2 CDs needs to be witnessed. The destruction of patient-returned CDs, whether they require denaturing or not, does not require witnessing by an authorised person.

Table 17 summarises the denaturing, witness requirements and record keeping requirements for patient-returned and expired or obsolete Controlled Drugs.

In prisons, to maintain a robust audit trail, use of Schedule 3 CDs (e.g. buprenorphine) should be recorded in the CD register. Therefore, any destruction should also be recorded. It is also recommended that a robust audit trail is maintained for Schedule 4 CDs, such as diazepam and chlordiazepoxide.

Various individuals and classes of person (e.g. police constables) are authorised to witness the destruction of CDs. This authority is derived from the Home Secretary. It can also be derived from the Secretary of State for Health or from an accountable officer (see section 3.6.1). An accountable officer has the power to authorise other persons to witness the destruction of CDs. However, the 2001 Regulations prevent an accountable officer from being an authorised person directly. Persons authorised by the accountable officer are usually senior members of staff who are not involved in the day-to-day management or use of CDs.

NB: If a pharmacy is engaged in manufacturing, compounding, importing or exporting Schedule 3 or 4 CDs then record keeping arrangements apply. Therefore, destruction of these requires an authorised witness.

Table 17: Denaturing and witness requirements for patient-returned and expired Controlled Drugs

	Is denaturing required?	Is an authorised witness required?	Record keeping
Patient returned Controlled Drug	Yes, if Schedule 2, 3 or 4 (Part 1)	No. However it is preferable for denaturing to be witnessed by another member of staff familiar with CDs (preferably a registered health professional)	A record should not be made in the CD register but records of patient-returned Schedule 2 CDs and their subsequent destruction should be recorded in a separate record for this purpose
Expired / obsolete/ unwanted stock	Yes, if Schedule 2, 3 or 4 (Part 1)	Yes, if Schedule 2. For Schedule 3 medicines it would be good practice to have another member of staff witness the denaturing	An entry should be made in the CD register for Schedule 2 CDs

METHODS OF DENATURING CONTROLLED DRUGS

All medicines should be disposed of in a safe and appropriate manner. Medicines should be disposed of in appropriate waste containers that are then sent for incineration. They should not be disposed of into the sewerage system.

The following generic advice has been agreed with the Home Office. All CDs in Schedule 2, 3 and 4 (Part 1) should be destroyed by being denatured and rendered irretrievable before being placed into pharmaceutical waste containers and sent for incineration.

The context of destruction by denaturing and rendering irretrievable is to guard against the misuse of drugs, harm to the environment or people and prevent the supply of easily retrievable CDs to waste carriers. These methods are not expected to render the detection of active ingredients with specialist equipment impossible, or to modify the chemical composition or properties of CDs.

For all forms of denaturing, and particularly if grinding or crushing tablets or breaking containers is involved individuals should work in a well-ventilated area and wear suitable protective gloves, a face mask and goggles as appropriate; following good Health and Safety practice.

Table 18 contains generic advice on methods of denaturing which have been agreed with the Home Office as likely to be compatible with legislative requirements. If additional product specific information is needed speak to the manufacturer of the product or your local Controlled Drug accountable officer.

Table 18: Destruction of Controlled Drugs

Dosage form	Method of destruction
Solid dosage forms, e.g. capsules and tablets	Grind or crush the solid dose formulation before adding to the CD denaturing kit to ensure that whole tablets or capsules are not retrievable. The use of a small amount of water whilst grinding or crushing may assist in minimising particles of dust being released into the air.
	Where a CD denaturing kit is not available, an alternative method of denaturing is to crush or grind the solid dose formulation and place it into a small amount of warm, soapy water stirring sufficiently to ensure the drug has been dissolved or dispersed. The resulting mixture is poured onto an appropriate amount of suitable product* and added to an appropriate waste disposal bin supplied by the waste contractor.

Dosage form	Method of destruction
Liquid dosage forms	Pour into an appropriately-sized CD denaturing kit.
	Where a CD denaturing kit is not available, an alternative method is to pour the liquid onto an appropriate amount of suitable product* and add this to an appropriate waste disposal bin.
	When a bottle containing a liquid CD has been emptied, small amounts of the pharmaceutical can remain.
	Bottles can be rinsed and the liquid disposed using the denaturing kit and then as the correct category of pharmaceutical waste. You may only dispose of rinsings contaminated with pharmaceuticals via the sewerage system IF you have a relevant Trade Effluent Consent from the relevant sewerage undertaker. Clean empty bottles are disposed of into the recycling or general waste (remember to remove or obliterate any labels). Disposal of irretrievable amounts of CD does not need to be recorded.
Ampoules and vials	For liquid containing ampoules, open the ampoule and empty the contents into a CD denaturing kit, or dispose of in the same manner as liquid dose formulations above. Dispose of the ampoule as sharps pharmaceutical waste.
	For powder containing ampoules, open the ampoule and add water to dissolve the powder inside. The resulting mixture can be poured into the CD denaturing kit and the ampoule disposed of as sharps pharmaceutical waste.
	An alternative but less preferable, disposal method is where the ampoules are crushed with a pestle inside an empty plastic container. Once broken, a small quantity of warm soapy water (for powder ampoules) or suitable product* (for liquid ampoules) is added. If these methods are used, care should be taken to ensure that the glass does not harm the person destroying the CD. The resulting liquid mixture should then be disposed of in a CD denaturing kit or in the bin that is used for disposal of liquid medicines.
Patches	Remove the backing and fold the patch over on itself. Place into a waste disposal bin or a CD denaturing kit.
Aerosol formulations	Expel into water and dispose of the resulting liquid in accordance with the guidance above on destroying liquid formulations.
	If this is not possible because of the nature of the formulation, expel into an absorbent material and dispose of this as pharmaceutical waste.
	Alternatively consider if it would be safe to open or to otherwise compromise the container to release the CD safely. The resulting liquid mixture should then be disposed of in a CD denaturing kit and disposed of as pharmaceutical waste.

*A risk assessment should be carried out to determine whether a product is suitable. A suitable product should render the CD irretrievable without compromising patient safety, the safety of the person carrying out the destruction, or the environment.

CD denaturing kits are widely available and should be used in preference to other materials that were historically used such as cat litter. It is the responsibility of the manufacturer or supplier of the kit to ensure that the kit and the instructions for use are fit-for purpose. Pharmacists are responsible for using a kit that has been obtained from a reputable source and to use those kits in accordance with the manufacturers' instructions – generic advice is also available in Table 18.

FURTHER READING

Department of Health and Social Care
Safe management of healthcare waste. 2013.
www.gov.uk

National Institute for Health and Care Excellence
Controlled Drugs: Safe use and management.
NICE guideline. 2016.
www.nice.org.uk

Water UK
National guidance for healthcare waste water discharges. 2014.
www.water.org.uk

3.6.11
RECORD KEEPING AND CONTROLLED DRUGS REGISTERS

A Controlled Drugs register must be used to record details of any Schedule 1 and Schedule 2 CDs received or supplied by a pharmacy.

Pharmacists are also required to keep records of Sativex (which is a Schedule 4 Part 1 CD). The Home Office strongly recommends the use of a CD register for making records relating to Sativex.

For Controlled Drugs received, the following must be recorded:

- Date supply received
- Name and address from whom received
- Quantity received.

For Controlled Drugs supplied, the following must be recorded:

- Date supplied
- Name and address of recipient
- Details of authority to possess – prescriber or licence holder's details
- Quantity supplied
- Details of person collecting Schedule 2 CD – patient, patient's representative or healthcare representative (if the latter, also record their name and address)
- Whether proof of identity was requested of the person collecting
- Whether proof of identity was provided.

These are the minimum fields of information that must be recorded; additional relevant information can be added.

THE NATURE OF THE REGISTER

Legislation requires that the class, strength and form be specified at the head of each page of the CD register. The register is required to be a bound book register (see box overleaf titled Electronic Controlled Drugs register for alternative to bound). It is also a requirement that different classes are kept in a separate part of the register and that, within each class, a separate page is used for different strengths and formulations of each drug. Multiple registers for the same class of CD are allowable if approved by the Home Office.

Prisons have one legally compliant register that records all the details as specified. However, since there are often several areas in each prison where CDs are stored, administered or issued, each of these areas should maintain a CD record book (similar to those used by hospital wards). Also recommended is that the movement of CDs between these areas be recorded by internal requisition so that robust audit trails are maintained.

THE NATURE OF THE ENTRIES

All entries made in CD registers should be:

- Entered chronologically

- Entered promptly – entries must be made on the day of the transaction or on the following day

- In ink or indelible – entries and corrections must be in ink or indelible (or computerised – see below)

- Unaltered – entries must not be cancelled, obliterated or altered. Corrections must be made by dated marginal notes or footnotes. The register should be marked to show who the amendments made are attributable to (e.g. name, initials/signature, GPhC number if applicable).

RECORD KEEPING

The following points regarding record keeping should be adhered to when maintaining CD registers:

- Location – each register should be kept at the premises to which it applies

- Duration – registers should be kept for two years from the date of the last entry

- Form – records can be kept in their original form or copied and kept in an approved computerised form

- Inspection – a copy of the register, and other details of stock, receipts and supplies, must be made available to authorised persons (e.g. a GPhC inspector or CD liaison officer) upon request.

ELECTRONIC CONTROLLED DRUGS REGISTERS

Electronic CD registers are permitted as an alternative to having a bound-book CD register. Legislation requires that computerised entries must be:

- Attributable

- Capable of being audited

- Compliant with best practice.

An electronic CD register must also be accessible from the premises and capable of being printed. Registers may only be kept in computerised form if safeguards are incorporated into the software to ensure all of the following:

- The author of each entry is identifiable

- Entries cannot be altered at a later date

- A log of all data entered is kept and can be recalled for audit purposes.

Access control systems should be in place to minimise the risk of unauthorised or unnecessary access to the data. Adequate backups must be made of computerised registers. Arrangements should be made so that inspectors can examine computerised registers during a visit with minimum disruption to the dispensing process.

RUNNING BALANCES AND STOCK CHECKS

The aim of a running balance is to ensure that irregularities or discrepancies are identified as quickly as possible. For most organisations the frequency of stock checks should be at least once a week* but these may be more or less frequent based on risk assessment, volume of CDs dispensing, frequency of past irregularities or incidents, or if there are several different pharmacists in charge over short periods. Liquid balances should be checked visually with periodic volume checks, and checks to confirm the balance on completion of a bottle. Stock checks should be recorded, signed and dated by the healthcare professional carrying out the check and if possible, two people should carry out stock checks.

Once a week, not necessarily required to be on the same day every week

It is also appropriate to visually check the running balance each time a CD is dispensed (i.e. where the calculated balance in the register visually matches the quantity you can see. If it does not match, you should investigate in more detail).

Some common reasons for stock to be at zero balance could be due to the drug not being reordered, destruction of the drug (i.e. expired and obsolete, see section 3.6.10 for destruction of CDs) or discontinuation of the drug by the manufacturer. Pharmacists can exercise their professional judgement to help decide whether the weekly running balance check for these CDs that have been zero balance for some time should be continued or suspended. Referring to relevant SOP(s) could form part of this process.

A running balance should be maintained as a matter of good practice and is a recommendation from the Shipman Inquiry. (It is intended that once electronic registers are in common use this will become a legal requirement.)

PRACTICE ISSUES

- The pharmacist has overall responsibility for maintaining running balances and dealing with discrepancies. However, these tasks can be delegated to competent staff, where appropriate

- If a discrepancy can be resolved following checks, a marginal note or footnote should be made in the register and the discrepancy corrected

- Running balances for liquid CDs can be affected by overage, residue and spillage

- Where a CD register entry has been made for a Schedule 2 CD, the usual requirement to make a record in the POM register does not apply.

3.6.12
EXTEMPORANEOUS METHADONE

The GPhC has published guidance on the preparation of unlicensed medicines, which sets out the key areas that need to be considered by the pharmacy owner and superintendent pharmacist in any registered pharmacy where unlicensed medicines are prepared by a pharmacist or under the supervision of a pharmacist. Every patient has every right to expect that when an unlicensed medicine is prepared, it is of equivalent quality to a licensed medicine.

This guidance also applies when unlicensed methadone is extemporaneously prepared. The guidance explains that pharmacies preparing unlicensed medicines must mitigate risks to patients and meet the GPhC's standards for registered pharmacies.

FURTHER READING

General Pharmaceutical Council
Guidance for registered pharmacies preparing unlicensed medicines. 2018.
www.pharmacyregulation.org

3.6.13
CANNABIS AND CANNABIS-BASED PRODUCTS

Cannabis contains more than 400 chemical constituents, including cannabinoids, terpenoids and phenolic compounds, many of which have potential for medicinal use. The most common of the cannabinoids are the psychoactive compound tetrahydrocannabinol (THC) and the non-psychoactive compound cannabidiol (CBD).

There are a wide range of cannabis-based products used for medicinal purposes, with varying constituents and covered by different aspects of legislation. These can be broadly categorised as:

Licensed products
- THC combined with CBD (Sativex)
- Nabilone
- CBD (Epidyolex)

Synthetic compounds
- Dronabinol

Cannabis-based products for medicinal use (CBPMS)
- As set out in the 2018 Regulations

LICENSED PRODUCTS

Name	Contains	Legal category	Uses
Sativex	Cannabis extracts containing THC and CBD	Schedule 4 CD	Moderate to severe spasticity in multiple sclerosis
Nabilone	A synthetic, non-natural cannabinoid	POM	Nausea and vomiting caused by cytotoxic chemotherapy, unresponsive to conventional antiemetic treatments
Epidyolex	Cannabidiol	Schedule 5 CD	Seizures associated with Lennox-Gastaut Syndrome or Dravets Syndrome (adjunctive treatment with clobazam)

SYNTHETIC COMPOUNDS

Name	Contains	Legal category	Uses
Dronabinol	A synthetic, nature-identical, version of THC	Schedule 2 CD	Available as a special (approved by the US Food and Drug Administration): to treat loss of appetite in people with AIDS, and to treat severe nausea and vomiting caused by cancer chemotherapy in patients with inadequate response to conventional antiemetic treatments

CANNABIS-BASED PRODUCTS FOR MEDICINAL USE (CBPM)

Regulations introduced in 2018 widened access to cannabis moving cannabis-based products for medicinal use in humans from Schedule 1 CD to Schedule 2 CD of the Misuse of Drugs Regulations 2001.

This allows defined cannabis-based products for medicinal use, restricts routes of access, and limits the prescribing of these products to specialist doctors on the GMC's Specialist Register.

CBMP definition

There are three broad requirements that a product should satisfy:

- The product is or contains cannabis, cannabis resin, cannabinol or a cannabinol derivative
- It is produced for medicinal use in humans; and
- It is a product that is regulated as a medicinal product, or an ingredient of a medicinal product.

The definition is necessarily broad to take account of the range of preparations which are cannabis-based that have been used for therapeutic purposes. Note that this definition does not include cannabidiol-based products, or any other cannabinoids than those derived from cannabinol.

This area is still evolving following the changes in the legislation. Product choice, suitability for prescribing and supply arrangements are being put in place nationally.

Prescribing CBPMs

Currently the only CBPMs are unlicensed medicines. As with prescribing any other unlicensed medicine, it is a clinician who will decide the most appropriate medicine or course of treatment to prescribe for a patient, having taken into account the patient, the clinical condition, the clinical evidence of effectiveness and safety, that cannot be met by a licensed medicine. The decision to commence treatment should be a joint decision between the prescriber and the patient and/or carer.

- CBPMs are Schedule 2 CDs and staff must follow all the legal and CD requirements for Schedule 2 CDs, including any Trust CD requirements (see section 3.6.7).

- Prescribing is currently restricted to clinicians listed on the Specialist Register of the GMC (www.gmc-uk.org)

- The decision to prescribe must be in line with guidance from NHS England or other country specific guidance (see Further reading section) and consideration given to guidance issued by Royal Colleges, and the Trust's unlicensed medicines and CD policies. Patients and/carers must be involved in the treatment decision.

- Patients should be made aware that the product being prescribed is unlicensed and a note of this should be made in the patient's medical records.

Supplying CBPMs against prescriptions

Private prescriptions for CBPMs must meet legal requirements for Schedule 2 CDs, be on the specially designated forms **(FP10PCD (England), PPCD(1) (Scotland), WP10PCD (Wales))** and specify the private prescriber's six digit identification number (see section 3.6.7).

- There is limited domestic availability of these products. However, several specialist importers have imported a range of products on a named patient basis. Products currently available via import come in a variety of forms (flos, oils, granules) and variety of CBD/THC ratios. The pharmacy should be able to advise on available products and routes of supply.

- Patients should be informed that there may be a small delay in obtaining the product as there are a limited number of THC containing products that are available in this country and so may have to be imported and the process for the supply of unlicensed medicines followed. Further advice should be sought from specialist importers.

CANNABIDIOL (CBD) OIL

CBD oil is typically extracted from strains such as industrial hemp, which contain high concentrations of CBD and low concentrations of the psychoactive tetrahydrocannbinol (THC).

CBD oil products available are marketed as food supplements and are classed as 'novel foods'. Novel foods, including CBD food products, are regulated by the Food Standards Agency and need to be safety evaluated, authorised and approved before they can be placed on the market. Information on CBD products authorised for sale as a novel food item can be found on the Food Standards Agency website (www.food.gov.uk).

The sale of CBD products is enforced by local trading authorities.

Note that if any medicinal claims are made these products will fall under medicines legislation.

Such products **must not** contain THC which remains a controlled substance, under Home Office legislation.

The Home Office has warned that pure CBD is 'very difficult' to isolate and that if a product contains THC it is 'highly likely' to be a Controlled Drug. Further information on CBD oils can be found in the RPS practical guide on www.rpharms.com CBD oil.

Note: A licensed preparation containing a highly purified liquid containing cannabidiol is available as Epidyolex. Epidyolex is used for seizures associated with Lennox-Gastaut Syndrome or Dravets Syndrome (adjunctive treatment with clobazam) – see above.

FURTHER READING

Royal Pharmaceutical Society
Cannabis-based medicines – a quick reference guide.
www.rpharms.com

Royal Pharmaceutical Society
Cannabis oils and cannabidiol oils.
www.rpharms.com

Royal Pharmaceutical Society
Practical guide on CBD oil.
www.rpharms.com

Home Office

Drug licensing factsheet – Cannabis, CBD and other cannabinoids.

www.gov.uk

Medicines and Healthcare products Regulatory Agency

Guidance on the supply, manufacture, importation and distribution of unlicensed cannabis-based products for medicinal (CBPMs) use as a 'special'.

www.gov.uk

Medicines and Healthcare products Regulatory Agency

A guide to what is a medicinal product: MHRA guidance note 8.

www.gov.uk

NHS England

Guidance to clinicians: Cannabis-based products for medicinal use.

www.england.nhs.uk

NHS website

Medical cannabis (and cannabis oils).

www.nhs.uk

National Institute for Health and Care Excellence

Cannabis-based medicinal products: NICE guideline NG 144.

www.nice.org.uk

Scottish Government

Letter for Clinicians: Cannabis-based products for medicinal use.

www.sehd.scot.nhs.uk

Welsh Government

Health Professional Letter: The rescheduling of cannabis for medicinal purposes.

https://gov.wales

3.7 Additional legal and professional issues

3.7.1   EXPIRY DATES

Where a product states 'Use by' or 'Use before', this means that the product should be used before the end of the previous month. For example, 'Use by 06/2023' means that the product should not be used after 31 May 2023.

MHRA's advice to pharmaceutical manufacturers is: the term 'expiry date' should be taken to mean that the product should not be used after the end of the month stated. Therefore, an expiry date of 12/2023 means that the product should not be used after 31 December 2023.

3.7.2
WASTE MEDICINES

Table 19 outlines the arrangements for disposing of pharmaceutical waste in England, Scotland and Wales. For information regarding denaturing of CDs, see section 3.6.10.

Table 19: Waste arrangements in England, Scotland and Wales

	England and Wales	Scotland
Enforcement body	Environment Agency www.gov.uk	Scottish Environment Protection Agency (SEPA) www.sepa.org.uk
Can pharmacies receive waste medicines?	Yes. Generally, activities relating to waste require a licence. However, there are certain exemptions in place that allow these activities to occur without a licence. Some exemptions need to be registered while others do not Under the Non-Waste Framework Directive (temporary storage at a collection point), pharmacies do not need to register an exemption to receive waste as long as the terms of the exemption are complied with.	Yes. The Waste Management Licensing (Scotland) Regulations 2011 allow registered pharmacies to accept returned medicines from patients or individuals and care services.
Sources of additional information	Further information is available in the Department of Health and Social Care publication *Health Technical Memorandum 07-01: safe management of healthcare waste* (www.gov.uk). Other sources of information include the Environment Agency (www.gov.uk) and Pharmaceutical Services Negotiating Committee (www.psnc.org.uk) - information is specific to England but of use in Wales.	Further information for Scotland is available in the Department of Health and Social Care publication *Health Technical Memorandum 07-01: safe management of healthcare waste* (www.gov.uk) and the NHS *Scotland Scottish Health Technical Note 3 Waste management guidance Part B: Waste management policy template* (www.scot.nhs.uk). Other sources of information include the Scottish Environment Protection Agency (www.sepa.org.uk).
Where should waste medicines be stored?	Waste medicines must be kept in secure waste containers in a designated area preferably away from medicines that are fit for use. If sharps are accepted, they should be stored in a sharps container.	
Dealing with confidential information	Ensure that any patient identifiable information is destroyed or totally obscured.	
Tablets and capsules	Blister strips can be removed from their inert outer packaging but tablets and capsules should not be de-blistered. *NB: An exemption applies to CD tablets and capsules, which require denaturing –* see section 3.6.10	

3

	England and Wales	Scotland
Sharps	Dispose of syringes and needles in a sharps container	
Liquids	The whole bottle (including empty bottles that may contain residue) should be placed into a pharmaceutical waste container because the mixing of different medicines could be hazardous. *NB: Exceptions apply to CD liquids, which require denaturing – see section 3.6.10*	
Advice for patients	Patients should be advised that unused, unwanted medicines should be returned to a pharmacy for safe disposal	

3.7.3
REQUESTS FOR POISONS AND CHEMICALS

Amendments to the Poisons Act 1972 have changed how poisons and some chemicals are classified and regulated. These require pharmacies to report suspicious transactions, significant stock loss and theft to the local police (dial 101) or the anti-terrorism hotline (dial 0800 789321). There is also a requirement for the public to present a valid licence issued by the Home Office before being able to purchase the most dangerous poisons or chemicals which could be used as explosive precursors. Where a licence is required, pharmacy teams will need to check that the licence is valid, unaltered and matches the request. Transaction details must be added to the licence, substances must be suitably labelled and regulated poisons require additional record keeping in a poisons register. Where licences are not required, the pharmacist should consider whether requests are suspicious and whether commercial alternatives or commercial retailers are appropriate to refer to.

Further information and details, including lists of regulated and reportable poisons and explosive precursors are available from the RPS guidance *Poisons and chemicals from pharmacy:*
www.rpharms.com

Information on REACH (Registration, Evaluation, Authorisation and restriction of CHemicals), the CLP Regulation (Classification, Labelling and Packaging of substances and mixtures) and COSHH Regulations (Control of Substances Hazardous to Health) are available from the Health and Safety Executive: www.hse.gov.uk

3.7.4
DELIVERY AND POSTING OF MEDICINES TO PATIENTS (INCLUDING ABROAD)

The following are professional and practical points to help you decide whether or not to deliver/post medicines (prescribed/sold) to patients (this list is not exhaustive):

- Patient consent for delivery or posting

- Patient confidentiality during the delivery or posting process

- Whether it is necessary for face-to-face contact with the patient to ensure that the medicine can be safely, effectively and appropriately used

- Whether it is necessary to interview the patient

- Whether the patient has been assessed or directly interviewed by the prescriber

- Medicines and medical devices are not ordinary items of commerce and must be handled and supplied to the patient safely. An adequate audit trail must be in place for delivery and receipt from the point at which the medicine leaves the pharmacy and is received by the patient/patient representative or returned to the pharmacy in the event of delivery failure. Wherever possible a signature should be obtained to indicate safe receipt of medicines

- Storage requirements during transit

- When posting – will the postal carrier agree to transport the medicinal product (check terms of carriage, prohibited and restricted goods)

- When posting abroad – are there legal restrictions in the destination country which would prevent you from posting? (E.g. guidance produced by the U.S. Food and Drug Administration (FDA) makes it clear that it is illegal for a foreign pharmacy to ship prescription medicines that are not approved by the FDA to the United States)

- When posting abroad – are there UK legal restrictions which would prevent you dispensing in the first instance? (e.g. is the prescriber recognised as an appropriate practitioner (see section 3.1.3) for the medicinal product in the UK?).

FURTHER READING

General Pharmaceutical Council
Guidance for registered pharmacies providing pharmacy services at a distance, including on the internet. 2022.
www.pharmacyregulation.org

International Narcotics Control Board
Lists of narcotic and psychotropic drugs under international control.
www.incb.org

Royal Mail
Prohibited and restricted items.
www.royalmail.com

3.7.5
SECURE ENVIRONMENTS

Secure environments include prisons, police custody suites, secure hospitals, immigration removal centres and other places where persons are detained. Medicines and other health legislation may not refer specifically to the particular environment, and where this is the case then consideration should be given to best practice in either primary or secondary care, as appropriate, acting within the confines of the relevant legislation.

When medicines are dispensed from an 'in-house' pharmacy for administration or supply to patients within a prison, the pharmacy does not need to be registered with the GPhC. Nonetheless, general pharmaceutical legal and good practice guidelines should be followed.

If provision of a pharmacy service to another prison is being considered from an in-house pharmacy, advice should be obtained from the GPhC and MHRA to discuss whether the pharmacy premises would require registration or whether a Wholesale Dealer's Licence will be required.

FURTHER READING

Royal Pharmaceutical Society
Professional standards for optimising medicines for people in secure environments.
www.rpharms.com

Royal Pharmaceutical Society
*Professional Standards for Hospital Pharmacy.
For providers of pharmacy services in or to acute hospital, mental health, private, community service, prison, hospice and ambulance settings.*
www.rpharms.com

3.7.6
CHILD-RESISTANT PACKAGING

Suitable, child-resistant packaging should be used for supplying all solid, all oral and external liquid dose preparations unless there is a good reason for not doing so. Such reasons may include:

- **Specific request**
  The patient, carer or representative requests a packaging that is not child resistant, perhaps due to difficulty in opening it. The request may be met by supplying a non-child-resistant lid

- **Original pack**
  The original pack may not be child resistant and there may be reasons underpinning why the medicine should remain in the original container. It may also be the case that no child-resistant packaging exists for a particular liquid medicine so it is not possible to change the container

Where appropriate, the patient should be counselled to keep medicines away from the reach and sight of children.

3

3.7.7
HOMEOPATHIC AND HERBAL REMEDIES

DIFFERENCES BETWEEN HOMEOPATHIC AND HERBAL PRODUCTS

The public can confuse homeopathic with herbal products as homeopathic products are often derived from herbs and are called by their botanical name, e.g. Aloe, and also because a single manufacturer may produce both homeopathic and herbal products. Pharmacists can help the public understand the difference between homeopathy and herbal products using information in our guide on *Homeopathy* www.rpharms.com

Homeopathy has been defined as a holistic complementary and alternative therapy based on the concept of 'like to treat like' and involves the administration of dilute and ultradilute products prepared according to methods given in homeopathic pharmacopoeias.

Herbal preparations contain plant-derived materials, either as raw or processed ingredients which may be from one or more plants.

EVIDENCE FOR HOMEOPATHY

There is no scientific or clinical evidence to support the efficacy of homeopathic products above the placebo effect, although anecdotal reports of their effectiveness have been published, particularly when used as part of individualised homeopathic treatment by a homeopathic practitioner.

Given the lack of clinical and scientific evidence to support homeopathy, the RPS does not endorse homeopathy as a form of treatment or support the prescribing of homeopathic products on the NHS.

ADVICE FOR PATIENTS

If a patient requests advice on homeopathy, you should advise on the lack of evidence on the efficacy of homeopathic products, discuss the formulation and composition of the product, and provide advice relevant to the patient's condition. You should also ensure that patients do not stop taking their prescribed medication if they take a homeopathic product.

REFERRAL

Pharmacists will be in a position to identify serious, underlying undiagnosed medical conditions requiring the patients to be referred to another healthcare professional. Homeopathic products should only be used for the treatment of minor, self-limiting conditions, and must never be used for the treatment of serious medical conditions.

LICENSING

For the purpose of licensing, the MHRA does not currently require homeopathic products to demonstrate efficacy, only quality and safety.

Herbal remedies must either have a full marketing authorisation based upon safety, quality and efficacy or a traditional herbal registration (THR) based upon safety, quality and evidence of traditional use.

FURTHER READING

Royal Pharmaceutical Society
Homeopathy guide.
www.rpharms.com

Royal Pharmaceutical Society
The Traditional Herbal Medicine Registration Scheme.
www.rpharms.com

Medicines and Healthcare products Regulatory Agency
Herbal and homeopathic medicines: Detailed information.
www.gov.uk

3.7.8
CHARITABLE DONATION OF MEDICINES

The World Health Organization (WHO) in co-operation with major international agencies involved with humanitarian and developmental aid (including the International Pharmaceutical Federation (FIP), International Federation of the Red Cross and Red Crescent Societies) has published guidance titled *Guidelines for medicine donations* that provides clear guidelines for the donation of medicine. We encourage any pharmacist considering donating medicines to read the document and adhere to the guidelines.

Pharmacists should be aware that if a pharmacy, in the course of its business, supplies a medicine to another business who obtains it for further supply, the supplying pharmacy will require a Wholesale Dealer's Licence (WDA(H)). This is regardless of whether the medicine is stock surplus to the requirements of the pharmacy or general stock that is to be donated for charitable use or in times of conflict. See section 3.4 for further information on Wholesale distribution.

CONSIDER ALTERNATIVES

WHO encourages, in the acute phase of an emergency, that standardised health kits of medicines are donated. These kits are permanently stocked by major international suppliers such as Médecins Sans Frontières and the United Nations Children's Fund.

After the acute phase, WHO encourages the donation of cash that can be used to purchase essential medicines and is usually more useful than donations of medicines. Pharmacists and patients who want to help should be advised to donate money to charitable organisations to enable them to purchase supplies.

These cash donations may then be used by charitable organisations to obtain reduced price purchases from manufacturers (where available) who are able to supply suitable medicines for the target area, in appropriate quantities and with viable shelf life.

PATIENT RETURNS

The WHO guidelines specifically advise that patient-returned medicines should not be donated and describes these types of donation as an example of a double standard. This is because most countries do not allow the reuse of patient returned medicines within their own country. The WHO guidelines describe how these donations also frustrate management efforts to administer medicine stocks in a rational way and as a result, donation of patient-returned medicines is forbidden in an increasing number of countries. In the past, unsuitable medicines have been donated, leading to situations where stocks could not be used within their remaining shelf life and as a result the receiving country has faced costly and inconvenient destruction procedures. Most charitable organisations supporting the developing world or providing disaster or emergency relief will find it very difficult to use the miscellaneous collection of medicines that is received from the donation of patient-returned medicines.

Pharmacies accept patient returned medicines in the course of their business for destruction. MHRA has advised that if a pharmacy takes in a patient returned medicine and supplies it to another legal entity which then makes a further supply of the medicine, the pharmacy will be wholesaling the patient returned medicine. Wholesale distribution of medicines requires a WDA(H).

FURTHER READING

World Health Organization
Guidelines for medicines donations
(3rd edition). Revised 2010.
www.who.int

3

3.7.9

COLLECTION AND PURCHASE OF MEDICINES BY CHILDREN

Pharmacists may be asked to supply dispensed medicines to a child for themselves, on behalf of another person, such as a parent, other relative or neighbour, or for persons whom they care for.

The decision on whether a supply is appropriate will need to be dealt with on a case by case basis and will involve considering the individual circumstances. Table 20 shows the factors that can be considered.

FURTHER READING

Royal Pharmaceutical Society
Children collecting medicines from a pharmacy.
www.rpharms.com

Table 20: Collection and purchase of medicines by children: factors to consider

1 **Knowledge of the child**	• Is the child known to the pharmacy? • What information is known?
2 **Maturity of the child**	• Are you satisfied the child is capable and competent to understand the importance of the medicines they are collecting and there are no further concerns with them delivering the medicines? • Are you confident the child will not misuse or tamper with the medicine?
3 **Nature of the medicine(s) supplied**	• What are the medicines being collected or supplied? • Can the medicine be misused? E.g. CDs or laxatives.
4 **Prior arrangement**	• Does the child regularly collect medicines from the pharmacy? • Is there an arrangement in place for this child to collect medicines for themselves/others, for example has this been previously discussed and agreed with a parent/guardian/representative (and recorded appropriately)?
5 **Reason for collection**	• Is there a good reason why the child is collecting or purchasing the medicine in the circumstances? • Is the person who the medicine is for housebound or unable to collect for an acceptable reason? • Is the child/young person a carer for the person that the medicine is for? • Is the child expected to self-medicate, such as with an inhaler?
6 **Advise on the use of medicines**	• Is any additional information required for the person taking the medicine? How will this be communicated? • Would the child understand any important information and are you confident these instructions will be passed on to the person the medicine is for? • Do you need to consider contacting an appropriate adult if special instructions for use are required?
7 **Local policies**	• Is there a local policy in place in your area? • You could contact your local Primary Care Organisation (CCG, LHB, HB etc.) • Does your organisation have a policy on children collecting medicines? Is there an SOP in place? • Consider making appropriate records.
8 **Proof of identity**	• Collecting Schedule 2 CDs require proof of identity which children may not have. You can use your professional judgement on making a supply without ID.

3.7.10
MEDICAL DEVICES

A medical device is described in the Medical Devices Regulations 2002 (SI 2002 No 618) as *any instrument, apparatus, appliance, software, material or other article, whether used alone or in combination, including the software necessary for its proper application intended by the manufacturer to be used on human beings for the purpose of:*

- *diagnosis, prevention, monitoring, treatment or alleviation of disease*
- *diagnosis, monitoring, treatment, or alleviation of or compensation for an injury or handicap*
- *investigation, replacement or modification of the anatomy or of a physiological process*
- *control of conception*

and which does not achieve its principal intended action in or on the human body by pharmacological, immunological or metabolic means, but which may be assisted in its function by such means.

Examples of medical devices (not exhaustive) available from a pharmacy include dressings, thermometers, needles, syringes, blood pressure monitors, stoma care products, condoms, test kits (e.g. cholesterol test kits, pregnancy test kits, etc.), inhalers, glucose meters and test strips, screening tests, some emollients, some eye drops, etc.

All medical devices are regulated by the MHRA.

All devices are required to carry the CE or UKCA mark denoting compliance with the medical devices regulations and indicating that the device performs as intended, is fit for purpose with all associated risks reduced as far as possible.

Medical devices which are similar or identical in appearance to licensed medicines (e.g. some prefilled syringes, some eye drops) can also be considered, following appropriate risk assessment, within the principles covered in the RPS Safe and secure handling of medicines (see RPS website www.rpharms.com)

FURTHER READING

Royal Pharmaceutical Society
Medical devices.
www.rpharms.com

Royal Pharmaceutical Society
Professional guidance for the procurement and supply of specials. 2015. (Includes guidance and case study on medical devices.)
www.rpharms.com

General Medical Council
Good practice in prescribing and managing medicines and devices.
www.gmc-uk.org

Medicines and Healthcare products Regulatory Agency
Medical devices regulation and safety.
www.gov.uk

Medicines and Healthcare products Regulatory Agency
Report a problem with a medicine or medical device.
www.gov.uk

3.7.11
MULTI-COMPARTMENT COMPLIANCE AIDS

Although multi-compartment compliance aids (MCA), (also known as monitored dosage systems (MDS)) may be of value to help some patients with problems managing their medicines and maintaining independent healthy living, they are one option following a comprehensive assessment of a patient's ability to safely manage their medicines. They may not be the best intervention for everyone and many alternative interventions are available. Evidence indicates that MCA should not automatically be the intervention of choice for all patients.

Not all medicines are suitable for inclusion in MCA and pharmacists should be aware that the re-packaging of medicines from a manufacturer's original packaging may often be off-licence and involves risks and responsibility for decisions made. The decision to supply a MCA needs to be reviewed and reassessed regularly to ensure its use continues to meet the need and is in the best interest of the user.

With the limited evidence base currently indicating a lack of patient benefit outcomes with the use of MCA, the RPS recommends that the use of original packs of medicines, supported by appropriate pharmaceutical care, should be the preferred intervention for the supply of medicines in the absence of a specific need identified by individual assessment for a MCA in all settings.

We have published a repository of MCA information where key resources can be accessed including patient assessment tools and our guidance *Improving patient outcomes: The better use of multi-compartment compliance aids*. This can be viewed on our website at www.rpharms.com.

Pharmacists are encouraged to be aware of the risks associated with MCA use on a population basis without individual assessments, to be aware of the alternatives and to share this knowledge with other health and social care professionals. Alternatives may include:

- Medicines administration record (MAR) charts
- Labels with pictograms
- Large print labels
- Information sheets
- Reminder alarms
- IT solutions and new technology such as phone apps and telemedicine

All of these interventions have a place in ensuring patients take or receive the correct medicines at the right time. The use of an MCA is just one additional intervention in a range of intervention options.

UK Medicines Information provide some information on the stability of medicines in compliance aids which can be accessed by all pharmacy staff via the Specialist Pharmacy Services website www.sps.nhs.uk.

3.7.12
DRUGS AND DRIVING

BACKGROUND
Section 4 of the Road Traffic Act 1988 includes an offence of driving whilst impaired through drugs, regardless of whether or not the drugs are being used legitimately. This means that if a patient driving is found to be impaired by medicines, even if he or she is taking them as prescribed or as recommended in the product information, he or she may still be prosecuted.

Additionally, it is an offence to drive with certain specified drugs in the body which are above an accepted limit – this is regardless of whether the driving is impaired. Table 21 lists the specified drugs: the first group are commonly abused drugs for which low limits have been set, the second group consists mainly of licensed medicines that have a significant liability to be abused and the specified limits have been set higher than those of the first group.

STATUTORY MEDICAL DEFENCE
A 'statutory medical defence' exists to protect patients who may test positive for these specified drugs (see Table 21) as a result of taking medicines in accordance with advice from a healthcare professional or the patient information leaflet.

Diagram 19 illustrates when the statutory medical defence can be raised.

The statutory medical defence may be raised at any point providing that the drug was:

- Lawfully prescribed, supplied or purchased over-the-counter, for medical or dental purposes; and
- Taken in accordance with advice given by the prescriber or supplier, and in accordance with any accompanying written instructions (provided these are consistent with any advice given by the prescriber).

Patient specific advice provided by a healthcare professional may sometimes differ from the general information given in the patient information leaflet of a medicine. In these cases, the advice provided by the healthcare professional may be used as a basis for the patient's statutory 'medical defence'.

Table 21: Specified drugs

First group		Second group	
	Cannabis (delta-9-tetrahydrocannabinol [THC])		Amfetamine
	Cocaine (and a cocaine metabolite, benzoylecgonine [BZE])		Clonazepam
			Diazepam
	Heroin/diamorphine metabolite (6-monoacetylmorphine [6-MAM])		Flunitrazepam
			Lorazepam
	Ketamine		Methadone
	Lysergic acid diethylamide (LSD)		Morphine or opiate and opioid-based drugs, e.g. codeine, tramadol
	MDMA (ecstasy)		Oxazepam
	Methylamfetamine		Temazepam

Diagram 19: Summary of how the statutory medical defence fits in with existing legislation

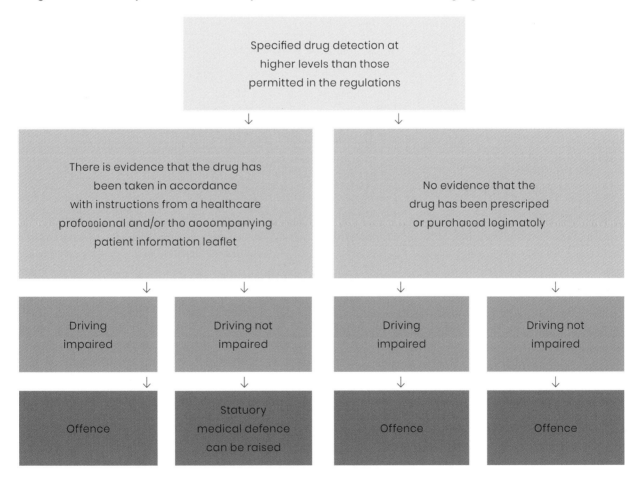

Pharmacists should be mindful of any new medicines added to a patient's regime that may interact with their existing therapies, affecting the metabolism of one of the specified drugs. They should also be cautious if there is a developing medical condition that could increase the risk of side effects from a medicine (e.g. during the development of a serious illness with significant weight loss).

ADVICE FOR PATIENTS

Reminder of the advice that should be provided to all patients receiving medicines that may impair driving ability:

- You must not drive if you feel sleepy, dizzy, are unable to concentrate or make decisions, have slowed thinking, or if you experience sight problems. If the medicine is one that could affect your driving ability, you should not drive until you know how the medicine affects you as an individual, particularly when starting a new medicine or following a dose change

- If you start a new medicine, even if it is one that does not directly affect your driving you should check with your pharmacist if it could have an effect on any of the medicines you are already taking, that could in turn affect your driving

- Remember that alcohol taken in combination with medicines, even in small amounts can greatly increase the risk of accidents

- An untreated medical condition may itself cause driving impairment and so it is important that you do not stop taking your medicines.

In addition to this, patients who are taking any of the drugs specified in Table 21 should also receive the following information and advice:

- There are limits on the amounts of certain drugs that you can have in your bloodstream whilst driving. There is a 'medical defence' for those who are taking medicines in line with a healthcare professional's advice, **provided that their driving is not impaired**

- Keep some suitable evidence with you when driving to show that you are taking your medicine as prescribed or supplied by a healthcare professional. Examples of evidence could include a repeat prescription slip for a prescribed medicine or the patient information leaflet for a P or general sale medicine.

It is important to note that if the individual's driving is impaired, they can still be prosecuted under the existing offence of driving whilst impaired through drugs, for which there is no statutory 'medical defence'. It remains the responsibility of all drivers to consider whether their driving is or could be impaired by their medicines.

MEDICAL CONDITIONS AND DRIVING

In addition to the drugs and driving offences described in this section there are also rules on fitness to drive requirements for patients with certain medical conditions. Further information on medical conditions, disabilities and driving is available on the Driving and Vehicle Licensing (DVLA) website: www.gov.uk

FURTHER READING

Royal Pharmaceutical Society
Drugs and driving legislation.
www.rpharms.com

Department for Transport
Guidance for healthcare professionals on drug driving. 2014.
www.gov.uk

Electronic Medicines Compendium
Information about whether a medicine is affected by the new legislation is included in its 'Summary of Product Characteristics'.
www.medicines.org.uk

Road Traffic Act
SI 2014/2868 The Drug Driving (Specified Limits) (England and Wales) Regulations. 2014
www.legislation.gov.uk

Road Traffic Act
SI 2015/911 The Drug Driving (Specified Limits) (England and Wales) (Amendment) Regulations. 2015.
www.legislation.gov.uk

Road Traffic Act
SI 2019/83 The Drug Driving (Specified Limits) (Scotland) Regulations. 2019.
www.legislation.gov.uk

Scottish Government
Drug driving and medicine: Advice for healthcare professionals.
www.gov.scot

3.7.13
RETENTION OF PHARMACY RECORDS

MEP refers to record keeping requirements throughout. In addition, East and South East England Specialist Pharmacy Services has published a document *Recommendations for Retention of Pharmacy Records*: www.sps.nhs.uk. This document includes guidance for all pharmacy settings as well as some sector-specific information.

FURTHER READING

NHS Digital
Records Management Code of Practice for Health and Social Care. 2016.
www.digital.nhs.uk

3.7.14
NEW PSYCHOACTIVE SUBSTANCES

The UK Psychoactive Substances Act (PSA) 2016 has described compounds commonly known as new psychoactive substances (NPS) as 'substances' that are 'capable of producing a psychoactive effect'.

WHY YOU SHOULD KNOW ABOUT NPS?

Pharmacists may encounter NPS products (such as tablets, capsules, powders, oils or herbs/seeds) in a range of settings including urgent and emergency care, secure environments, community pharmacies, pharmacists working in GP practices and in mental health units.

Although the PSA does not criminalise simple possession of NPSs, it is an offence to possess them within custodial institutions, or anywhere with intent to supply them to another. It is also an offence to import them (e.g. by buying them from a foreign website).

It is important that pharmacists are aware that the labels on NPS are not compliant with legal and professional requirements, as is the case with pharmaceuticals (e.g. requirements of Good Manufacturing Practices (GMP)). Furthermore, NPS products may contain unclaimed Schedule 1 or 2 substances (The Misuse of Drugs Regulations 2001), for which legal requirements apply.

Pharmacists need to be aware of possible NPS /POM interactions, some of which are documented, such as interactions with anti-retrovirals (www.neptune-clinical-guidance.co.uk). In addition, pharmacists need to be aware of interactions arising from unclaimed active ingredients present in NPS. Furthermore, research has shown that NPS have not replaced the current repertoire of traditional drugs of abuse (e.g. amphetamine, cocaine, heroin, ecstasy) but rather have supplemented it, with or without alcohol, resulting upon co-administration in a high risk of synergistic or additive pharmacological effects.

NPS may also have an impact on the enforcement of the drug-driving laws. For example, if a patient takes an NPS that inhibits the metabolism of a prescribed Schedule 2 POM, a road-side test may show greater concentrations of the Schedule 2 drug than that allowed whilst driving, which may result in the arrest of the patient. NPS are not included in the drug-driving lists.

Pharmacists should be aware of the 're-classification' of OTC and P medicines to NPS when used for recreational purposes e.g. the diverted use of OTC and P medicines.

The use of NPS may induce addiction and psychosis, therefore, there are legal (under the Mental Health Act 2007), professional, clinical and cost implications.

FURTHER READING

Royal Pharmaceutical Society
New psychoactive substances – guide and factsheet.
www.rpharms.com

European Monitoring Centre for Drugs and Drug Addiction
Various resources available. These include risk assessment reports on high-risk NPS, which have induced severe harm or fatalities.
www.emcdda.europa.eu/publications

3.7.15
WORKING DURING A PANDEMIC

During a global pandemic, pharmacists and pharmacy teams need to adapt quickly and efficiently to ensure continuation of pharmacy services.

CHANGES IN LEGISLATION DURING A PANDEMIC

Legislation is already in place which relaxes the emergency supply requirements in the event of a pandemic or imminent pandemic being declared. It allows pharmacists to make an emergency supply of a medicine without the need to interview the patient.

Provisions are also in place to allow the supply of medicines against a protocol from designated collection points when a disease is pandemic or imminently pandemic and there is a serious or potentially serious risk to human health. Further information is available in Regulations 226 and 247 of the Human Medicines Regulations 2012 (www.legislation.gov.uk)

The Government also has 'emergency powers' to respond rapidly during a public emergency such as a pandemic by introducing new legislation or enacting existing legislation. Any changes made under 'emergency powers' are temporary, apply to specific circumstances, and are kept under review. Some of these changes in legislation are effective immediately – other changes are introduced in anticipation of a particular need and require a Government minister to 'switch on' the changes before they are used.

Do not assume that because legislation has changed that any new provision is in force immediately:

- Changes may need to be activated or 'switched on'
- They may be effective for a specific time period only
- Changes may apply in a particular geographic region – not necessary across GB
- Always read the guidance carefully

If you have any doubts check with RPS Support.

WORKING OUTSIDE YOUR SPECIALITY/ SCOPE

During a pandemic you may be asked to work outside your speciality; for example, providing cover in a new area such as critical care. This is reasonable and practical during a pandemic. However, you should always work within your competence.

If you do not feel competent or have concerns about what you are being asked to do speak to your manager.

If you find yourself having to prescribe outside your competence in an emergency, you should provide the safest care you are able to, based on evidence and best practice. The aim should be to provide overall benefit for the patient.

Our guidance *Ethical, professional decision making in the COVID-19 pandemic* www.rpharms.com will assist with making difficult decisions and ensure safe and effective care. It contains guidance on structured decision making and includes some examples specific to the current pandemic. This framework can be used by all sectors of the profession.

FURTHER INFORMATION

Key sources of information during a pandemic include

RPS
www.rpharms.com

Government websites
www.gov.uk, www.gov.wales, www.gov.scot (includes information on public health agencies)

NHS websites
www.nhs.uk, www.scot.nhs.uk, www.wales.nhs.uk

World Health Organization
www.who.int

3.7.16
NEEDLE SYRINGE PROVISION

Pharmacists delivering needle exchange services or Injectable Equipment Provision (IEP) services should be aware of National and Local guidelines.

When delivering these services pharmacists are expected to behave in a non judgemental manner using the appropriate language, maintaining confidentiality and remembering the importance of harm reduction for the service users.

Pharmacists should consider training available for themselves and staff to provide these services competently and effectively.

FURTHER READING

National Institute for Health and Care Excellence
Needle and Syringe Programmes (March 2014)
www.nice.org.uk

National Services Scotland
Guidance on Injecting Equipment Provision (IEP) Draft
www.nss.nhs.scot

3

The Responsible Pharmacist

A pharmacist must be in charge of a registered pharmacy as the responsible pharmacist, in order to lawfully conduct a retail pharmacy business.

There can only be one responsible pharmacist in charge at any one time, and the pharmacist can only be in charge of one registered premises at any one time.

Legislation introducing the role and responsibilities of the Responsible Pharmacist are set out in full in the Medicines Act 1968 (as amended by the *Health Act 2006*) and the *Medicines (Pharmacies) (Responsible Pharmacist) Regulations 2008*.

Note: At the time of writing, the Rebalancing Medicines Legislation and Pharmacy Regulation Programme Board were reviewing pharmacy regulation and considering changes to the role and responsibilities of superintendent and responsible pharmacist.
www.gov.uk/government/groups/
pharmacy-regulation-programme-board

WHAT BEING A RESPONSIBLE PHARMACIST INVOLVES

A Responsible Pharmacist will need to:

Secure the safe and effective running of the pharmacy

↓

Display a notice

↓

Complete the pharmacy record

↓

Establish, maintain and review pharmacy procedures

SECURING THE SAFE AND EFFECTIVE RUNNING OF A REGISTERED PHARMACY

The responsible pharmacist is responsible for the safe and effective running of the pharmacy and should establish the scope of the responsibilities before taking on a role. If unsure about anything reasonable measures can be taken to clarify
with the pharmacy owner, superintendent pharmacist or other delegated person.

Further material on how a responsible pharmacist can secure the safe and effective running of a registered pharmacy can be found on the RPS Responsible Pharmacist Toolkit on RPS website at www.rpharms.com.

If a responsible pharmacist believes the pharmacy is not safe or patients are at risk then steps should be taken to secure the safe and effective running of the pharmacy. If this is not possible then the pharmacy may need to be closed.

DISPLAYING A NOTICE

A responsible pharmacist is required to display a notice that is clearly visible to patients and the public with the information below for as long as she/he is a responsible pharmacist.

This needs to include:

- The name of the responsible pharmacist
- The GPhC registration number
- The fact that the responsible pharmacist is in charge of the pharmacy at the time

If the responsible pharmacist is temporarily absent from the pharmacy (see further on under "Absence") but remains the responsible pharmacist, the notice should not be removed even if there is a second pharmacist in the pharmacy.
However, if the responsible pharmacist changes throughout the day, so too should the name and registration number on the notice.

COMPLETING THE PHARMACY RECORD

The pharmacy record is an important legal document. It shows who the responsible pharmacist is at any given date and at any time.

The pharmacy record may be kept in the following formats:

- In writing
- Electronically
- Or in both forms

THE RECORD SHOULD:

- Be recorded accurately and reflects who the responsible pharmacist is and was at any given date and time (including any absences).
- Should be made contemporaneously personally by the responsible pharmacist. An entry may be made remotely as long as the record complies with all the relevant and professional requirements.
- Any alterations or amendments made for both paper-based and electronic pharmacy records need to identify when and by whom the alteration/amendment was made.
- For electronic records appropriate measures should be made to back up the record and be kept on the pharmacy premises, available for GPhC inspection if required.

THE FOLLOWING DETAILS MUST BE RECORDED IN THE PHARMACY RECORD:

- The responsible pharmacist's name
- The responsible pharmacist's registration number
- The date and time at which the pharmacist became the responsible pharmacist
- The date and time at which the responsible pharmacist stopped being the responsible pharmacist
- If you are absent from the premises:
  - The date of absence
  - The time which the responsible pharmacist left the pharmacy premises
  - The time at which the responsible pharmacist returned to the pharmacy premises

The pharmacy owner or superintendent pharmacist must keep the pharmacy record for a period of FIVE years. The record must be available at the pharmacy to which it relates to.

4

PHARMACY PROCEDURES

A responsible pharmacist must establish, maintain and review the pharmacy procedures in the pharmacy she/he is working in.

Regulation 4 of The Medicines (Pharmacies) (Responsible Pharmacist) Regulations 2008 outlines the pharmacy procedures must cover the following:

1   The arrangements to secure that medicinal products are:

- Ordered
- Stored
- Prepared
- Sold by retail
- Supplied in circumstances corresponding to retail sale
- Delivered outside the pharmacy and
- Disposed of in a safe and effective manner

2   The circumstances in which a member of pharmacy staff who is not a pharmacist may give advice about medicinal products

3   The identification of members of pharmacy staff who are, in the view of the Responsible Pharmacist, competent to perform certain tasks relating to the pharmacy business

4   The keeping of records about the arrangements

5   The arrangements which are to apply during the absence of the Responsible Pharmacist from the premises

6   The steps to be taken when there is a change of Responsible Pharmacist at the premises

7   The procedure which is to be followed if a complaint is made about the pharmacy business

8   The procedure which is to be followed if an incident occurs which may indicate that the pharmacy business is not running in a safe and effective manner and

9   The manner in which changes to the pharmacy procedures are to be notified to pharmacy staff

- In writing
- Electronically (consider any backups required)
- Or in both forms

Adequate back-ups of the contents of the procedures should be made.

THE PHARMACY PROCEDURE SHOULD:

- Be available for inspection by the person who owns the pharmacy business, the superintendent pharmacist, the responsible pharmacist, the pharmacy staff and GPhC inspectorate.

- Be reviewed regularly. They can be reviewed once every two years or following an incident which may indicate that the pharmacy may not be running safely and effectively (such as a dispensing error).

  - Identify the responsible pharmacist who reviewed the procedure
  - Identify which procedures are in place
  - Identify which procedures were previously in place

A responsible pharmacist can use her/his professional judgement to make a temporary amendment to the pharmacy procedures if the circumstances in the pharmacy change (for example a key member of staff if off sick, etc).

If temporary amendments are made the responsible pharmacist should maintain an audit trail to identify:

- Which procedures are in place
- Which procedures were previously in place
- The responsible pharmacist who amended the procedure
- The date on which the amendment was made

The responsible pharmacist needs to be satisfied the pharmacy staff are aware of and understand the pharmacy procedures which are in place.

ABSENCE

Legislation allows the responsible pharmacist to be absent for up to a maximum period of two hours during the pharmacy's business hours between midnight and midnight.

If there is more than one responsible pharmacist in charge of the pharmacy during the pharmacy's business hours, the total period of absence for all the responsible pharmacists must not exceed two hours.

Note: The requirements of the NHS Pharmaceutical Regulations should be considered before the responsible pharmacist is absent.

If the responsible pharmacist is absent, the following arrangements must be in place:

- Only be absent if the pharmacy can continue to run safely and effectively

- Remain contactable with the pharmacy staff, where this is reasonably practical and be able to return with reasonable promptness.

- If the responsible pharmacist cannot remain contactable and return with reasonable promptness, she/he must arrange for another pharmacist to be contactable and available to provide advice (this does not need to be another responsible pharmacist).

If a responsible pharmacist is absent from the premises as a minimum she/he must record:

- The date of absence

- The time which the responsible pharmacist left the pharmacy premises

- The time at which the responsible pharmacist returned to the pharmacy premises

Further information on how a responsible pharmacist can deal with an absence can be found on the RPS Responsible Pharmacist Toolkit at www.rpharms.com.

WHICH ACTIVITIES REQUIRE A RESPONSIBLE PHARMACIST?

The operational activities that may take place in the registered pharmacy when a responsible pharmacist is in charge of the pharmacy depend on the level of supervision provided and whether or not she/he is absent from the registered pharmacy. Examples of operational activities and the level of supervision required can be found in tables below

Table 22 : Activities that can take place with a responsible pharmacist in charge of the pharmacy under the supervision of a pharmacist and the supervising pharmacist will need to be physically present at the pharmacy

Activity	Other points to consider
Professional check (clinical and legal check) of a prescription	This check is required under the NHS pharmaceutical legislation www.legislation.gov.uk
Sale/supply of P medicines	'Supervision' in this context requires physical presence and pharmacist being able to advise and intervene
Sale/supply of POMs (e.g. handing dispensed medicines to patient, patient representative or a delivery person)	'Supervision' in this context requires physical presence and pharmacist being able to advise and intervene
Supply of medicines under a patient group direction (PGD)	'Supervision' in this context requires physical presence
Wholesale of medicines	'Supervision' in this context requires physical presence and pharmacist being able to advise and intervene
Emergency supply of a medicine(s) at the request of a patient or healthcare professional	'Supervision' in this context requires physical presence and pharmacist being able to advise and intervene

Activity	Other points to consider
The assembly process (including assembly of compliance aids (monitored dosage systems): • Generating a dispensing label • Taking medicines off the dispensary shelves • Assembly of the item (e.g. counting tablets) • Labelling of containers with the dispensing label • Accuracy checking	'Supervision' in this context may not require the physical presence of a pharmacist. The level of supervision required of the suitable trained staff who undertake this work will depend on what is regarded as good practice within the pharmacy profession.

EXPLANATION OF 'ASSEMBLY'

The assembly of medicines against a prescription is controlled by Section 10 of the Medicines Act 1968 defining medicinal product 'assembly'.

Section 10 of the Medicines Act 1968 requires that the assembly process takes place under the 'supervision' of a pharmacist.

Supervision is not defined in the Act, and since the time the legislation was written the nature of assembly has changed in many instances such as the introduction of patient packs.

The courts have considered the issue of the nature of 'supervision' required for the purposes of sale or supply of medicines and have concluded that, where supervision by a pharmacist is required, the actual transaction cannot take place without the physical presence of a pharmacist who is able to advise and intervene, even though s/he will not need to carry out the transaction themselves. However, the level of supervision required for assembly activities is less clear, and so for these activities, reference has to be made to more general case law of what 'supervision' means in the context of professional supervision. The general position (derived from the Court of Appeal's judgement in Summers v Congreve Horner and Co [1992] 2 EGLR 152) is that supervision, in the context of professional supervision, means the degree of supervision required by what is regarded as good practice within the profession, having regard to the qualifications and experience of the person being supervised, but actual physical presence may not be necessary.

Applying that to the present context, it means that if the pharmacist responsible for supervising assembly of a medicinal product is absent, pharmacy support staff may continue to carry out activities which are considered to be 'assembling' activities for the purposes of the definition set out above, without breaching the legislation, provided it is recognised good practice within the pharmacy profession that they be allowed to do so. The RPS publishes good practice guidance, but it is important to emphasise that no single solution fits all circumstances. What may be good practice for one type of assembling activity may not be good practice for other types of assembling activities, and all such activities must be 'supervised' at an appropriate level. It is also important to emphasise that this does not affect the position that the supply of assembled medicines against a prescription is prohibited unless the pharmacist is physically present in the registered pharmacy and in a position to advise and intervene. However, 'supervision' is not a 'one size fits all circumstances' legal concept, and the courts have recognised this.

Table 24 : Activities that can take place with a responsible pharmacist in charge of the pharmacy (but does not require supervision of a pharmacist)

Activity	Other points to consider
Sale of general sale medicines	Undertaken by suitable trained staff and operating within an agreed documented operating procedure.
Processing waste stock medicines or patient returned medicines	Undertaken by suitable trained staff and operating within an agreed documented operating procedure. There are also medicines disposal obligation in NHS pharmaceutical services legislation. Responsible Pharmacists and Superintendents should give consideration to processing stock or patient returned medicines which are CDs.

Table 25 : Activities that can take place without a responsible pharmacist to be in charge of the pharmacy but requires the support staff undertaking the activity to be appropiately trained

Activity	Other points to consider
Ordering stock from pharmaceutical wholesalers	Undertaken by suitable trained staff and operating within an agreed documented operating procedure.
Receiving stock from pharmaceutical wholesalers into the building	Undertaken by suitable trained staff and operating within an agreed documented operating procedure. Responsible Pharmacists and superintendents should give consideration to how the pharmacy receives orders containing CDs taking into account the Misuse of Drugs Regulations 2001.
Putting medicinal stock received from the wholesaler away onto the pharmacy shelves	Undertaken by suitable trained staff and operating within an agreed documented operating procedure. Responsible Pharmacists and Superintendents should give consideration to how the pharmacy handles CDs taking into account the Misuse of Drugs Regulations 2001.

Activity	Other points to consider
Date checking	Undertaken by suitable trained staff and operating within an agreed documented operating procedure. Responsible Pharmacists and Superintendents should give consideration to how the pharmacy date checks CDs taking into account the Misuse of Drugs Regulations 2001.
Stocking pharmacy with consumables	Undertaken by suitable trained staff and operating within an agreed documented operating procedure.
Cleaning of the pharmacy	Undertaken by suitable trained staff and operating within an agreed documented operating procedure. Responsible Pharmacists and Superintendents should give consideration to how access to the registered pharmacy premises is controlled, especially if cleaning of the pharmacy takes place overnight when the pharmacy is closed and/or if the cleaning services are contracted out.
Responding to enquiries (about medicine issues)	Undertaken by suitable trained staff and operating within an agreed documented operating procedure.
Accessing the PMR	Undertaken by suitable trained staff and operating within an agreed documented operating procedure. Responsible Pharmacists and Superintendents should give consideration to how access to confidential information is protected in accordance with Data Protection and confidentiality requirements. Further information can be found in the GPhC Guidance on Confidentiality 2017 on GPhC website at www.pharmacyregulation.org
Receiving prescription directly from EPS systems (England only) patients or collecting from a surgery	Undertaken by suitable trained staff and operating within an agreed documented operating procedure. Obligations under NHS pharmaceutical legislation to ensure that prescriptions are dispensed with reasonable promptness.

Activity	Other points to consider
Processing of prescription forms that have been dispensed (eg. Counting number of items dispensed, sorting prior submission for reimbursement)	Undertaken by suitable trained staff and operating within an agreed documented operating procedure. NHS reimbursement covered under NHS legislation.
Delivery person conveying medicines to patient	Undertaken by suitable trained staff and operating within an agreed documented operating procedure. Responsible Pharmacists and Superintendents should give consideration to what will happen to undelivered medicines especially relating to CDs.
Receiving patient returned medicines	Undertaken by suitable trained staff and operating within an agreed documented operating procedure. Responsible Pharmacists and Superintendents should give consideration to how the pharmacy handles receipt of patient returned medicines which are CDs in accordance with the Misuse of Drugs Regulations 2001. Also see section 3.6 for further guidance on CDs.

FURTHER READING

Royal Pharmaceutical Society
Responsible pharmacist.
www.rpharms.com

General Pharmaceutical Council
Information for employers: Responsible pharmacist.
www.pharmacyregulation.org

Pharmaceutical Services Negotiating Committee
Responsible pharmacist. Includes a series of FAQs.
www.psnc.org.uk

Rebalancing Medicines Legislation and Pharmacy Regulation Programme Board
www.gov.uk

4

Royal Pharmaceutical Society code of conduct

The Code of Conduct for members of the RPS has been reproduced below and is available online in appendix A of the RPS regulations www.rpharms.com (search 'how we are run')

CODE OF CONDUCT

Assembly may create, and from time to time amend or rescind, a Code of Conduct to be observed by all members of the Society. Breaches of the Code may, upon proper investigation under the process set out in the appropriate Regulations, lead to a Conduct Panel hearing which may, in turn, depending on the nature of the breach, ultimately lead to expulsion from the Society.

ALL MEMBERS

Being a member of the RPS is a mark of professionalism and members, as ambassadors of the Society, should do nothing that might detract from the high standing of the profession. This includes any aspect of a member's personal conduct which could have a negative impact upon the profession. On admission to, and annually on renewal of membership, all members must therefore:

- Be in good standing professionally, including with the Society and any other professional body or regulator of which they are a member or registrant

- Conduct themselves in a manner that upholds and enhances the reputation of the Society

- Further the interests of and maintain the dignity and welfare of the Society and the profession

- Exercise their professional skills and judgement to the best of their ability, discharge their professional responsibilities with integrity and do all in their power to ensure that their professional activities do not put the health and safety of others at risk

- When called upon to give a professional opinion, do so with objectivity and reliability
- Be truthful and honest in dealings with clients, colleagues, other professionals and all they come into contact with in the course of their duties
- Never engage in any activity that will impair the dignity, reputation or welfare of the Society, fellow members or their profession
- Never knowingly engage in any corrupt or unethical practice
- Not implicate the Society, through direct reference or use of membership status, in any statement that may be construed as defamatory, discriminatory, libellous, offensive, slanderous, subversive or otherwise damaging to the Society
- If convicted of a criminal or civil offence anywhere in the world inform the Society promptly, and provide such information concerning the conviction as the Institution may require. *NB this does not included Fixed Penalty Notice offences.*
- Observe the Policies of the Society
- Comply with the Society's Regulations and all applicable laws

CONDUCT

If a member generally becomes aware of, or has reasonable grounds for believing, that another member is engaged in or has engaged in conduct which is in breach of the Regulations and/or Code of Conduct of the Society, they shall inform the Society in writing of that belief, but shall not maliciously or recklessly injure or attempt to injure, directly or indirectly, the reputation, practice, employment or livelihood of another member.

Complaints about the opinions expressed by a member or content shared by a member publicly on a social media platform should be reported to the social media platform directly or, where relevant, to the police. RPS will not routinely take action to undermine any Members right to challenge and/or criticise any action of RPS. RPS will only consider complaints about such content under the Conduct Scheme where the member is holding themselves out as a representative of RPS on such a platform or where at the reasonable discretion of the CEO the content may infringe common standards of decency or place an

individual at risk of harm in which case the complaint may be dealt with under the Conduct Scheme. Fellows are held to the same standard as ordinary members in this respect.

Complaints about the professional practice, performance or conduct of a member should be referred to the General Pharmaceutical Council, and any action by the Society shall be postponed until the outcome of the Council's proceedings is known.

If the complaint is summarily dismissed by the General Pharmaceutical Council, the procedures set out in the Conduct Scheme for Members will be followed.

If the complaint is the subject of proceedings before a court or other regulatory authority, any action by the Society shall be postponed until the outcome of those proceedings is known, but is not obliged to do so. The Society is entitled to conduct its own investigations and implement its own decisions in accordance with the Society's Regulations and conduct procedures independently from the General Pharmaceutical Council, courts or any other authority.

In exceptional circumstances, the Society may take action in advance of a decision of a court or regulatory authority, in which case the complaint shall be referred to the Chairman of the Membership Committee, and the procedures set out in the Conduct Scheme for Members will be followed.

BULLYING OR HARASSMENT

The Society aims to create an environment which respects the dignity of all individuals, including but not limited to individuals who are Members, members or employees, those who provide services to the Society or conduct business on behalf of the Society or who come into contact with anyone connected to the Society.

Bullying, harassment, or victimisation of any will not be tolerated.

Bullying is offensive, intimidating, malicious or insulting behaviour, and/or misuse or an abuse or misuse of power that is meant to undermine, humiliate or injure the person on the receiving end.

Harassment is any unwanted physical, verbal or non-verbal conduct which has the purpose of violating another person's dignity or creating an intimidating, hostile, degrading, humiliating or offensive environment for another person, or is reasonably considered by that person to have the effect of violating their dignity or creating such an environment, even if this effect was not intended by the person responsible for the conduct. A single incident or a pattern of multiple incidents of this type of behaviour can amount to harassment and/or bullying. It also includes treating someone less favourably because they have submitted or refused to submit to such behaviour in the past.

Any of these behaviours will always be viewed extremely seriously and may result in disciplinary action being taken including, or where appropriate, summary dismissal, removal from office, termination of a contract to provide services or membership of the Society.

Pharmacist Support

Pharmacist Support is an independent, trusted charity, providing a wide variety of free and confidential support services to pharmacists and their families, former pharmacists, Foundation trainee pharmacists, and MPharm and OSPAP students.

The charity supports people through a wide variety of challenges. From student financial struggles and exam anxiety, to practical support with managing debt, finances and employment issues and supporting those going through the GPhC fitness to practise proceedings. Pharmacist Support provides assistance to alleviate stress and pressure so you can focus on your pharmacy studies, trainee foundation placement or job, ensuring you don't have to face challenging times alone.

Pharmacist Support offer a range of free and confidential support including:

· An information and enquiry service

· Wardley Wellbeing Service

· Counselling and Peer Support

· Financial assistance

· Specialist advice in the areas of debt, benefits and employment law

· Addiction support programme (covering alcohol and drug dependencies, gambling and eating disorders).

Please visit Pharmacist Support website www.pharmacistsupport.org to find out more about the services and how you can access them.

COMMITTED TO PHARMACY WELLBEING

Over the past ten years the charity has taken a more proactive approach to its support. They have established services and a major wellbeing campaign to help to prevent those across the profession from reaching crisis point in the first place.

The charity has lots of guidance, information and practical support available on their website for pharmacists to help understand the signs and symptoms of stress and to prioritise and manage wellbeing.

Pharmacist Support's mission is to champion wellbeing within pharmacy. As part of this commitment, they have provided the following guidance to minimise the risk of reaching crisis point, and outline some of the steps you can take should you find yourself struggling or in difficulty.

STRESS IN THE WORKPLACE

Pressures, anxieties, doubts, and worries are all part of normal life. However, they can quickly turn into stress when they are excessive, persistent and uncontrollable.

Healthcare professionals face enormous pressures in their work lives and, as a result, many struggle with high levels of stress and burnout. In the 2020 Workforce Wellbeing Survey hosted jointly between RPS and Pharmacist Support, almost nine in ten pharmacists working in Great Britain said that they're at high risk of burnout.

Living in a constant state of stress can take an enormous toll on your emotional and physical wellbeing. When you can't get stressful thoughts out of your head and they interfere with your everyday life, it's time to take action.

There are many practical techniques you could use to manage day to day worries and stress, including talking about your concerns and pressures with someone you trust, creating a daily 'worry period' when you allow yourself to think proactively about your concerns, interrupting the worry cycle by engaging in another activity such as exercise or socialising, and practicing mindfulness. Pharmacist Support's website has many resources dedicated to helping you through times of worry and stress. The charity's free Wellbeing Learning Platform for individual wellbeing learning and training Is also a great way to access and follow a range of free online wellbeing workshops at a time that suits you.

The charity's now annual ACTNow campaigns, running at three separate times in the year and targeting the wellbeing needs of students, trainees and pharmacists, also look to address some of the mental health issues highlighted through research around workplace culture and stigma. Through ACTNow the charity shall be looking beyond what individuals can do, and towards what we can all do to create positive environments to allow people to thrive. Through the campaigns, the charity wants to further support organisations to embed wellbeing practices into the workplace and place of study. To find out more visit the Pharmacist Support website www.pharmacistsupport.org.

FURTHER INFORMATION FROM PHARMACIST SUPPORT

Managing stress (self-learning module)

Information about their counselling and peer support service pharmacistsupport.org

Practical fact sheets on identifying stress triggers and how to tackle them

Stories from colleagues across the country who share their own learning and tips on overcoming stress

Wellbeing Learning Platform pharmacistsupportclcmoodle.org

ADDICTION (DRUG/ALCOHOL)

Pharmacist Support recognise that those working in pharmacy face extreme work responsibilities and can suffer intense work-related stress and anxiety. Like many people outside of their profession, this can lead pharmacists to turn to alcohol or drugs as a coping mechanism. Others may turn to mood altering substances for other reasons.

Learning how substance abuse and addiction develops and understanding how to notice behavioural changes in ourselves or others is an important first step to recovery. After all, addiction is a cunning illness, persuading people that 'things are not that bad … I can stop when the time is right'.

While recovery from addiction can seem daunting, with the right strategies, treatment and support, change is possible, even if you have tried and failed before. If you're struggling to manage dependency issues, Pharmacist Support encourage you to reach out and take advantage of their free and confidential addiction support service.

FURTHER INFORMATION FROM PHARMACIST SUPPORT

Addiction Support Programme

Case study:
How Pharmacist Support supported a pharmacist struggling with addiction

Help with alcoholism

Help with drug abuse

DEBT

Debt can happen to anyone, even those who are prudent with their finances. Unemployment, redundancy, a change in household circumstances, poor physical or mental health, and poor fiscal decisions can all lead to people falling into debt.

Worrying about finances and how to manage money can take a serious toll on mental health and wellbeing. Debt can be a considerable burden, especially if you are dealing with it alone and feel unsupported by loved ones and creditors. However, with the right support and strategies, you can regain control of your finances. Take a look at the resources below to see how Pharmacist Support can support you.

FURTHER INFORMATION FROM PHARMACIST SUPPORT

Financial assistance

Help with debt

Managing your money

Specialist advice

HEALTH AND WELLBEING

As the profession's charity, Pharmacist Support understand the stresses and pressures you face. In your dedication to provide care for others and the day-to-day challenges you need to tackle, self-care is often put at the bottom of the list. How often have you carried on, despite feeling sick yourself?

Even if the term might sound indulgent, self-care is vital for maintaining stable wellbeing. Wellbeing is the state of having good mental health, high life satisfaction, a sense of meaning or purpose,

and the ability to manage stress. It's important to realise that wellbeing is a much deeper concept than moment-to-moment happiness, and we must invest in it if we want to have sustained happiness, control of our emotions, higher productivity, and good physical health.

Self-care is not selfish either: if you're taking good care of yourself, you'll be in a better position to take care of others. Pharmacist Support encourage everyone in the pharmacy family to prioritise their health and wellbeing and have included some resources below to help you start that journey.

FURTHER INFORMATION FROM PHARMACIST SUPPORT

Being positive (self-learning module)

Wardley Wellbeing hub – looking after your body

FITNESS TO PRACTICE

Pharmacist Support understand the profound impact a fitness to practice investigation and possible outcome can have on a pharmacist's health and wellbeing. If you are facing a fitness to practice issue, please read through the information below or contact us to see how Pharmacist Support could support you.

FURTHER INFORMATION FROM PHARMACIST SUPPORT

Case study: How Pharmacist Support supported someone during their investigation

Investigations and hearings

We'd like to thank Pharmacist Support for their help in writing this Chapter.

For further information about the charity and how they can support you, please visit pharmacistsupport.org. You can also contact them via email at info@pharmacistsupport.org or call one of the freephone numbers on 0808 168 2233 or 0808 168 5133.

Appendices

The appendices are key regulatory standards and guidance that have been reproduced with the permission of the GPhC. These documents are subject to change and review by the GPhC and the latest versions can be obtained from the GPhC website www.pharmacyregulation.org

Additional standards and guidance have not been reproduced in the appendices (see also Section 1) and can be obtained from the GPhC website www.pharmacyregulation.org

The GPhC Standards Team can be contacted at:

STANDARDS TEAM
General Pharmaceutical Council
25 Canada Square
London E14 5LQ
Tel: 020 3713 8000
Email: standards@pharmacyregulation.org

GPhC inspection reports and learning from inspections can be found on the GPhC inspections website at inspections.pharmacyregulation.org.

Appendix 1
GPhC standards for pharmacy professionals

MAY 2017

INTRODUCTION

1   Pharmacy professionals' (pharmacists and pharmacy technicians) play a vital role in delivering care and helping people to maintain and improve their health, safety and wellbeing. The professionalism they demonstrate is central to maintaining trust and confidence in pharmacy.

2   Patients and the public have a right to expect safe and effective care from pharmacy professionals. We believe it is the attitudes and behaviours of pharmacy professionals in their day-to-day work which make the most significant contributions to the quality of care, of which safety is a vital part.

3   The standards for pharmacy professionals describe how safe and effective care is delivered through 'person-centred' professionalism.
The standards are a statement of what people expect from pharmacy professionals and also reflect what pharmacy professionals have told us they expect of themselves and their colleagues.

4   At the heart of the standards is the principle that every person must be treated as an individual. Pharmacy professionals have an important role in involving, supporting and enabling people to make decisions about their health, safety and wellbeing. For example, what is important to one person managing their short or long-term condition may not be important to another.

5   There are nine standards that every pharmacy professional is accountable for meeting. The standards apply to all pharmacists and pharmacy technicians. We know that pharmacy professionals practise in a number of sectors and settings and may use different ways to communicate with the people they provide care to. The standards apply whatever their form of practice. And even when pharmacy professionals do not provide care directly to patients and the public, their practice can indirectly have an impact on the safe and effective care that patients and the public receive, and on the confidence of members of the public in pharmacy as a whole.

6   The standards need to be met at all times, not only during working hours. This is because the attitudes and behaviours of professionals outside of work can affect the trust and confidence of patients and the public in pharmacy professionals.

7   The meaning of each of the standards is explained, and there are examples of the types of attitudes and behaviours that pharmacy professionals should demonstrate. The examples may not apply in all situations.

8   The standards include the term 'person centred care' and refer to a 'person' throughout. This means 'the person receiving care'. The term may also apply to carers or patients' representatives depending on the situation.

THE STANDARDS AND PHARMACY STUDENTS AND TRAINEES

9   The standards for pharmacy professionals are relevant to all pharmacy students and trainees while they are on their journey towards registration and practice. The standards explain the knowledge, attitudes and behaviours that will be expected of students and trainees if they apply to join the register.

10 They should be interpreted in the context of education and training and used as a tool to prepare students and trainees for registration as a pharmacy professional.

11   Pharmacy students and trainees should consider the standards as they move closer to registration and professional practice, and should read them alongside other relevant documents that are provided by initial education and training providers.

THE STANDARDS AND REGISTRATION

12   The standards are designed to reflect what it means to be a pharmacy professional. They are also at the heart of initial education and training, registration and renewal as a pharmacy professional, and continuing fitness to remain registered.

APPLYING THE STANDARDS

13   Pharmacy professionals are personally accountable for meeting the standards and must be able to justify the decisions they make.

14   We expect pharmacy professionals to consider these standards, their legal duties and any relevant guidance when making decisions.

15   The standards and supporting explanations do not list the legal duties pharmacy professionals have, as all pharmacy professionals must keep to the relevant laws. Relevant guidance is published by a number of organisations, including professional leadership bodies, other regulators, the NHS, National Institute for Health and Care Excellence and Scottish Intercollegiate Guidelines Network, as well as by the GPhC.

16   There will be times when pharmacy professionals are faced with conflicting legal and professional responsibilities. Or they may be faced with complex situations that mean they have to balance competing priorities. The standards provide a framework to help them when making professional judgements. Pharmacy professionals must work in partnership with everyone involved, and make sure the person they are providing care to is their first priority.

STANDARDS FOR PHARMACY PROFESSIONALS

All pharmacy professionals contribute to delivering and improving the health, safety and wellbeing of patients and the public. Professionalism and safe and effective practice are central to that role. Pharmacy professionals must:

1   Provide person-centred care

2   Work in partnership with others

3   Communicate effectively

4   Maintain, develop and use their professional knowledge and skills

5   Use professional judgement

6   Behave in a professional manner

7   Respect and maintain the person's confidentiality and privacy

8   Speak up when they have concerns or when things go wrong

9   Demonstrate leadership

PHARMACY PROFESSIONALS MUST PROVIDE PERSON-CENTRED CARE

PHARMACY PROFESSIONALS MUST WORK IN PARTNERSHIP WITH OTHERS

APPLYING THE STANDARD

Every person is an individual with their own values, needs and concerns. Person-centred care is delivered when pharmacy professionals understand what is important to the individual and then adapt the care to meet their needs – making the care of the person their first priority. All pharmacy professionals can demonstrate 'person-centredness', whether or not they provide care directly, by thinking about the impact their decisions have on people. There are a number of ways to meet this standard, and below are examples of the attitudes and behaviours expected.

People receive safe and effective care when pharmacy professionals:

- Obtain consent to provide care and pharmacy services

- Involve, support and enable every person when making decisions about their health, care and wellbeing

- Listen to the person and understand their needs and what matters to them

- Give the person all relevant information in a way they can understand, so they can make informed decisions and choices

- Consider the impact of their practice whether or not they provide care directly

- Respect and safeguard the person's dignity

- Recognise and value diversity, and respect cultural differences – making sure that every person is treated fairly whatever their values and beliefs

- Recognise their own values and beliefs but do not impose them on other people

- Take responsibility for ensuring that person-centred care is not compromised because of personal values and beliefs

- Make the best use of the resources available

APPLYING THE STANDARD

A person's health, safety and wellbeing are dependent on pharmacy professionals working in partnership with others, where everyone is contributing towards providing the person with the care they need. This includes the person and will also include other healthcare professionals and teams. It may also include carers, relatives and professionals in other settings – such as social workers and public health officials. There are a number of ways to meet this standard and below are examples of the attitudes and behaviours expected.

People receive safe and effective care when pharmacy professionals:

- Work with the person receiving care

- Identify and work with the individuals and teams who are involved in the person's care

- Contact, involve and work with the relevant local and national organisations

- Demonstrate effective team working

- Adapt their communication to bring about effective partnership working

- Take action to safeguard people, particularly children and vulnerable adults

- Make and use records of the care provided

- Work with others to make sure there is continuity of care for the person concerned

PHARMACY PROFESSIONALS MUST COMMUNICATE EFFECTIVELY

APPLYING THE STANDARD

Communication can take many forms and happens in different ways. Effective communication is essential to the delivery of person-centred care and to working in partnership with others. It helps people to be involved in decisions about their health, safety and wellbeing. Communication is more than giving a person information, asking questions and listening. It is the exchange of information between people. Body language, tone of voice and the words pharmacy professionals use all contribute to effective communication. There are a number of ways to meet this standard and below are examples of the attitudes and behaviours expected.

People receive safe and effective care when pharmacy professionals:

- Adapt their communication to meet the needs of the person they are communicating with

- Overcome barriers to communication

- Ask questions and listen carefully to the responses, to understand the person's needs and come to a shared decision about the care they provide

- Listen actively and respond to the information they receive in a timely manner

- Check the person has understood the information they have been given

- Communicate effectively with others involved in the care of the person.

STANDARD 4

PHARMACY PROFESSIONALS MUST MAINTAIN, DEVELOP AND USE THEIR PROFESSIONAL KNOWLEDGE AND SKILLS

APPLYING THE STANDARD

People receive safe and effective care when pharmacy professionals reflect on the application of their knowledge and skills and keep them up-to-date, including using evidence in their decision making. A pharmacy professional's

knowledge and skills must develop over the course of their career to reflect the changing nature of healthcare, the population they provide care to and the roles they carry out. There are a number of ways to meet this standard and below are examples of the attitudes and behaviours expected.

People receive safe and effective care when pharmacy professionals:

- Recognise and work within the limits of their knowledge and skills, and refer to others when needed

- Use their skills and knowledge, including up-to-date evidence, to deliver care and improve the quality of care they provide

- Carry out a range of continuing professional development (CPD) activities relevant to their practice

- Record their development activities to demonstrate that their knowledge and skills are up to date

- Use a variety of methods to regularly monitor and reflect on their practice, skills and knowledge

STANDARD 5

PHARMACY PROFESSIONALS MUST USE THEIR PROFESSIONAL JUDGEMENT

APPLYING THE STANDARD

People expect pharmacy professionals to use their professional judgement so that they deliver safe and effective care. Professional judgement may include balancing the needs of individuals with the needs of society as a whole. It can also include managing complex legal and professional responsibilities and working with the person to understand and decide together what the right thing is for them – particularly if those responsibilities appear to conflict. There are a number of ways to meet this standard and below are examples of the attitudes and behaviours expected.

People receive safe and effective care when pharmacy professionals:

- Make the care of the person their first concern and act in their best interests

- Use their judgement to make clinical and professional decisions with the person or others

- Have the information they need to provide appropriate care

- Declare any personal or professional interests and manage these professionally

- Practise only when fit to do so

- Recognise the limits of their competence

- Consider and manage appropriately any personal or organisational goals, incentives or targets and make sure the care they provide reflects the needs of the person

STANDARD 6
PHARMACY PROFESSIONALS MUST BEHAVE IN A PROFESSIONAL MANNER

APPLYING THE STANDARD

People expect pharmacy professionals to behave professionally. This is essential to maintaining trust and confidence in pharmacy. Behaving professionally is not limited to the working day, or face-to-face interactions. The privilege of being a pharmacist or pharmacy technician, and the importance of maintaining confidence in the professions, call for appropriate behaviour at all times. There are a number of ways to meet this standard and below are examples of the attitudes and behaviours expected.

People receive safe and effective care when pharmacy professionals:

- Are polite and considerate

- Are trustworthy and act with honesty and integrity

- Show empathy and compassion

- Treat people with respect and safeguard their dignity

- Maintain appropriate personal and professional boundaries with the people they provide care to and with others

STANDARD 7
PHARMACY PROFESSIONALS MUST RESPECT AND MAINTAIN A PERSON'S CONFIDENTIALITY AND PRIVACY

APPLYING THE STANDARD

People trust that their confidentiality and privacy will be maintained by pharmacy professionals, whether in a healthcare setting – such as a hospital, primary care or community pharmacy setting – in person, or online. Maintaining confidentiality is a vital part of the relationship between a pharmacy professional and the person seeking care. People may be reluctant to ask for care if they believe their information may not be kept confidential. The principles of confidentiality still apply after a person's death. There are a number of ways to meet this standard and below are examples of the attitudes and behaviours expected.

People receive safe and effective care when pharmacy professionals:

- Understand the importance of managing information responsibly and securely, and apply this to their practice

- Reflect on their environment and take steps to maintain the person's privacy and confidentiality

- Do not discuss information that can identify the person when the discussions can be overheard or seen by others not involved in their care

- Ensure that everyone in the team understands the need to maintain a person's privacy and confidentiality

- Work in partnership with the person when considering whether to share their information, except where this would not be appropriate

PHARMACY PROFESSIONALS MUST SPEAK UP WHEN THEY HAVE CONCERNS OR WHEN THINGS GO WRONG

APPLYING THE STANDARD

The quality of care that people receive is improved when pharmacy professionals learn from feedback and incidents, and challenge poor practice and behaviours. This includes speaking up when they have concerns. At the heart of this standard is the requirement to be candid with the person concerned and with colleagues and employers. This is usually called the 'duty of candour' – which means being honest when things go wrong. There are a number of ways to meet this standard and below are examples of the attitudes and behaviours expected.

People receive safe and effective care when pharmacy professionals:

- Promote and encourage a culture of learning and improvement

- Challenge poor practice and behaviours

- Raise a concern, even when it is not easy to do so

- Promptly tell their employer and all relevant authorities (including the GPhC) about concerns they may have

- Support people who raise concerns and provide feedback

- Are open and honest when things go wrong

- Say sorry, provide an explanation and put things right when things go wrong

- Reflect on feedback or concerns, taking action as appropriate and thinking about what can be done to prevent the same thing happening again

- Improve the quality of care and pharmacy practice by learning from feedback and when things go wrong

PHARMACY PROFESSIONALS MUST DEMONSTRATE LEADERSHIP

APPLYING THE STANDARD

Every pharmacy professional can demonstrate leadership, whatever their role. Leadership includes taking responsibility for their actions and leading by example. Wherever a pharmacy professional practises, they must provide leadership to the people they work with and to others. There are a number of ways to meet this standard and below are some examples of the attitudes and behaviours expected.

People receive safe and effective care when pharmacy professionals:

- Take responsibility for their practice and demonstrate leadership to the people they work with

- Assess the risks in the care they provide and do everything they can to keep these risks as low as possible

- Contribute to the education, training and development of the team or of others

- Delegate tasks only to people who are competent and appropriately trained or are in training, and exercise proper oversight

- Do not abuse their position or set out to influence others to abuse theirs

- Lead by example, in particular to those who are working towards registration as a pharmacy professional

Appendix 2
GPhC standards for registered pharmacies

REVISED JUNE 2018

INTRODUCTION

The purpose of these standards is to create and maintain the right environment, both organisational and physical, for the safe and effective practice of pharmacy. The standards apply to all pharmacies registered with the General Pharmaceutical Council.

We recognise that for anyone operating a registered pharmacy there will always be competing demands. These may be professional, managerial, legal or commercial. However, medicines are not ordinary items of commerce. Along with pharmacy services, the supply of medicines is a fundamental healthcare service. Pharmacy owners must take account of this when applying these standards.

Pharmacy owners are responsible for ensuring the safe and effective provision of pharmacy services at or from a registered pharmacy. They are accountable for making sure that the standards for registered pharmacies are met. If the pharmacy is owned by a 'body corporate', the directors must assure themselves that the standards for registered pharmacies are being met.

Although registered pharmacies may have different ownership structures, it is important that the culture and processes within the pharmacy deliver safe and effective care to patients and the public.

In a limited, or public limited company, the board of directors has a significant role in making sure people receive safe and effective care from registered pharmacies. The Companies Act, and other relevant legislation, sets out the legal responsibilities for directors. In a pharmacy where healthcare is being delivered to the public, there is further guidance[1] for directors about their extra responsibilities in delivering a public service. This applies whether they are in a private or a voluntary organisation.

As a pharmacy owner you should consider the context of each individual pharmacy. This includes:

- The range of services provided

- The skill mix and number of staff in the pharmacy team

- Most importantly, the needs of patients and people who use pharmacy services

As well as meeting our standards, the pharmacy owner must make sure they comply with all legal requirements including those covering medicines legislation, health and safety, employment, data protection and equalities legislation.

Pharmacy owners must make sure that all staff, including non-pharmacists, involved in the management of pharmacy services are familiar with the standards and understand the importance of their being met. We also expect them to be familiar with all relevant guidance. All registered professionals working in a registered pharmacy should also be familiar with these standards; and pharmacists and pharmacy technicians must understand that they have a professional responsibility to raise concerns if they believe the standards are not being met.

The standards can also be used by patients and the public so that they know what they should expect when they receive pharmacy services from registered pharmacies. Throughout this document we use the term 'pharmacy services'. This covers all pharmacy-related services provided by a registered pharmacy including the management of medicines, provision of advice and referral, clinical services such as vaccination services, and services provided to care homes.

Throughout this document we use the term 'staff '. This includes agency and contract workers, as well as employees and other people who are involved in the provision of pharmacy services by a registered pharmacy. Where we use the term 'you,' this means the pharmacy owner.

---

[1] www.assets.publishing.service.gov.uk/government/uploads/system/uploads/attachment_data/fi le/481535/6.1291_CO_LAL_Ethical_standards_of_public_life_report_Interactive__2_.pdf

In some limited circumstances (for example, following death or bankruptcy), a representative can take the role of the pharmacy owner. In these cases, the appointed representative will be responsible for making sure these standards are met.

We have grouped the standards under five principles. The principles are the backbone of our regulatory approach and are all equally important.

THE PRINCIPLES

Principle 1 The governance arrangements safeguard the health, safety and wellbeing of patients and the public.

Principle 2 Staff are empowered and competent to safeguard the health, safety and wellbeing of patients and the public.

Principle 3 The environment and condition of the premises from which pharmacy services are provided, and any associated premises, safeguard the health, safety and wellbeing of patients and the public.

Principle 4 The way in which pharmacy services, including the management of medicines and medical devices, are delivered safeguards the health, safety and wellbeing of patients and the public.

Principle 5 The equipment and facilities used in the provision of pharmacy services safeguard the health, safety and wellbeing of patients and the public.

THE STANDARDS

The standards under each principle are requirements that must be met when you operate a registered pharmacy.

Responsibility for meeting the standards lies with the pharmacy owner. If the registered pharmacy is owned by a 'body corporate' the directors must assure themselves that the standards for registered pharmacies are being met.

APPLYING THE STANDARDS

The principles for registered pharmacies, and the standards that must be met, are all equally important. Therefore you should read all the standards in their entirety. Pharmacy owners

and other pharmacy professionals should also be familiar with the standards for pharmacy professionals.

We know that a pharmacy owner may be accountable for one, a few or a large number of registered pharmacies. We expect the pharmacy owner to make sure that these standards are met whatever the number of pharmacies they are accountable for.

PRINCIPLE 1

The governance arrangements safeguard the health, safety and wellbeing of patients and the public.
'Governance arrangements' includes having clear definitions of the roles and accountabilities of the people involved in providing and managing pharmacy services. It also includes the arrangements for managing risks, and the way the registered pharmacy is managed and operated.

STANDARDS

1.1   The risks associated with providing pharmacy services are identified and managed.

1.2   The safety and quality of pharmacy services are reviewed and monitored.

1.3   Pharmacy services are provided by staff with clearly defined roles and clear lines of accountability.

1.4   Feedback and concerns about the pharmacy, services and staff can be raised by individuals and organisations, and these are taken into account and action taken where appropriate.

1.5   Appropriate indemnity or insurance arrangements are in place for the pharmacy services provided.

1.6   All necessary records for the safe provision of pharmacy services are kept and maintained.

1.7   Information is managed to protect the privacy, dignity and confidentiality of patients and the public who receive pharmacy services.

1.8   Children and vulnerable adults are safeguarded.

PRINCIPLE 2

Staff are empowered and competent to safeguard the health, safety and wellbeing of patients and the public.

The staff you employ and the people you work with are key to the safe and effective practice of pharmacy. Staff members, and anyone involved in providing pharmacy services, must be competent and empowered to safeguard the health, safety and well being of patients and the public in all that they do.

STANDARDS

2.1 There are enough staff, suitably qualified and skilled, for the safe and effective provision of the pharmacy services provided.

2.2 Staff have the appropriate skills, qualifications and competence for their role and the tasks they carry out, or are working under the supervision of another person while they are in training.

2.3 Staff can comply with their own professional and legal obligations and are empowered to exercise their professional judgement in the interests of patients and the public.

2.4 There is a culture of openness, honesty and learning.

2.5 Staff are empowered to provide feedback and raise concerns about meeting these standards and other aspects of pharmacy services.

2.6 Incentives or targets do not compromise the health, safety or wellbeing of patients and the public, or the professional judgement of staff.

PRINCIPLE 3

The environment and condition of the premises from which pharmacy services are provided, and any associated premises, safeguard the health, safety and wellbeing of patients and the public.

It is important that patients and the public receive pharmacy services from premises that are suitable for the services being provided and which protect and maintain their health, safety and wellbeing. To achieve this you must make sure that all premises where pharmacy services are provided are safe and suitable. Any associated premises, for example non-registered premises used to store medicines, must also comply with these standards where applicable.

STANDARDS

3.1 Premises are safe, clean, properly maintained and suitable for the pharmacy services provided.

3.2 Premises protect the privacy, dignity and confidentiality of patients and the public who receive pharmacy services.

3.3 Premises are maintained to a level of hygiene appropriate to the pharmacy services provided.

3.4 Premises are secure and safeguarded from unauthorised access.

3.5 Pharmacy services are provided in an environment that is appropriate for the provision of healthcare.

PRINCIPLE 4

The way in which pharmacy services, including the management of medicines and medical devices, are delivered safeguards the health, safety and wellbeing of patients and the public.

'Pharmacy services' covers all pharmacy-related services provided by a registered pharmacy including the management of medicines, advice and referral, and the wide range of clinical services pharmacies provide. The management of medicines includes arrangements for obtaining, keeping, handling, using and supplying medicinal products and medical devices, as well as security and waste management.

Medicines and medical devices are not ordinary commercial items. The way they are managed is fundamental to ensuring the health, safety and wellbeing of patients and the public who receive pharmacy services.

STANDARDS

4.1 The pharmacy services provided are accessible to patients and the public.

4.2 Pharmacy services are managed and delivered safely and effectively.

4.3 Medicines and medical devices are:

- Obtained from a reputable source

- Safe and fit for purpose

- Stored securely

- Safeguarded from unauthorised access

- Supplied to the patient safely

- Disposed of safely and securely.

4.4 Concerns are raised when it is suspected that medicines or medical devices are not fit for purpose.

PRINCIPLE 5

The equipment and facilities used in the provision of pharmacy services safeguard the health, safety and wellbeing of patients and the public.

The availability of safe and suitable equipment and facilities is fundamental to the provision of pharmacy services and is essential if staff are to safeguard the health, safety and wellbeing of patients and the public when providing effective pharmacy services.

STANDARDS

5.1 Equipment and facilities needed to provide pharmacy services are readily available.

5.2 Equipment and facilities are:

- Obtained from a reputable source

- Safe to use and fit for purpose

- Stored securely

- Safeguarded from unauthorised access

- Appropriately maintained.

5.3 Equipment and facilities are used in a way that protects the privacy and dignity of the patients and the public who receive pharmacy services.

Appendix 3
GPhC in practice: guidance on confidentiality

REVISED JUNE 2018

ABOUT THIS GUIDANCE

This guidance explains to pharmacy professionals (pharmacists and pharmacy technicians) the importance of maintaining confidentiality, and their relevant responsibilities. Pharmacy professionals should use their professional judgement in applying this guidance.

Pharmacy professionals should satisfy themselves that all members of the team are familiar with the issues raised within this guidance and understand their own responsibilities in relation to confidentiality.

If a pharmacy professional is not sure about what they should do in a specific situation, they should always ask for advice from their employer, professional indemnity insurance provider, union, professional body or other pharmacy organisation, or get independent legal advice.

This guidance should be read alongside the standards for pharmacy professionals which all pharmacy professionals must meet. This guidance covers standard 7 of the standards for pharmacy professionals, which says:

Pharmacy professionals must respect and maintain a person's confidentiality and privacy

APPLYING THE STANDARD

People trust that their confidentiality and privacy will be maintained by pharmacy professionals, whether in a healthcare setting – such as a hospital, primary care or community pharmacy setting – in person, or online. Maintaining confidentiality is a vital part of the relationship between a pharmacy professional and the person seeking care. People may be reluctant to ask for care if they believe their information may not be kept confidential. The principles of confidentiality still apply after a person's death. There are a

number of ways to meet this standard and below are examples of the attitudes and behaviours expected.

People receive safe and effective care when pharmacy professionals:

- Understand the importance of managing information responsibly and securely, and apply this to their practice

- Reflect on their environment and take steps to maintain the person's privacy and confidentiality

- Do not discuss information that can identify the person, when the discussions can be overheard or seen by others not involved in their care

- Ensure that everyone in the team understands the need to maintain a person's privacy and confidentiality

- Work in partnership with the person when considering whether to share their information, except where this would not be appropriate

This guidance is not intended to cover every aspect of confidentiality and it does not give detailed legal advice. However, it reflects the law in Great Britain at the time of publication.

Pharmacy professionals must make sure that they keep up to date and comply with data protection legislation, for example: UK domestic data protection legislation, the **General Data Protection Regulation ((EU) 2016/679) (GDPR)** eur-lex.europa. eu/eli/reg/2016/679/oj and the **Human Rights Act 1998 (HRA)** www.equalityhumanrights.com/en/ human_rights/human-rights-act.
The common law duty of confidentiality also applies, as do any NHS or employment policies on confidentiality that apply to their particular area of work.

UK data protection legislation covers personal information, including data about the physical or mental health or condition of a person (called a 'data subject' in data protection legislation).
The **Information Commissioner's Office (ICO)** ico.org.uk/for-organisations/ enforces data protection legislation and produces advice and guidance on it.

The HRA incorporates the European Convention on Human Rights (ECHR) into UK law. This, and the Charter of Fundamental Rights of the European Union, gives individuals a right to respect for their private life.

The charter also gives them a right to the protection of their personal data[1]. These issues can be complex and pharmacy professionals should get legal advice, if they need it.

Pharmacy professionals providing NHS services must also follow NHS codes of practice, and the guidance on handling information in health and care.

We have a range of guidance on our website to help pharmacy professionals apply our standards. In particular, when reading this guidance, please also see our *In practice: Guidance on consent*.

1
THE IMPORTANCE OF MAINTAINING CONFIDENTIALITY

1.1 Maintaining confidentiality is a vital part of the relationship between a pharmacy professional and a person under their care. A person may be reluctant to ask for advice, or give a pharmacy professional the information they need to provide proper care, if they believe that the pharmacy professional may not keep the information confidential. When pharmacy professionals do not handle confidential information appropriately it can damage public trust and confidence in the pharmacy professions and other healthcare professions.

2
DUTY OF CONFIDENTIALITY

2.1 Pharmacy professionals have a professional and legal duty to keep confidential the information they obtain during the course of their professional practice. The duty of confidentiality applies to information about any person, whatever their age (see our *In practice: Guidance on consent*), and continues to apply after a person's death.

2.2 A duty of confidentiality arises when one person discloses information to another in circumstances where it is reasonable to expect that the information will be held in confidence. This duty applies to all information that pharmacy professionals obtain during the course of their professional practice.

2.3 Confidential information includes:

- Electronic and hard copy data

- Personal details

- Information about a person's medication (prescribed and non-prescribed)

- Other information about a person's medical history, treatment or care that could identify them, and

- Information that people share that is not strictly medical in nature, but that the person disclosing it would expect to be kept confidential

2.4 Confidential information does not include:

- Anonymous information – information from which individuals cannot reasonably be identified

- Pseudonymised information – information from which individuals cannot reasonably be identified, but which allows information about different people receiving care to be distinguished (for example, to identify drug side effects)

- Information that is already legitimately in the public domain

3
PROTECTING INFORMATION

3.1 It is essential that pharmacy professionals take steps to protect the confidential information they are given either in the course of their professional practice or because they are a pharmacy professional They must:

- Take all reasonable steps to protect the confidentiality and security of information they receive, access, store, send or destroy, including protection against unauthorised or unlawful processing and against intrusion, destruction or damage

- Take steps to make sure that, when processing personal data, it is accurate and, where necessary, kept up to date

---

[1] The rights under Article 8 of the HRA are complicated and there are conditons and exceptions. For more information on Article 8 see: www.equalityhumanrights.com/en/human-rights-act/article-8-respect-your-private-and-family-life

- Take steps to prevent accidental disclosure of confidential information

- Access confidential information and records only as part of providing treatment and care for a person, or for another permitted purpose that meets one of the conditions for lawfully processing personal data set out in legislation

- Make sure that everyone they work with in their pharmacy, hospital, practice or other setting knows about their responsibility to maintain confidentiality

- Raise concerns with the person who is responsible for data control (the data controller) where they work, or with any other appropriate authority, if they find that the security of personal information there is not appropriate

- Continue to protect a person's confidentiality after they have died, subject to disclosures required by law or when it is in the public interest (see below)

- Store hard copy and electronic documents, records, registers, prescriptions and other sources of confidential information securely for no longer than is necessary for the purposes for which the personal data are processed

- Not leave confidential information where it may be seen or accessed by people receiving care, the public or anyone else who should not have access to it

- Not discuss information that can identify people receiving care if the discussions can be overheard or seen by others not involved in their care

- Not disclose information on any websites, internet chat forums or social media that could identify a person (see our guidance on demonstrating professionalism online).

4
DISCLOSING CONFIDENTIAL INFORMATION

4.1 Decisions about disclosing confidential information can be complex. In most situations pharmacy professionals will not have to disclose information immediately. However, there will be limited situations where to delay is not practical, for example if this may cause a risk to another person. Pharmacy professionals should take the necessary steps to satisfy themselves that any disclosure being asked for is appropriate and meets the legal requirements covering confidentiality, and the conditions for lawfully processing personal data in data protection legislation.
If it is practicable, pharmacy professionals may find it useful to get advice on what to do from appropriate sources (without identifying the person under their care).

4.2 Maintaining confidentiality is an important duty, but there are circumstances when it may be appropriate to disclose confidential information. These are when a pharmacy professional:

- Has the consent of the person under their care

- Has to disclose by law

- Should do so in the public interest, and/or

- Must do so in the vital interests of a person receiving treatment or care, for example if a patient needs immediate urgent medical attention

4.3 In the course of their professional practice pharmacy professionals may receive requests for confidential information about people under their care from a variety of people (for example a person's relative, partner or carer) or organisations (for example the police or a healthcare regulator). Decisions about disclosing information should be made on a case-by-case basis and after fully considering all relevant factors.

4.4 If a person with capacity (see our *In practice: Guidance on consent* for more information on capacity) refuses to give consent for information to be shared with other healthcare professionals involved in providing their care, it may mean that the care they can be provided with is limited. Pharmacy professionals must respect that decision, but tell the person receiving care about the potential implications for their care or treatment.

4.5 Pharmacy professionals must respect the wishes of a person with capacity under their care who does not consent to information about them being shared with others, unless the law says they must disclose the information or it is in the public interest to make such a disclosure.

4.6 If a pharmacy professional decides to disclose confidential information about a person, they should:

- Pseudonymise information or make it anonymous, if they do not need to identify the person receiving care

- Get the person's consent to share their information. But they do not need to do this if:

  - Disclosure is required by law, or

  - the disclosure can be justified in the public interest[1], or

  - To do so is impracticable, would put the pharmacy professional or others (including the person receiving treatment or care) at risk of serious harm, or would prejudice the purpose of the disclosure, for example to prevent a crime

- Disclose only the information needed for the particular purpose

- Make sure that, if they disclose confidential information, the people receiving the information know that it is confidential and is to be treated as such

- Make appropriate records to show:

  - Who the request came from

  - Whether they obtained the consent of the person under their care, or their reasons for not doing so

  - Whether consent was given or refused

  - What they disclosed

  - How it was ensured that the disclosure was made securely, and

  - What the lawful authority or provision was under which the request and/or disclosure was made

- Be prepared to justify the decisions and any actions they take

- Release the information promptly once they are satisfied what information should be disclosed and have taken all necessary steps to protect confidentiality

- Retain a copy of the disclosure made

5
DISCLOSING INFORMATION WITH CONSENT

5.1 Pharmacy professionals should get the person's consent to share their information unless that would undermine the purpose of disclosure (see 4.6 above).

5.2 They should make sure the person in their care understands:

- What information will be disclosed

- Why information will be disclosed

- Who it will be disclosed to

- The likely consequences of disclosing and of not disclosing the information.

5.3 When the reason for sharing confidential information is one that the person receiving care would not reasonably expect, pharmacy professionals must get their explicit consent before disclosure.

---

[1] When considering whether disclosing confidential information without consent may be justified in the public interest, pharmacy professionals must be satisfied that the disclosure would comply with data protection legislation. Please see the ICO's website for more information.

5.4 If a pharmacy professional is unsure whether they have the person's consent to share their information, they should contact them and obtain their consent.

5.5 Pharmacy professionals should also take data protection legislation into account in these circumstances, as those requirements also need to be followed. Under data protection legislation, information can be shared when express consent (specific permission to do something) is given. Consent to share information under the duty of confidentiality may not be valid for the purposes of data protection legislation.

6
DISCLOSING INFORMATION WITHOUT CONSENT

6.1 Pharmacy professionals should make every effort to get consent to disclose confidential information. However, if that would undermine the purpose of disclosure (for example, when there is a risk to others) or is not practicable, then they should use the guidance in this section.

6.2 Before disclosing information without the consent of the person receiving care, a pharmacy professional should:

- Be satisfied that the law says they have to disclose the information, or that disclosure can be justified as being in the public interest and also meets the requirements of data protection legislation. (This would be through an exemption or condition that would apply for the information to be processed and disclosed.)

- If they are unsure about the basis for the request, ask for clarification from the person making the request

- Ask for the request in writing.

6.3 If necessary, pharmacy professionals should get advice from a relevant body, for example their indemnity insurance provider, union, professional body or other pharmacy organisation, or an independent legal adviser. The ICO can give advice, and has issued guidance, on the requirements of data protection legislation.

7
DISCLOSURES REQUIRED BY LAW

7.1 There are circumstances when the law says a pharmacy professional must disclose information that they hold. These circumstances include when a person or body is using their powers under the law to ask for the information, for example:

- The police or another enforcement, prosecuting or regulatory authority

- A healthcare regulator, such as the GPhC or the GMC

- An NHS counter-fraud investigation officer

- A coroner, procurator fiscal, judge or relevant court which orders that the information should be disclosed

7.2 These individuals and organisations do not have an automatic right to access all confidential information about people receiving care. Pharmacy professionals must be satisfied they have a legitimate reason for requesting the information.

7.3 If necessary, pharmacy professionals should get advice from a relevant body, for example their indemnity insurance provider, union, professional body or other pharmacy organisation, the ICO, or an independent legal adviser.

8

DISCLOSURES MADE IN THE PUBLIC INTEREST

8.1   These decisions are complex and must take account of both the person receiving care and public interest in either maintaining or breaching confidentiality.

8.2   A pharmacy professional may disclose confidential information when they consider it to be in the public interest to do so, for example if the information is required to prevent:

- A serious crime

- Serious harm to a person receiving care or to a third party, or

- Serious risk to public health

8.3   Pharmacy professionals must carefully balance the competing interests of maintaining the confidentiality of the information and the public interest benefit in disclosing the information.

8.4   Pharmacy professionals must consider the possible harm that may be caused by not disclosing the information against the potential consequences of disclosing the information. This includes considering how disclosing the information may affect the care of the person and the trust that they have in pharmacy professionals.

8.5   When considering whether disclosing confidential information without consent may be justified in the public interest, pharmacy professionals must be satisfied that the disclosure would comply with the requirements of data protection law.

8.6   If necessary, pharmacy professionals should get advice from a relevant body, for example their indemnity insurance provider, union, professional body or other pharmacy organisation, the ICO, or an independent legal adviser.

GPhC in practice: guidance on consent

REVISED JUNE 2018

ABOUT THIS GUIDANCE

This guidance explains to pharmacy professionals (pharmacists and pharmacy technicians) the importance of consent and their relevant responsibilities. Pharmacy professionals should use their professional judgement in applying this guidance.

Pharmacy professionals should satisfy themselves that all members of the team are familiar with the issues raised within this guidance and understand their own responsibilities in relation to consent. If a pharmacy professional is not sure about what they should do in a specific situation, they should always ask for advice from their employer, professional indemnity insurance provider, union, professional body or other pharmacy organisation, or get independent legal advice.

This guidance should be read alongside the *standards for pharmacy professionals* which all pharmacy professionals must meet. This guidance covers standard 1 of the standards for pharmacy professionals, which says:

Pharmacy professionals must provide person-centred care

APPLYING THE STANDARD

Every person is an individual with their own values, needs and concerns. Person-centred care is delivered when pharmacy professionals understand what is important to the individual and then adapt the care to meet their needs – making the care of the person their first priority. All pharmacy professionals can demonstrate 'person-centredness' – whether or not they provide care directly – by thinking about the impact their decisions have on people.

There are a number of ways to meet this standard, and below are examples of the attitudes and behaviours expected.

People receive safe and effective care when pharmacy professionals:

- Obtain consent to provide care and pharmacy services

- Involve, support and enable every person when making decisions about their health, care and wellbeing

- Listen to the person and understand their needs and what matters to them

- Give the person all relevant information in a way they can understand, so they can make informed decisions and choices

- Consider the impact of their practice – whether or not they provide care directly

- Respect and safeguard the person's dignity

- Recognise and value diversity, and respect cultural differences – making sure that every person is treated fairly whatever their values and beliefs

- Recognise their own values and beliefs but do not impose them on other people

- Take responsibility for ensuring that person centred care is not compromised because of personal values and beliefs

- Make the best use of the resources available

This guidance is not intended to cover every aspect of consent, and it does not give legal advice. However, it reflects the law in Great Britain at the time of publication.

Pharmacy professionals must make sure that they keep up to date and comply with the law, and with any NHS or employment policies on consent that apply to their particular area of work.

Pharmacy professionals work in many different settings. So how relevant this guidance is to a pharmacy professional, and how consent is obtained, may vary depending on their role and the type of contact they have with people receiving care.

We have a range of guidance on our website to help pharmacy professionals apply our standards. In particular, when reading this guidance please also see our *In practice: Guidance on confidentiality*.

1
WHAT IS CONSENT?

1.1 The Oxford English Dictionary defines 'to consent' as 'to express willingness, give permission, agree'.

1.2 People have a basic right to be involved in decisions about their healthcare. Obtaining consent is a fundamental part of respecting a person's rights.

1.3 Obtaining consent is also essential in forming and maintaining effective partnerships between pharmacy professionals and the people receiving care.

1.4 Pharmacy professionals have a professional and legal duty to get a person's consent for the professional services, treatment or care they provide, and for using a person's information.

1.5 Pharmacy professionals must know and comply with the law and the good practice requirements about consent which apply to them in their day-today practice.

2
TYPES OF CONSENT

2.1 There are two types of consent:

- Explicit (or 'express') consent: when a person gives a pharmacy professional specific permission, either spoken or written, to do something

- Implied consent: when a person gives their consent indirectly, for example by bringing their prescription to a pharmacy professional to be dispensed. This is not a lesser form of consent but it is only valid if the person knows and understands what they are consenting to. If a pharmacy professional is not sure whether they have implied consent, they should get explicit consent.

2.2 Pharmacy professionals must use their professional judgement to decide what type of consent to get. Pharmacy professionals should take into account legal requirements and NHS service requirements, and the policies where they work that may set this out.

2.3 When appropriate, pharmacy professionals should record the fact that the person receiving care has given explicit consent and what they have consented to.

2.4 Consent may be used as a condition for processing a person's information under data protection legislation, including: UK domestic data protection legislation, the General Data Protection Regulation ((EU) 2016/679) (GDPR) and the Human Rights Act 1998 (HRA) . Consent would be required to allow a person's information to be shared with third parties if there was no other legal basis for doing so. When consent is used as a condition for processing, a person needs to have taken positive action and shown that they agreed to their personal data being processed. This cannot be inferred or taken as understood from a lack of action – such as a failure to object or to tick an 'opt-out' box. Please also see our *In practice: Guidance on confidentiality* for more information. For more guidance on data protection and on consent in the context of GDPR see the Information Commissioner's Office (ICO) website.

3
OBTAINING CONSENT

3.1 For consent to be valid the person must:

- Have the capacity to give consent (see section 4 for an explanation of 'capacity')

- Be acting voluntarily – they must not be under any undue pressure from a pharmacy professional or anyone else to make a decision

- Have sufficient, balanced information to allow them to make an informed decision. This includes making sure the person receiving care knows about any material risks involved in the recommended treatment, and about any reasonable alternative treatments.

Material risks are those a reasonable person would think are significant in the circumstances, but also those the particular person would find significant. Material risks must be disclosed unless to do so would be seriously detrimental to the person's health[1] (See also Section 16 – Emergencies, for when it may be allowable not to obtain consent)

- Be capable of using and weighing up the information provided.

- Understand the consequences of not giving consent

3.2 The information a pharmacy professional provides to the person must be clear, accurate and presented in a way that the person can understand. For example, pharmacy professionals must consider any disabilities, and literacy or language barriers.

3.3 Pharmacy professionals should not make assumptions about the person's level of knowledge and they should give them the opportunity to ask questions.

3.4 Pharmacy professionals are responsible for making sure that a person has given valid consent. Pharmacy professionals must use their professional judgement to decide whether they themselves should get consent from the person, or whether this task can properly be delegated. If the pharmacy professional does delegate the task of obtaining consent they must make sure they delegate it to a competent and appropriately trained member of staff.

3.5 Getting consent is an ongoing process between a pharmacy professional and the person receiving care. Consent cannot be presumed just because it was given on a previous occasion. Pharmacy professionals must get a person's consent on each occasion that it is needed, for example when there is a change in treatment or service options. Consent must be recorded.

3.6 People with capacity are entitled to withdraw their consent at any time. (See section 7 – When a competent adult refuses to give consent.)

---

[1] Montgomery v Lanarkshire Health Board. [2015] UKSC 11. www.supremecourt.uk/cases/docs/uksc-2013-0136-judgment.pdf

4

WHAT IS CAPACITY?

4.1 In England and Wales, under the Mental Capacity Act 2005, a person lacks capacity if at the time the decision needs to be made, they are unable to make or communicate the decision because of an impairment or disturbance that affects the way their mind or brain works.

4.2 In Scotland, under the Adults with Incapacity (Scotland) Act 2000, a person lacks capacity if they cannot act, make decisions or communicate them, or understand or remember their decisions because of a mental disorder or physical inability to communicate in any form.

5

ASSESSING CAPACITY

5.1 A pharmacy professional must base an assessment of capacity on the person's ability to make a specific decision at the time it needs to be made. A person receiving care may be capable of making some decisions but not others.

5.2 In general, to make an informed decision the person should be able to:

- Understand the information provided

- Remember the information provided

- Use and weigh up the information provided, and

- Communicate their decision to the pharmacy professional (by any means).

5.3 Pharmacy professionals must not assume that because a person lacks capacity on one occasion, or in relation to one type of service, that they lack capacity to make all decisions.

5.4 A person's capacity to consent may be temporarily affected by other factors, for example: fatigue, panic, or the effects of drugs or alcohol. This should not lead to an automatic assumption that the person does not have the capacity to consent. Instead, pharmacy professionals should use their professional judgement to make a decision based on the individual circumstances.

5.5 Pharmacy professionals must not assume that a person lacks capacity based just upon their age, disability, beliefs, condition or behaviour, or because they make a decision that the pharmacy professional disagrees with.

5.6 Pharmacy professionals must take all reasonable steps to help and support people to make their own decisions, or to be as involved as they can be in a decision. They should, for example:

- Time the discussion for when the person's understanding may be better

- Use appropriate types of communication, simple language or visual aids

- Get someone else to help with communication such as a family member, support worker or interpreter.

5.7 If a pharmacy professional is unsure about a person's capacity they must get advice from other healthcare professionals or from people involved in their care.

5.8 If a pharmacy professional is still unsure they must get legal advice.

5.9 Any advice they get or assessments carried out should be properly recorded, along with the outcome.

5.10 Pharmacy professionals can find more guidance on how people should be helped to make their own decisions, and how to assess capacity, in the Codes of Practice that accompany the Mental Capacity Act 2005 and Adults with Incapacity (Scotland) Act 2000.

6

ADULTS WITH CAPACITY

6.1 Every adult is presumed to have the capacity to make their own decisions (that is, that they are competent) and to give consent for a service or treatment unless there is enough evidence to suggest otherwise.

7

WHEN A COMPETENT ADULT REFUSES TO GIVE CONSENT

7.1 If an adult with capacity makes a voluntary, informed decision to refuse a service or treatment, pharmacy professionals must respect their decision – even when they think that their decision is wrong or may cause the person harm. This does not apply when the law says otherwise, such as when compulsory treatment is authorised by mental health legislation.[2]

7.2 Pharmacy professionals should clearly explain the consequences of the decision, but must make sure that they do not pressure the person to accept their advice.

7.3 Pharmacy professionals should make a detailed record if a person refuses to give consent. This should include the discussions that have taken place and the advice given.

7.4 If a pharmacy professional believes that the person is at risk of serious harm because of their decision to refuse a service or treatment, they must raise this issue with relevant healthcare or pharmacy colleagues or with people involved in the person's care, and with their own employer (if they have one). They should also consider getting legal advice if necessary.

8

ADULTS WITHOUT CAPACITY

8.1 If the person is not able to make decisions for themselves, pharmacy professionals must work with people close to the person receiving care and with other members of the healthcare team.

8.2 The Mental Capacity Act 2005 and Adults with Incapacity (Scotland) Act 2000 set out the criteria and the processes to be followed in making decisions and providing care services when a person lacks the capacity to make some or all decisions for themselves. They also give legal authority to certain people to make decisions on behalf of people receiving care who lack capacity.

8.3 If pharmacy professionals believe that a person lacks capacity to make decisions for themselves, they should consult the Codes of Practice that accompany the Mental Capacity Act 2005 or Adults with Incapacity (Scotland) Act (2000). These set out who can make decisions on the person's behalf, in which situations, and how they should go about this.

9

YOUNG PEOPLE AND CHILDREN

9.1 The capacity to consent depends more on the person's ability to understand and consider their decision than on their age.

9.2 In this guidance 'a young person' means anyone aged 16 or 17, and 'a child' means anyone aged under 16. However, people gain full legal capacity in relation to medical treatment at a different age in Scotland than in England and Wales.

9.3 As with any person receiving care, a young person or child may have the capacity to consent to some services or treatments but not to others. Therefore it is important that pharmacy professionals assess the maturity and understanding of each person individually, and keep in mind the complexity and importance of the decision to be made.

---

[2] Mental Health Act 1983 (as amended by the Mental Health Act 2007), and the Mental Health (Care and Treatment) (Scotland) Act 2003

9.4 If a person with parental responsibility has to give consent, pharmacy professionals may need to get legal advice if: they are in any doubt about who has parental responsibility for the person, or those that have parental responsibility cannot agree whether or not to give consent.

9.5 Young people and children should be involved as much as possible in decisions about their care, even when they are not able to make decisions on their own.

10
YOUNG PEOPLE WITH CAPACITY

10.1 Young people are presumed to have the capacity to make their own decisions and give consent for a service or treatment, unless there is enough evidence to suggest otherwise.

10.2 To decide whether a young person has the capacity to consent to a service or treatment, pharmacy professionals should use the same criteria as for adults (see section 5 – Assessing capacity).

10.3 Pharmacy professionals should encourage young people to involve their parents in making important decisions. However, pharmacy professionals should respect a competent young person's request for confidentiality.

11
CHILDREN WITH CAPACITY

11.1 Children are not presumed to have the capacity to consent. They must demonstrate their competence.

11.2 A child can give consent if the pharmacy professional is satisfied that the treatment is in their best interests, and that they have the maturity and ability to fully understand the information given and what they are consenting to. In this case pharmacy professionals do not also need consent from a person with parental responsibility.

12
WHEN COMPETENT YOUNG PEOPLE AND CHILDREN REFUSE TO GIVE CONSENT

ENGLAND AND WALES

12.1 In some circumstances, the courts can override the refusal of consent of a young person or child. Pharmacy professionals should get legal advice on this issue if needed.

12.2 The law is complex when a competent young person or child refuses to give consent for a treatment or service and someone with parental responsibility wants to override their decision. Pharmacy professionals should get legal advice if they are faced with this situation.

SCOTLAND

12.3 When a young person or child has capacity to make a decision, then their decision should be respected. This applies even if the decision differs from the pharmacy professional's view, or from the views of those with parental responsibility.

12.4 However, this position has not yet been fully tested in the Scottish courts. Nor has the issue of whether a court can override a young person's or child's decision. Pharmacy professionals should therefore get legal advice if they are faced with this situation.

13
YOUNG PEOPLE WITHOUT CAPACITY

13.1 A person with parental responsibility for a young person without capacity can give consent on behalf of that young person to investigations and treatment that are in the young person's best interests.

13.2 The rights of a person with parental responsibility to make decisions on behalf of a child end when the child reaches the age of 16.

13.3 Young people who do not have the capacity to consent should be treated as though they are adults and in line with the Adults with Incapacity (Scotland) Act 2000.

14
CHILDREN WITHOUT CAPACITY

14.1 When a child lacks capacity to give consent, any person with parental responsibility for that child, or the court, can give consent on their behalf.

15
ADVANCE DECISIONS

15.1 People who understand the implications of their choices can say in advance how they want to be treated if they later suffer loss of mental capacity.

15.2 An unambiguous advance refusal for a treatment, procedure or intervention which is voluntarily made by a competent, informed adult is likely to have legal force.

15.3 An advance refusal of treatment cannot override the legal authority to give compulsory treatment under the mental health laws.

15.4 Any advance decision is superseded by a competent decision by the person concerned, made at the time consent is sought.

15.5 Advance decisions are covered by the Mental Capacity Act 2005. For an advance refusal of treatment to be legally valid, it must meet certain criteria set out in the Mental Capacity Act 2005.

15.6 If an advance decision does not meet these criteria, it is not legally binding but can still be used in deciding the person's best interests.

15.7 Pharmacy professionals must follow an advance decision if it is valid and applicable to current circumstances.

15.8 The Adults with Incapacity (Scotland) Act 2000 does not specifically cover advance decisions. However, it says that health professionals must take account of the person receiving care's past and present wishes, however they were communicated.

15.9 It is likely that pharmacy professionals would be bound by a valid and applicable advance decision. However, there have been no specific cases yet considered by the Scottish courts. If in any doubt, pharmacy professionals should get legal advice.

16
EMERGENCIES

16.1 In an emergency, when a person needs urgent treatment, if a pharmacy professional cannot get consent (for example, if the person is unconscious and unable to make a decision) they can provide treatment that is in the person's best interests and is needed to save their life or prevent deterioration in their condition. This applies to children, young people and adults.

16.2 There is an exception to 16.1 above if a pharmacy professional knows that there is a valid and applicable advance decision to refuse a particular treatment. For more information pharmacy professionals should see the relevant incapacity legislation and its code of practice, or ask their professional indemnity insurance provider or a legal adviser.

Appendix 5
GPhC in practice: guidance on raising concerns

MAY 2017

1
THE IMPORTANCE OF RAISING CONCERNS

1.1 Every pharmacy professional has a duty to raise any concerns about individuals, actions or circumstances that may be unacceptable and that could result in risks to people receiving care and public safety.

1.2 Pharmacy professionals have a professional responsibility to take action to protect the wellbeing of people receiving care and the public. Raising concerns about individual pharmacy professionals, the members of the pharmacy team they work with (including trainees), employers and the environment they work in is a key part of this.

1.3 This includes raising and reporting any concerns pharmacy professionals have about the people they come into contact with during the course of their work, including pharmacists, pharmacy technicians, pharmacy owners, managers and employers, other healthcare professionals or people responsible for providing care and treatment for others, such as carers, care home staff or key workers. It includes concerns about behaviours, competency, the working environment and any action that may compromise an individual's safety.

1.4 We recognise that pharmacy professionals may be reluctant to raise a concern for a variety of reasons. For example, they may be worried that:

- They will cause trouble for their colleagues

- There may be a negative impact on their career

- It may lead to difficult working relationships with their colleagues

- They could face reprisals

- Nothing will be done as a result of the concern being raised.

1.5 Raising concerns at an early stage can help to identify areas of practice that can be improved. It allows employers, regulators and other authorities to take correct action as quickly as possible and before any direct harm comes to people receiving care and the public.

1.6 Pharmacy professionals must remember that:

- Their professional duty to safeguard the people they are providing care for and public safety must come before any other loyalties or considerations

- Failing to raise concerns about poor practice could result in harm to people receiving care

- The Public Interest Disclosure Act 1008 (PIDA) protects employees who raise genuine concerns and expose 'malpractice' in the workplace

- If they do not report any concerns they may have about a colleague or others it may be out of line with our standards for pharmacy professionals, and this may call into question their own fitness to practise.

2

HOW TO RAISE A CONCERN

2.1 Pharmacy professionals have a professional responsibility to raise genuine concerns. They have this responsibility whether they are an employer, employee, a locum or temporary staff. Pharmacy professionals should normally raise their concern with their employer first, before taking it to a regulator or other organisations. If they are not sure whether or how to raise their concern they should get advice from one of the organisations listed in the other sources of information section. How pharmacy professionals raise a concern will vary, depending on:

- The nature of their concern

- Who or what they are concerned about, and

- Whether they consider there is a direct or immediate risk of harm to the public or to people receiving care.

2.2 **FIND OUT THE ORGANISATION'S POLICY**
Pharmacy professionals should find out their employer's policy on raising concerns or 'whistle blowing' and follow this whenever possible.

2.3 **REPORT WITHOUT DELAY**
If pharmacy professionals believe that people receiving care are, or may be, at risk of death or serious harm they should report their concern without delay.

2.4 **REPORT TO THE IMMEDIATE SUPERVISOR**
The person pharmacy professionals report their concerns to will vary depending on the nature of the concern. In most situations they will be able to raise their concerns with their line manager.

2.5 **REPORT TO ANOTHER SUITABLE PERSON IN AUTHORITY OR AN OUTSIDE BODY**
There may be some situations when it isn't possible for pharmacy professionals to raise their concerns with their line manager. For example, they may be the cause of the concern or may have strong loyalties to those who are the cause of the concern. In these situations pharmacy professionals may need to speak to:

- A person who has been named as responsible for handling concerns

- A senior manager in the organisation for example a chief pharmacist, pharmacy owner or superintendent pharmacist or non-pharmacist manager

- The primary care organisation (including the accountable officer if the concern is about controlled drugs)

- The health or social care profession regulator [1]

- The relevant systems regulator for the organisation. [2]

2.6 **KEEP A RECORD**
Pharmacy professionals should keep a record of the concerns they have, who they have raised them with and the response or action that has been taken as a result of their action.

2.7 **MAINTAIN CONFIDENTIALITY**
If a concern raised by a pharmacy professional is about a specific person, for example a person receiving care or colleague, they should, where possible, maintain confidentiality and not disclose information without consent.

3

THE LAW

3.1 The PIDA sets out a step-by-step approach to raising and escalating concerns. It aims to protect employees from unfair treatment or victimisation from their employer if they have made certain disclosures of information in the public interest.

3.2 Under the PIDA pharmacy professionals should raise a concern about issues which have happened, or which they reasonably believe are likely to happen, and involve:

- A danger to the health or safety of an individual (for example, irresponsible or illegal prescribing, abuse of a person receiving care, or a professional whose health or fitness to practise may be impaired)

- A crime, or a civil offence (for example, fraud, theft or the illegal diversion of drugs)

- A miscarriage of justice

- Damage to the environment

- A cover-up of information about any of the above

3.3 This is not a full list. The other sources of information section gives contact details for other sources of information if pharmacy professionals have a concern and are unsure about whether or how they should raise it.

4
EXTRA GUIDANCE FOR EMPLOYERS

4.1 It is important that employees know about the procedures to follow if they have a concern about a colleague or the organisation they work in. There should also be procedures to identity concerns that should be referred to a regulatory body such as ourselves. Creating an open working environment where employees feel comfortable raising concerns will safeguard people's safety by helping to identify and therefore improve poor practice.

4.2 Employers should:

- Make sure they have fair and robust policies and procedures to manage concerns that are raised with them. These policies and procedures need to be accessible to all staff

- Encourage all staff, including temporary staff and locums, to raise concerns about the safety of people receiving care, including risks posed by colleagues

- Make sure that all concerns raised with them are taken seriously and the person who has raised them is not victimised

- Make sure that all concerns are properly investigated and that all staff, including temporary staff and locums, are kept informed of the progress

- Have systems in place to give adequate support to pharmacy professionals who have raised concerns, and treat any information they are given in confidence

- Take appropriate steps to deal with concerns that have been raised because of a failure to maintain standards

- Have systems in place to support pharmacy professionals who are the subject of the concern, whether it is due to their poor performance, health or behaviour

- Keep appropriate records of any concerns raised and the action taken to deal with them

- Pass records of concerns raised to the manager or superintendent pharmacist so that they can consider an overall assessment of the concerns

- Not stop anyone from raising a concern

- Report on the concerns they have received through the year. This may be internally to their own staff, through their annual report or on their website

- Have in place internal whistleblowing arrangements which are reviewed regularly to ensure they are operating effectively

- Train managers to handle whistleblowing concerns.

1 The healthcare regulators are: General Chiropractic Council; General Dental Council; General Medical Council; General Optical Council; General Osteopathic Council; Health and Care Professions Council; Nursing and Midwifery Council; General Pharmaceutical Council and Pharmaceutical Society of Northern Ireland. The social care regulators are the Care Council in Wales; Health and Care Professions Council in England; Northern Ireland Social Care Council and the Scottish Social Services Council.

2 These include, within the hospital setting, the Care Quality Commission in England, the Health Inspectorate Wales, Healthcare Improvement Scotland and the General Pharmaceutical Council if the concern is about registered pharmacy premises.

WHERE TO GO FOR MORE ADVICE

5.1 For more information on the PIDA and how to raise concerns under this employment legislation pharmacy professionals may want to contact the charity Public Concern at Work (PCaW). This is an independent charity that gives free, confidential legal advice to people who are not sure whether or how to raise concerns about 'malpractice' at work. If pharmacy professionals are not sure whether or how to raise their concern they should get advice from:

- Senior members of staff in their organisation

- The accountable officer, if the concern is about controlled drugs

- Their professional indemnity insurance provider, professional body or other pharmacy organisation

- The General Pharmaceutical Council or, if their concern is about a colleague in another healthcare profession, the appropriate regulatory body

- The charity Pharmacist Support

- Their union

Index

B

C

R

INDEX

S

T

Notes

Notes

Acknowledgements

We would like to thank the GPhC for permission to reproduce their regulatory standards and guidance within the MEP appendices. The most current versions of these documents will be on the GPhC website www.pharmacyregulation.org

We are also grateful to the following persons who have provided expert advice and information during the preparation of MEP 45 as part of the MEP advisory panel.

———————————————

The RPS welcomes members from all sectors and all stages of practices to volunteer their time to contribute to improving future editions of MEP. To volunteer to join the advisory panel please contact support@rpharms.com

ADVISORY PANEL

Catherine Baldridge
Carol Candlish
Judith Gajree
Roz Gittins
Amira Guirguis
Karen Harrowing
Dilesh Khandhia
Sally Lau
Babir Malik
Isaac Moore
Rob Morris
Abigail Oloo
Rachel Quinlan
Dibar Sabir
Ellen Schafheutle
Tsz To Sham
Jennifer Smith
David Tyas

RPS STAFF

Lead editor
Rakhee Amin

Editorial team
Regina Ahmed
Colin Babb
Angela Crawford
Sonia Garner
Wing Tang

Contributors
Yogeeta Bhupal
Alison Murray
Helena Rosado
Margaret Ryan
Sabes Thurairasa
Yen Truong

DESIGN

planningunit.co.uk